Unde
Hong

Understanding Criminal Justice in Hong Kong

Edited by

Wing Hong Chui and T. Wing Lo

WILLAN
PUBLISHING

Published by

Willan Publishing
Culmcott House
Mill Street, Uffculme
Cullompton, Devon
EX15 3AT, UK
Tel: +44(0)1884 840337
Fax: +44(0)1884 840251
e-mail: info@willanpublishing.co.uk
website: www.willanpublishing.co.uk

Published simultaneously in the USA and Canada by

Willan Publishing
c/o ISBS, 920 NE 58th Ave, Suite 300,
Portland, Oregon 97213-3786, USA
Tel: +001(0)503 287 3093
Fax: +001(0)503 280 8832
e-mail: info@isbs.com
website: www.isbs.com

First published 2008

ISBN 978-1-84392-300-8 paperback
978-1-84392-301-5 hardback

British Library Cataloguing-in-Publication Data

A catalogue record for this book is available from the British Library.

Project managed by Deer Park Productions, Tavistock, Devon
Typeset by GCS, Leighton Buzzard, Bedfordshire
Printed and bound by T.J. International Ltd, Padstow, Cornwall

Contents

Notes on contributors

Roderic Broadhurst is presently Honorary Professor at the Key Centre for Ethics, Law, Justice & Governance, Griffith University and Visiting Fellow at the College of Asia and the Pacific, Australian National University. He was former head of the School of Justice, Queensland University of Technology and Associate Professor with the Department of Sociology, University of Hong Kong. He received his PhD in Criminal Justice from the School of Law, University of Western Australia (UWA) and a MPhil from the Institute of Criminology, Cambridge University. He is an Associate Fellow of the Australian Institute of Criminology, Honorary Professor of the University of Hong Kong, and Honorary Research Fellow of the Crime Research Centre, UWA. He is founding editor of the *Asian Journal of Criminology* (published by Springer). With over 30 years of experience in the criminal justice system, his recent research has focused on cyber crime, crime victimization, lethal violence and transnational crime.

Ching Yee Chan is currently a Fellow of the Centre for Criminology, University of Hong Kong (HKU). She received her MPhil and PhD from the Departments of History and Sociology, HKU, in collective violence in China during the Cultural Revolution and lethal aggression in Hong Kong. She also has a Masters in forensic psychology from Leicester University. She currently teaches a variety of criminology courses at HKU. Her recent research has focused on the response of the criminal justice system to social changes with a focus on the use of custodial sentence in Hong Kong.

Wai To Chan worked in the Social Welfare Department (1977–85) with a variety of posts including Group and Community Work, Probation Officer, Aftercare Officer and Training Officer. He has been a Senior Lecturer of the Division of Social Studies, City University of Hong Kong since 1991 after serving the Hong Kong Polytechnic University as a Lecturer in Social Work for six years. He has Masters degrees in social science (socio-legal studies) from the University of Birmingham, England and in education from the Chinese University of Hong Kong. He has been appointed by the government to sit on Criminal and Law Enforcement Injuries Compensation Boards (1977–2003) and the Release under Supervision Board since 2003. He is the Secretary of the Executive Committee of the Society of Rehabilitation and Crime Prevention, Hong Kong.

Wing Hong Chui has recently been appointed as an Associate Professor in the Department of Social Work and Social Administration at the University of Hong Kong. Prior to this, he was Associate Professor in the School of Law at the Chinese University of Hong Kong. He completed his Masters and doctoral studies at the Institute of Criminology at the University of Cambridge. His areas of interest include youth studies, criminology and criminal justice, problem gambling, and migration studies. He has published several articles in the *Asian Journal of Criminology, Australian and New Zealand Journal of Criminology, European Journal of Criminology, Howard Journal of Criminal Justice, International Journal of Law, Crime and Justice* and *International Journal of Offender Therapy and Comparative Criminology*. He is co-editor of four books: *Moving Probation Forward* (with Mike Nellis 2003), *Social Work and Human Services Best Practice* (with Jill Wilson 2006), *Experiences of Transnational Chinese Migrants in the Asia-Pacific* (with David Ip and Ray Hibbins 2006), and *Research Methods for Law* (with Mike McConville 2007).

I. Grenville Cross SC has been the Director of Public Prosecutions of the Hong Kong Special Administrative Region since 1997. A graduate of the University of Southampton, he was called to the Bar by the Middle Temple. Mr Cross was appointed Queen's Counsel in 1990, and Senior Counsel in 1997. He is co-author of *Sentencing in Hong Kong* (5th edn) (with Patrick W.S. Cheung and Elaine Y.L. Tsui 2007), and Sentencing Editor of *Archbold Hong Kong*. Mr Cross is Adjunct Professor of Law, China University of Political Science and Law, Beijing.

Raymond W.K. Lau is an Associate Professor at the School of Arts and Social Sciences, The Open University of Hong Kong, teaching courses that range from Policing in Chinese Societies to Media, Culture and Society. In recent years, his research interests lie in criminal justice studies, social theory, and media sociology. He has published in refereed journals such as *International Journal of the Sociology of Law, Sociology* and *Media, Culture & Society*. He is currently planning a book on 'Fetishistic forms of rationality in contemporary modernity'.

King Wa Lee is currently a Research Fellow at the Centre for Criminology, University of Hong Kong. He received his PhD in criminology from the Department of Sociology in the same university. His research has focused on crime against businesses, comparative crime victimization, restorative justice, and organized crime. He has taught a variety of criminology and sociology courses in the University of Hong Kong and the Chinese University of Hong Kong. He is also a visiting scholar at the School of Justice, Queensland University of Technology.

T. Wing Lo is a Professor at the Department of Applied Social Studies, City University of Hong Kong, where he teaches criminology and social work. He graduated with a MPhil from the University of Hull and a PhD from the University of Cambridge. He has published articles in the *International Journal of Offender Therapy and Comparative Criminology, Social and Legal Studies, Asian Journal of Criminology, International Social Work, Journal of Youth Studies, Youth and Society, International Journal of Human Rights, Trends in Organised Crime*, and *Groupwork*. He is the author of *Corruption and Politics in Hong Kong and China* (1993) and *Fighting Youth Crime: A Comparative Study of Two Little Dragons in Asia* (with Alfred Choi, 2004), and has co-edited *Alternatives to Prosecution: Rehabilitative and Restorative Models of Youth Justice* (with Dennis Wong and Gabrielle Maxwell 2005) and *Youth Empowerment and Volunteerism: Principles, Policies and Practices* (with Elaine S.C. Au and Michael J. Holosko 2008). His research interests include corruption, youth justice, gang work, and group counselling.

Rebecca Ong is currently an Assistant Professor with the School of Law, City University of Hong Kong. She is a graduate of the University of London with a Masters in Law from both King's College, London and University of Strathclyde, Glasgow. She was called to the Bar by Lincoln's Inn and practised as an Advocate and

Solicitor in the High Court of Malaya for a number of years before joining academia. She has published in a number of refereed journals including the *International Journal of Law and Information Technology*, *Journal of Information Technology Law*, *International Review of Law and Information Technology*, and *International Journal of Intellectual Property Management*.

Tony Upham is admitted to practise as a solicitor in England and Wales and Hong Kong but is not currently in practice in either jurisdiction. He is currently an Associate Professor in the School of Law at City University of Hong Kong where he teaches Criminal Law, Criminal Procedure, Evidence and the Criminal Justice System. Before joining City University he was a Magistrate in the Judiciary of Hong Kong and prior to that he spent some 14 years as a solicitor in private practice in England. He is a contributor to *Archbold Hong Kong 2007* and co-author of *Criminal Litigation* (2nd edn) (with Christopher Knight 2002).

Simon N.M. Young is an Associate Professor in the Faculty of Law, University of Hong Kong (HKU) and Director of the Centre for Comparative and Public Law. Previously he was a Crown prosecutor for the Ministry of the Attorney General for Ontario in Toronto. He is a member of the Hong Kong Law Reform Commission sub-committees on hearsay in criminal proceedings and double jeopardy. His publications include *Hong Kong Evidence Casebook, The Essential Statutes on Hong Kong Criminal Law and Procedure 2007–8*, and two chapters in *Archbold Hong Kong 2007* on the law of human rights and hearsay. He is a practicing member of the Hong Kong Bar. The work described in his chapter was supported by a grant from the Central Policy Unit of the Government of the Hong Kong Special Administrative Region and the Research Grants Council of the Hong Kong Special Administrative Region, China (Project No. HKU 7023-PPR-20051).

Lena Y. Zhong is an Assistant Professor at the Department of Applied Social Studies, City University of Hong Kong where she teaches courses in criminology and applied sociology. Her research interests include Chinese policing, community crime prevention, and social capital. She is the author of *Communities, Crime and Social Capital in Contemporary China* (2008), and is currently conducting a study on cocaine abuse in Hong Kong. She is a member of the editorial board of *Asian Journal of Criminology*.

Preface and acknowledgements

The principal aim of initiating this book project is to provide students reading criminal justice, criminal procedure, police studies, public administration, and social work with an updated account on selected issues surrounding the administration of justice in Hong Kong. We are aware of the growth of criminological and criminal justice literature in Hong Kong in the last few years. However, our edited volume draws together a diverse group of talented academics and active researchers, each of whom brings a wealth of knowledge and experience in various practice areas and aspects of criminal justice. They are Roderic Broadhurst of Griffith University, Rebecca Ong, Wai To Chan, Tony Upham, and Lena Zhong of City University of Hong Kong, Raymond Lau of The Open University of Hong Kong, and Simon Young, King Wa Lee, and Ching Yee Chan of the University of Hong Kong. We are especially humbled by the contribution to this collection from the Director of Public Prosecution, I. Grenville Cross, in spite of his busy schedule. We sincerely hope that the outcome of our work is helpful to practitioners and students alike in the fields of criminal justice, social work, and law.

The impetus of this book was stimulated by a professional colleague and friend, Mark Israel, who is currently Professor in the School of Law at Flinders University, Adelaide. In his capacity as an external examiner of a law course entitled Criminal Justice between 2003 and 2005, he commented on the lack of indigenous teaching materials in delivering the course and drew attention to the utilization of dated textbooks – *Crime and Justice in Hong Kong* (edited by Jon Vagg and Harold Traver) and *Introduction to the Criminal Justice System* (edited by Mark S. Gaylord and Harold Traver) – which were published in 1991 and 1994 respectively. In this respect, another aim of this book is to analyze the changing nature and context of crime and its control in Hong Kong by referring to local news reports, research data, and authorities whenever and wherever possible.

Each chapter includes an introduction, structured coursework on a particular topic, concluding remarks by contributors, links to external resource information, review questions, and a chapter bibliography. While each contributor had a primary objective for their chapter, we have made every effort to ensure that the contributors applied a common style and provided cross-referencing across chapters. We have striven to ensure consistency and high quality in the material of the book, despite the fact that this was a challenging and time-consuming task. We do hope that readers find the book accessible and coherent.

Last but not the least, we are grateful to Dr Tina Rochelle, David Tuk Wai Leong and Sarah Laimayum who have assisted in proof-reading earlier drafts of various chapters. We also wish to express our deep gratitude to those contributors who were so diligent and willing to give their time and expertise in contributing to this publication. Without their support, the task of producing this book would have been neither fun nor enjoyable. Finally, we would like to thank Emma Gubb and Brian Willan for their encouragement in motivating us to complete this project.

Wing Hong Chui
T. Wing Lo

Chapter 1

Introduction and overview

Wing Hong Chui and T. Wing Lo

This book is an introduction to the administration of various agencies of the criminal justice system. It outlines some basic concepts in criminal law, which is a common approach of defining crime in Hong Kong, and analyzes the process of the criminal justice system, ranging from the report of a crime to the correctional system. Another aim of this book is to examine how the criminal justice personnel or actors work in practice, and how they deal with the offender and victim during the criminal justice process. This edited volume is designed as a prescribed or recommended text to both undergraduate and postgraduate students undertaking criminal justice and law as they embark on their studies. It may also be of interest to those individuals who would like to learn about arrangements for law enforcement, crime control, crime prevention, and methods for dealing with convicted offenders in Hong Kong. While this book is meant to be introductory, its ultimate goal is to persuade readers to adopt a more critical approach in order to understand the workings of the system and to encourage more empirical research on crime and justice. Instead of simply focusing on how different criminal justice organizations operate and function, throughout the text readers are encouraged to consider the arguments and debates that surround the controversial issues in the Hong Kong criminal justice system. For instance, how should we define crime? How can the legal system protect the rights of the victims? Should the police be given more powers to maintain law and order in society? How do judges make a decision in adjudicating the guilt of the defendant and sentencing? What is the best method of punishing criminals and preventing them from further offending? These issues are not only academic concerns but also 'the daily diet of much of our media' (Muncie and Wilson 2004: ix). In this introductory chapter, we will provide some background information about Hong Kong for the benefit of non-Hong Kong readers; Hong Kong is a former British colony and is now a special administrative region of the People's Republic of China (hereafter referred to as HKSAR). Selected themes and topics which subsequent chapters examine will be briefly considered in this opening chapter.

Administration of justice before and after 1 July 1997: an overview

At the outset, it should be emphasized that the following is a brief overview of the government structure in Hong Kong, and readers should consult some comprehensive textbooks on this area such as *Politics and Government: An Introduction* (Lam 1994) and *The Government and Politics of Hong Kong* (Miners 1998) for more details. Hong Kong, a special administrative region of the People's Republic of China, covers a small area of 423 square miles. However, by 2006 Hong Kong had an estimated population of over 6.9 million (Census and Statistics Department 2007). Hong Kong was a British colony for more than 150 years, from 1842 to 1997. The colonial status was a result of a series of Anglo-Chinese wars and their 'unequal' treaties, including the Treaty of Nanjing in 1842; Convention of Beijing in 1860; and the Second Convention of Beijing in 1898 (Lau 1997; Wesley-Smith 1998a; Tsang 2004). Hong Kong was governed by a British-appointed governor, assisted by senior civil servants, including a chief secretary, financial secretary, Attorney-General, and a group of secretaries responsible for various functions, such as education, health, social welfare, and transport (Lo 2000). Broadly speaking, there were two main branches of the government, namely the Executive and Legislative Councils. During the colonial rule, a large proportion of members of these two councils were primarily official and appointed unofficial members. The Executive Council functioned as the cabinet of the Governor, whereas the Legislative Council was responsible for making laws, debating issues of public interest, examining and approving public income and expenditure, and monitoring the work of the executive branches and administration of the government (Miners 1998). Two major constitutional documents handed down by the British Government were the Hong Kong *Letters Patent* and

Royal Instructions. These outlined the constitutional arrangements, including the powers and responsibilities of the Governor and the said Councils. In addition to the two branches, the judiciary, led by the Chief Justice, was independent of the central administration and legislature (Wesley-Smith 1998b). Jones with Vagg (2007) commented that in many respects law and organization of criminal justice in Hong Kong has a colonial origin, primarily from Great Britain, but they emphasized that the appointed Governor was given some latitude to address local customs and problems:

> In general terms, the key institutions and principles of English law were introduced and applied, but the introduction of the rule of law probably owed as much to the *realpolitik* of the colonial rule as the 'civilising mission' – experience elsewhere had taught the Colonial Office that the best means of establishing the *pax Britannica* was by attaching the native population to colonial rule through rule of law and associated institutions (2007: 3).

Despite the lack of democracy, the rule of law has been regarded as a cornerstone of Hong Kong's success as a leading international commercial and financial centre since colonial days. The rights and freedom of citizens were protected, and the rule of law was upheld by the independence of the Judiciary. The functioning of the capitalist system and way of life in Hong Kong indicates that the rule of law had worked very well before the resumption of the exercise of sovereignty over Hong Kong by the People's Republic of China.

In accordance with the principle of 'one country, two systems', the capitalist system of the HKSAR will retain its existing social and economic systems for 50 years from 1 July 1997. The *Basic Law of the Hong Kong Special Administrative Region of the People's Republic of China* (hereafter referred to as *Basic Law*) has replaced *Letters Patent* and *Royal Instructions* as the main constitutional document in Hong Kong. There are several principles enshrined under the *Basic Law*. For instance, Article 5 states that 'the socialist system and policies shall not be practised in the [HKSAR], and the previous capitalist system and way of life shall remain unchanged for 50 years'. Article 2 specifies that the governance of the HKSAR will exercise a high degree of autonomy, except in defence and foreign affairs, and enjoy executive, legislative, and independent judicial power. In many ways, the Hong Kong legal system has survived alongside the political, economic, and social systems. Article 8 states that the laws previously in force in Hong Kong, that is, the common law, rules of equity, ordinances, customary law shall be maintained, except for any that contravene the *Basic Law* and subject to any amendment by the legislature of the HKSAR. Several provisions are concerned with the rights and responsibilities of the Hong Kong residents. Articles 25 and 26 assure that all residents shall be equal before the law and permanent residents of the HKSAR shall have the right to vote and the right to stand for election in accordance with the law. Article 28 specifies that no one shall be subjected to arbitrary or unlawful arrest, detention, or imprisonment, and arbitrary or unlawful search of the body of any resident or deprivation or restriction of the freedom of the person shall be prohibited.

There were several significant changes in terms of the government structure in Hong Kong after the transfer of sovereignty. The following are some examples. Firstly, the Governor is replaced by the Chief Executive who is elected by a representative Election Committee in accordance with Annex I of the *Basic Law*, and the Chief Executive is appointed by the Central People's Government in Beijing. The Chief Executive is responsible for implementing the *Basic Law*, signing bills and budgets, promulgating laws, making decisions on government policies, and issuing Executive Orders. Secondly, the Attorney-General is now called the Secretary for Justice. Other features of the Government have remained basically the same. The Secretary for Justice, now appointed by the Central People's Government upon nomination by the Chief Executive, is the principal legal advisor to the Chief Executive, to the Government, and the individual government departments and agencies. Thirdly, the Court of Final Appeal was established to replace the United Kingdom's Privy Council as the highest appellate court which is headed by the Chief Justice (see Chapter 9). Despite these changes, the administration of criminal justice has remained unchanged. In addition to the Judiciary, several key government departments that are responsible for maintaining law and order, fighting crime, enforcing law, and rehabilitating offenders include: Department of Justice, Hong Kong Police Force, Immigration Department, Independent Commission Against Corruption, Customs and Excise Department, Labour Department, Fire Services Department, Legal Aid Department, Social Welfare Department, and Correctional Services Department. It is worth pointing out that while crime control is still very much the state's business and privatization of criminal justice organizations is not common in Hong Kong, there has been a birth of private policing in places such as banks, shopping malls and private residential areas.

Laws, crimes and victims

This book can be divided into two main parts. Chapters 2 to 4 deal with the nature of law, crimes, and victims, whereas the remaining chapters examine different themes and issues surrounding the criminal justice system in Hong Kong. While acknowledging the varied definitions of crime (Hagan 1987; Williams 2005), Rebecca Ong defines crime primarily from a legal perspective. Chapter 2 provides a general overview of criminal law in Hong Kong by examining the function and purposes of criminal law and elements for criminal liability. Using case law, three basic elements of crime, including *actus reus*, *mens rea*, and defence are discussed. The chapter then goes on to deal with a number of specific offences, including offences against the person, offences against property, offences against public order, offences against public interest, and offences against morals and public policy. It is a well-known fact that the formal legalist definition of crime is commonly adopted in most industrialized countries, and 'no matter how immoral, reprehensible, damaging or dangerous an act is, it is not a crime unless it is made by the authorities of the State' (Williams 2005: 12). In this respect, the legal conception of crime determines how we measure the level and volume of crime.

In Chapter 3, Roderic Broadhurst, King Wa Lee and Ching Yee Chan conclude that Hong Kong has become one of the world's safest metropolises. They argue that this is reflected in the low official crime and victimization rates – confirmed by both government and United Nations crime victim surveys. Various sources of official data such as police records and prison statistics were used to analyze crime trends. In addition to the United Nations crime victim surveys, several crime victimization surveys conducted by the Census and Statistics Department were also used as an alternative method of measuring the nature and extent of crime. Despite the low crime rate, Hong Kong's anti-crime efforts and support of law enforcement are reflected in the relatively high incarceration rate (176.8 per 100,000 in 2005) and a large police service (486.6 police per 100,000 in 2000). An average of 10 per cent of total public expenditure is devoted to security. The role of the Government and other factors in contributing to a relatively safe environment is discussed in this chapter. Cultural factors such as utilitarian familism, Confucianism and extended kinship structures are often cited as contributing factors to the low crime rates. Analysis indicates that most Hong Kong citizens are conformist and public attitudes favour a government that is hostile to crime and supportive of severe punishment to adult offenders.

Apart from studying the number of criminals and the volume of crime, Chapter 4 considers in what ways the victim plays an important role in the process of criminal justice. For example, the victim reports an offence to the police, makes a statement, attends identification parades, and gives their time by attending court as a witness. Regrettably, amid the criminal justice process, legal professionals are inclined to direct attention to details of an actual offence or the criminal's need by disposing lenient sentences. Consequently, the victims of crime do not get the proper attention they deserve, and which their role in the justice system affords them. Indeed, this chapter also examines whether criminal law processes are sufficiently dealing with the victim. Wai To Chan comments that the current provision of victim programmes in Hong Kong seems to be hampered by the absence of a sound philosophical basis for action. The suggested improvement of *The Victims of Crime Charter* (Department of Justice 2003) and the proposed use of mediation and reparation schemes could be the first step in the course of promoting restorative justice in society. It is hoped that crime victims have the right to be treated with courtesy and respect by criminal justice professionals and they are given a prompt and proper response to complaints of crime (Lo 2000).

Stages of the criminal justice system

The second part of the book covers various aspects of the criminal justice process, including law enforcement, criminal courts, the penal system, and crime prevention. Broadly speaking, these chapters are concerned with three stages of the justice system: the pre-trial stage, trial stage, and post-trial stage. The pre-trial stage refers to those actions or activities that take place after a crime is reported to the police and before the defendant is summoned to appear in court. The trial stage covers the process and procedures that take place within the judicial system. Attention has been paid to highlight the distinctions between what happens in lower and higher courts. The post-trial stage is concerned with the treatment of an offender after being convicted and sentenced. However, it is important to bear in mind that the linear and logical progression of justice from a crime being reported, through investigation or arrest, preparing for court, appearing in court, sentencing, and punishment may not necessarily follow one to another in real life. There are a number of decisions made along these three stages by the principal actors of the criminal justice system. Their decision-making process or use of discretion directly affects how a suspect is processed at various stages of the criminal justice system and whether a defendant will be convicted (Gelsthorpe and Padfield 2003).

Chapters 5 and 6 examine two major actors in the pre-trial stage of the criminal justice system, including the police and prosecutor. These two are referred to as 'gatekeepers' of the criminal justice system. Police officers are authorized to stop and search individuals in a public place, request to see the person's proof of identity, and arrest and interrogate a person if they have 'reasonable suspicion' (Whitford 2006). Among other powers, a senior police officer should decide whether there is sufficient evidence to lay a charge against the suspect, whether it is necessary to seek the advice of the Department of Justice in relation to their decision to initiate prosecution, and whether it is appropriate to exercise the discretionary power to divert a suspect from the formal criminal justice system.

In Chapter 5, Raymond Lau analyzes the changing police organization from a historical perspective. The Hong Kong Police Force (HKPF) was established in the mid-nineteenth century, following Britain's acquisition of Hong Kong as a crown colony from China in 1842. After hesitant beginnings, it soon developed into a classic paramilitary colonial force. This lasted well into the early 1970s. The colonial administration was always wary of the loyalty of the rank and file, following India's and Pakistan's independence in 1947, whereupon the South Asian rank and file returned home en masse. Thus the HKPF was composed overwhelmingly of locals. However, to its surprise, in the disturbances of the late 1960s, the local rank and file took an active part in the suppression of patriotic protesters. Corruption was always a problem, but it reached highly organized and epidemic proportions after the Second World War. After the late-1960s disturbances, the colonial administration engineered a radical shift in governance style, under which a determined effort to root out police corruption was made in the mid-1970s despite fierce police resistance. This initiated a shift of the HKPF from a force focused on maintaining public order to a double emphasis on both public order and crime fighting. In the early 1990s, following Britain's lead, the HKPF vowed to change from a force into a service. This chapter provides an analysis of the future prospects of the reform endeavour.

Chapter 6 investigates the general prosecution practice and policy in Hong Kong. More specifically, I. Grenville Cross introduces the role and function of the Department of Justice. The *Basic Law* provides that the Department of Justice shall control criminal prosecutions, free from any interference. At the same time, private prosecutions may be instituted by aggrieved persons. The courts are loathe to interfere with a decision to prosecute, but retain an inherent discretion to prevent an abuse of process. Throughout criminal proceedings, the role of the prosecutor is vital. No one should be prosecuted unless there is sufficient evidence and a prosecution is in the public interest. At court, the prosecutor must be firm and fair, and should not press for a conviction at all costs. The functions of the prosecutor and the investigator are separate and distinct. The prosecutor should safeguard the interests of victims and witnesses, for without their co-operation the guilty will escape justice. At trial, the prosecutor must assist the court to avoid appealable error. If there is an appeal against conviction or sentence, the duty of the prosecutor is to ensure that a just disposal of the appeal is achieved.

Chapters 7 to 9 are trial chapters which examine the role of criminal courts, sentencing options and policy, and the appellate courts in Hong Kong. Chapter 7 examines the role, powers, and responsibilities of Hong Kong's criminal trial courts, namely the Magistrates' Court, District Court, and Court of First Instance. Each of these courts takes its powers from its enabling ordinance. It is important to appreciate that if the enabling ordinance does not give the court power to do what it has done, the act is a nullity. All criminal cases start in the Magistrates' Court in the sense that this is where a defendant facing an allegation of crime will first appear. The case is either dealt with in the Magistrates' Court or transferred to the District Court or the Court of First Instance. Tony Upham examines how criminal proceedings usually commence, and provides an overview of the process and procedure of a criminal case through the three types of courts. In addition, this chapter also argues that a cornerstone of the common law is the jury. Trial by jury is reserved for the most serious criminal offences. As will be seen, some cases must be tried before a judge and jury in the Court of First Instance, while other cases may be tried there if the prosecution chooses. There is no jury either in the Magistrates' Court or in the District Court. The division of responsibility between the judge and the jury will be examined as well as the role, composition, and responsibility of the jury.

The two main functions of the court are to adjudicate whether the defendant is guilty and to impose appropriate sanctions or punishments on the convicted individual. Simon Young, in Chapter 8, outlines the purposes and principles which animate the law of sentencing in Hong Kong. It identifies and describes the range of options or measures available to the Hong Kong court when sentencing an individual for a criminal offence. Sentencing is the responsibility of the magistrate or judge. In trying to arrive at a just and appropriate sentence, the sentencing judge has a difficult task as the purposes and principles will often push the severity of the sentence in opposite directions. Hong Kong is a place with constitutional rights and remedies, and thus the law of sentencing must necessarily be informed by overarching constitutional values and principles. The sentence in every case must not only heed such fundamental rights but also be responsive to the interests of the victim and community.

The right to an appeal or a review for the conviction and sentence is also granted in the criminal justice system. The right is grounded in ordinance. Article 11(4) of the Hong Kong *Bill of Rights Ordinance* stipulates that everyone convicted of a crime shall have the right to his or her conviction and sentence being reviewed by a higher tribunal according to law. Tony Upham discusses the different avenues of appeal which are open to the convicted. The grounds for appeals against conviction and sentence are discussed, and the process of the application for review and prosecution appeals is described in Chapter 9. Three types of court with appellate jurisdiction over criminal matters in Hong Kong are the Court of First Instance, Court of Appeal, and Court of Final Appeal.

Once the sentence has been imposed on the criminal, he or she is expected to comply with the conditions imposed from the court. There are three main types of sentencing options, namely unsupervised (such as fines and binding over order), supervised (such as probation order and community service order) and custodial sentences (such as detention centre order and imprisonment). The ultimate goal of these sentences is to reintegrate offenders into the community and to turn them into becoming law-abiding citizens. Corporal punishment and the death penalty were abolished in Hong Kong in 1989 and 1993 respectively (Lo 2000). To determine an appropriate sentence for an offender, the court may obtain and consider information about his or her character, physical and mental conditions, schooling, employment, and family circumstances. This information is provided through a wide range of reports prepared by probation officers, prison officers, psychologists, psychiatrists, and medical officers. If necessary, the Young Offender Assessment Panel are asked to examine specific cases thoroughly and advise the court on the appropriate sentence for young offenders (Choi and Lo 2004).

A consistent theme emerging from Chapters 10 and 11 is that the ethos of rehabilitation is the dominant sentencing theory and the main intervention method of dealing with offenders. In the post-trial stage, two principal government departments that work with offenders in the community and prison are the Social Welfare Department and Correctional Services Department. In Chapter 10, Wing Hong Chui introduces the concept of community sentencing. In contrast to the custodial sentencing option, community sentence is a non-punitive approach targeting first-time, non-violent offenders who pose little threat to society. The theoretical underpinning of the probation order and community service order are discussed. Major justifications for community sentences are diversion or deinstitutionalization, reintegration (or rehabilitation) and reparation. He points out that the Social Welfare Department is primarily staffed by trained social workers who employ various treatment models and interventions to promote pro-social behaviour among those being given community sentences. The ingredients of effective intervention with offenders are highlighted drawing upon empirical evidence. The chapter points to the importance of developing a more systematic and evidence-based criminal justice social work intervention for offenders. Chapter 11 is concerned with the role and function of the Correctional Services Department (CSD), formerly the Prison Department. Lo describes that the CSD is a disciplinary force, administering a detention centre, drug addiction treatment centres, rehabilitation centres, training centres, and prisons for offenders aged 14 years of age or above. In addition, its halfway houses offer temporary shelter for young offenders during their adjustment period after release. Various examples of rehabilitative programmes within the prison are cited to illustrate the commitment of the CSD to achieve the goal of offender rehabilitation.

Consistent with what Roderic Broadhurst and others find, Lena Zhong opines that Hong Kong is among the safest cities around the world, both in terms of official crime statistics and crime victim surveys. Chapter 12 first introduces the definition of crime prevention, with special emphases placed on the multi-faceted nature of crime prevention and the multi-agency approach to crime prevention. Secondly, the three most commonly used typologies of crime prevention, namely the public health model, the social/situational model, and Tonry and Farrington's Four-level Model, are reviewed. Drawing on the definition and typologies, it reviews various locally initiated crime prevention measures, including some innovative ones. The chapter emphasizes that crime prevention measures in Hong Kong should be subject to more vigorous evaluations to assess their effectiveness.

Finally, we want to stress that it is beyond the scope of this introductory text to cover all aspects of criminal justice in Hong Kong. However, its coverage reflects what we believe is essential knowledge that students coming to the field for the first time should acquire. Despite there being 12 chapters and a wide range of topics examined, there are a number of areas that are not included. If space had allowed, we would have liked to discuss the rights of defendants, the role of defence lawyers, and the operation and specific function of various law enforcement organizations which also play an important role in fighting crime. Some examples of these organizations are the Independent Commission Against Corruption, Customs and Excise Department, Department of Immigration, and Labour Department. Also, a more detailed analysis of the specific criminal procedure for juvenile and mentally disordered offenders should have been discussed. In this respect, readers are advised to consult other textbooks such as Gaylord and Traver (1994), Wesley-Smith (1998a), Jackson (2003), Jiao (2007), Jones with Vagg (2007) and Whitford (2006) or the websites listed at the end of this chapter for further details.

References

Census and Statistics Department (2007) *Hong Kong 2006 Population By-census – Main Tables*. Hong Kong: Government Printer.

Choi, A. and Lo, T.W. (2004) *Fighting Youth Crime: A Comparative Study of Two Little Dragons in Asia* (2nd edn). Singapore: Eastern Universities Press.

Department of Justice (2003) *The Victims of Crime Charter*. Hong Kong: Government Printer. Available at: http://www.doj.gov.hk/eng/public/pub200004.htm

Gaylord, M.S. and Traver, H. (eds) (1994) *Introduction to the Hong Kong Criminal Justice System*. Hong Kong: Hong Kong University Press.

Gelsthorpe, L. and Padfield, N. (eds) (2003) *Exercising Discretion: Decision-making in the Criminal Justice System and Beyond*. Cullompton, Devon: Willan.

Hagan, J. (1987) *Modern Criminology: Crime, Criminal Behavior, and its Control*. New York: McGraw-Hill.

Jackson, M. (2003) *Criminal Law in Hong Kong*. Hong Kong: Hong Kong University Press.

Jiao, A.Y. (2007) *The Police in Hong Kong: A Contemporary View*. Lanham, MA: University Press of America.

Jones, C. with Vagg, J. (2007) *Criminal Justice in Hong Kong*. London: Routledge-Cavendish.

Lam, J.T.M. (1994) *Politics and Government: An Introduction*. Hong Kong: Writers' and Publishers' Cooperative.

Lau, C.K. (1997) *Hong Kong's Colonial Legacy: A Hong Kong Chinese's View of the British Heritage*. Hong Kong: The Chinese University Press.

Lo, T.W. (2000) 'An overview of the criminal justice system in Hong Kong', in O.N.I. Ebbe (ed.) *Comparative and International Criminal Justice Systems: Policing, Judiciary, and Corrections* (2nd edn) (pp. 113–28). Boston: Butterworth-Heinemann.

Miners, N. (1998) *The Government and Politics of Hong Kong* (5th edn). Hong Kong: Oxford University Press.

Muncie, J. and Wilson, D. (2004) 'Editors' introduction', in J. Muncie and D. Wilson (eds) *Student Handbook of Criminal Justice and Criminology* (pp. ix–xi). London: Cavendish.

Tsang, S. Y-S. (2004) *A Modern History of Hong Kong*. London: I.B. Tauris.

Wesley-Smith, P. (1998a) *Unequal Treaty, 1898–1997: China, Great Britain, and Hong Kong's New Territories* (Revised edn). Hong Kong: Oxford University Press.

Wesley-Smith, P. (1998b) *An Introduction to the Hong Kong Legal System* (3rd edn). Hong Kong: Oxford University Press.

Whitford, A. (2006) *Criminal Procedure in Hong Kong: A Guide for Students and Practitioners*. Hong Kong: LexisNexis.

Williams, K.S. (2005) *Textbook on Criminology* (5th edn). Oxford: Oxford University Press.

Legislations cited

Basic Law of the Hong Kong Special Administrative Region of the People's Republic of China

Hong Kong Bill of Rights Ordinance (Cap. 383)

Letters Patent (Hong Kong)

Royal Instructions (Hong Kong)

Relevant websites

Basic Law of the Hong Kong Special Administrative Region of the People's Republic of China	http://www.info.gov.hk/basic_law/flash.html
Customs and Excise Department	http://www.customs.gov.hk/
Correctional Services Department	http://www.csd.gov.hk/
Department of Justice	http://www.doj.gov.hk/
Fire Services Department	http://www.hkfsd.gov.hk/home/
Hong Kong Police Force	http://www.police.gov.hk/
Immigration Department	http://www.immd.gov.hk/index.html

Independent Commission Against Corruption	http://www.icac.org.hk/
Labour Department	http://www.labour.gov.hk/eng/news/content.htm
Legal Aid Department	http://www.lad.gov.hk/
Security Bureau	http://www.sb.gov.hk/
Social Welfare Department	http://www.swd.gov.hk/en/index/index.html

Chapter 2

Criminal law

Rebecca Ong

Introduction

Criminal law is a branch of law that deals with the punishment of an offender for wrongs committed against society. The 'wrong' or crime can be an act (stealing) or an omission to act (failure to drive carefully) that the courts consider punishable so as to deter others from committing the offence. The courts will deal with such cases by sentencing the offender to a term of imprisonment or by imposing other forms of non-custodial sentences such as ordering the offender to pay a fine, serve a community service order, or to be placed on probation. It can thus be said that the purpose of criminal law is not only to protect societal interests but also to maintain and regulate societal conduct and behaviour. Who therefore bears this responsibility of protecting the public? It is the government; which is why it is the government that generally initiates criminal proceedings (prosecutes) in the courts. For example, in *HKSAR v Wong*, it is the Hong Kong government against the person charged, Wong, who is also known as the defendant in the case. Before a defendant can be convicted, it is the prosecutor's duty to prove the defendant's guilt 'beyond reasonable doubt'. This is the standard of proof (see *Kwan Ping Bong v R* (1979) HKLR 1). If reasonable doubt is created in respect of any elements of the offence the defendant is charged with, the prosecution is said not to have made its case and the defendant will be acquitted. The standard of proof coupled with the presumption that a defendant is innocent unless proven guilty (presumption of innocence) imposes an onerous burden on the prosecutor.

Function of criminal law

Although criminal law can be seen as intrusive to the individual's civil liberties, criminal law is one of every nation's cornerstone laws, without which society would be in turmoil. This is because the function of criminal law is to regulate, maintain, and enforce social conduct by discouraging behaviour that is harmful to society as well as behaviour that challenges the government's authority and legitimacy, for instance riots and public disorder. With the aim of enforcing society's more favourable behaviour in mind, criminal law focuses on the use of criminal sanctions for penalizing (or punishing) the offender. Criminal sanctions are seen as serving the purposes of criminal law in that they tend to (a) incapacitate the offender from harming society during his or her period of imprisonment, (b) rehabilitate the offender, enabling him or her to change the behaviour of harming others, (c) retribute the offender for the harm done and (d) deter the offender from engaging in the prohibited conduct in the future. These sanctions vary from the most severe death penalty (although abolished in many jurisdictions) to imposition of fines and community service orders. Sanctions are imposed and effected through a combination of various organizations such as the courts, the police, the prison service, and the Social Welfare Department. The penal system differs from the way in which civil wrongs are dealt with. In a civil case, for example, an individual who has suffered injuries as a result of being supplied with defective products may bring an action in negligence which entitles the wronged person to be compensated (or paid damages). Negligence is a type of tort and is a civil wrong.[1] In addition to the difference in the 'remedy' afforded in criminal law and civil wrongs, it must be noted that in civil proceedings as opposed criminal proceedings, the burden of proving the case at hand is on the plaintiff. For example, in *Donoghue v Stevenson* [1932] All ER Rep 1] the House of Lords held that the plaintiff, Donoghue, had to prove that the manufacturer breached its duty of care in not ensuring that reasonable care had been taken in the preparation and manufacture of the product. This is especially so where it is intended that the product reaches and is consumed by the ultimate consumer in the same condition as it had left the manufacturer without any possibility of intermediate examination. The standard for which the plaintiff has to prove fault on the part of the defendant manufacturer however is lower, that is, on the balance of probabilities. Essentially, this means that the plaintiff has to prove that it is more likely than not that the manufacturer had breached his duty to take care.

Sources of criminal law

The main sources of Hong Kong criminal law are laws developed through the courts or judge-made law (common law) and law made by the Legislative Council (Ordinances). Common law is still very much part of Hong Kong law despite the return of sovereignty to the People's Republic of China (Articles 8 and 18 of the *Basic Law*). Its importance cannot be overlooked as older crimes such as murder and assault established by common law continue to be recognized. The same holds true for common law defences like insanity and duress. Notwithstanding this, offences established by ordinances are becoming the norm. In fact, these statutory offences are the most common form of offences. Some examples of statutory offences include noisy or disorderly behaviour in a public place, punishable by 12 months' imprisonment and a fine of HK$5,000: section 17B(2) of the *Public Order Ordinance* (Cap. 245); being a member of a triad society contrary to section 20(2) of the *Societies Ordinance* (Cap. 151), punishable on first conviction to 3 years' imprisonment and a fine of HK$100,000; possessing or using an identity card belonging to another, punishable on indictment by 10 years' imprisonment (or summarily by 2 years' imprisonment) and a fine of HK$100,000 (HK$50,000): section 7A(1A) of the *Registration of Persons Ordinance* (Cap. 177); and obtaining property by deception, punishable by an imprisonment of 20 years: section 17(1) of the *Theft Ordinance* (Cap. 210).

Categorization of offences

In Hong Kong, criminal offences are divided into categories according to their seriousness. Summary offences are the least serious offences which are dealt with by the Magistrates' Court summarily. Such offences include causing obstruction in a public place (section 4A of the *Summary Offences Ordinance*, Cap. 228) or careless driving (section 38 of the *Road Traffic Ordinance*, Cap. 374). Very serious offences such as murder, manslaughter, rape, and drug trafficking are dealt with on indictment. Where the accused has entered a plea of 'Not guilty' to these offences, they may be heard before a judge and a jury of seven lay people in the Court of First Instance (CFI) of the High Court (see also Chapters 7 and 9 of this volume for details). In a trial by jury (also known as a trial by your peers), the judge will urge the jury to reach a unanimous verdict on whether the defendant is guilty or not guilty. The jury may, in failing to reach unanimity, arrive at a majority verdict of five to two. Between summary and indictable offences is a hybrid offence categorized as offences triable either way. These offences can be dealt with either in the Magistrates' Court, in the District Court, or in the CFI depending on the seriousness of the offence.

Criminal liability and elements of crime

Criminal liability is based on the premise that an individual has committed an act prohibited by law. It is thus necessary to determine the prohibited act. This is done by looking at the elements of the offence at common law or under the relevant ordinance. For example, for the offence of theft, section 2(1) of the *Theft Ordinance* provides 'A person commits theft if he dishonestly appropriates property belonging to another with the intention of permanently depriving the other of it'. Sections 3–7 of the *Theft Ordinance* further provide the definitions of the essential elements that constitute the offence of theft as provided for in section 2 above, such as dishonesty, appropriation, property belonging to another, and the intention of permanently depriving. The individual is only criminally liable if the prosecution can prove the prohibited act (*actus reus*) coupled with the guilty state of mind (*mens rea*). Both these elements must co-exist; one without the other will not do. This can be seen from the principle '*actus non facit reum nisi mens sit rea*':[2] 'an act alone does not make a person criminally liable, the mind must also be legally blameworthy'. However, for offences of strict liability, the co-existence of both elements of *actus reus* and *mens rea* are not necessary. This is also the position in civil proceedings, for example in a breach of contract or tort. It is usually not necessary to prove a subjective mental element to establish liability in these cases, although if a breach is intentionally committed, it may lead to an increase in the measure of damages payable to the plaintiff as compensation.

Actus reus

The *actus reus* is the sum of all the elements of the offence other than the *mens rea*. As such, the whole *actus reus* must be proved to establish criminal liability. However, *actus reus* does not always have to be a positive act. Liability can also be imposed for the failure to act. This can arise where there is a legal duty to act as a result of a parent–child relationship or where the obligation to care for another is undertaken. Examples can be seen in *R v Stone and Dobinson* [1977] QB 354, where the defendant had undertaken to care for his anorexic sister but a failure to seek proper medical care resulted in her death, or where the defendant had created a dangerous situation and had failed to act. In *R v Miller* [1983] 2 AC 161, for example, the defendant was convicted of arson (criminal damage) for failing to take steps to extinguish a fire which he accidentally started. *Actus reus* is also established where the statute imposes a duty on the individual to act in a particular manner and the individual has failed to so act. Such instances include a failure to administer proper care resulting in injuries to a child (section 27 of the *Offences Against the Persons Ordinance* (Cap. 212), the failure to file a tax return (section 80(1) of the *Inland Revenue Ordinance* (Cap. 112) and the failure to report a motor vehicle accident (section 56(3) of the *Road Traffic Ordinance*).

It should also be noted that *actus reus* can include the act itself, which does not require proof of result, for example drink driving, or it can include the circumstances in which the act occurred, for example having intercourse with a person under 16 years. *Actus reus* may also just be the consequence of the act, for instance criminal damage.

Causation

The defendant is not liable unless the prosecution proves a causal link exists between the defendant's act and the prohibited consequences. It must be shown that the defendant's act is the operative, substantial, and effective cause of the consequence. As such, there is no *actus reus* if the defendant's course of conduct fails to bring about the prohibited consequences, for example there is no assault if the individual at whom the defendant is directing his fist, ducks. There may nevertheless be a charge of attempted assault. In *R v White* [1910] 1 KB 124, as the mother died of natural causes rather than as a result of the defendant's poisoning, the 'but for' test was not satisfied. The mother would have died anyway irrespective of the defendant's act of poisoning. The 'but for' test of causation can be illustrated by reference to the facts which arose in *R v Pagett* [1983] 76 Cr App R 279. In *Pagett*, a hostage used by the defendant as a shield was shot and killed by police. The shots fired by the police were in self-defence in response to the shots fired by the defendant. Unfortunately, when responding to the shots fired by the defendant, the police failed to see the hostage in the dark. Thus, the question in relation to the defendant's liability has to be answered by asking whether the hostage would have died *but for* the defendant's conduct? If a causal link does exist, for instance between the pulling of the trigger and the resulting injuries or death, then it matters not that the defendant's act is one of a number of causes of the prohibited consequence nor would it be an excuse for the defendant to claim that the victim hastened his own death by refusing medical treatment (a blood transfusion) as in *R v Blaue* [1975] 3 All ER 446.

Novus actus interveniens

As mentioned earlier, the defendant does not commit an offence if a causal link between his prohibited act and the prohibited consequences is not established. Accordingly, it is possible for an independent intervening act by a third party to break this causal link. The causal link, however, is not broken if the third party's intervening act was foreseeable by the defendant or if the medical treatment received by the victim was inadequate or negligent, as in *R v Smith* [1959] 2 All ER 193. In *Smith*, a soldier's death was the result of a combination of unfortunate events, including being dropped several times on the way to the medical station and wrong medical treatment. Smith, however, was convicted of murder since his act of stabbing the soldier with his bayonet was the operative and substantial cause of death.

Mens rea

As *mens rea* is the mental element of an offence, the commission of a prohibited act will not render the person guilty of an offence unless it is accompanied with a guilty mind – '*actus non facit reum nisi mens sit rea*'.[3] As such, once the defendant is found responsible for committing the physical elements (*actus reus*) of the offence, he or she must also be shown to have the necessary mental state for its commission. The mental state (*mens rea*) of an offence can include intention, recklessness, and negligence. Thus it must be proven that the defendant intended the consequences of the prohibited act or that he or she was reckless as to its consequences or that he or she cared not what the consequences were.

Mens rea varies with each offence. For example, for the offence of theft the prosecution needs to prove the defendant intended to dishonestly deprive the rightful owner permanently of his or her goods, while in manslaughter it is acting recklessly thereby causing death as in *Kong Cheuk-kwan v R* [1986] HKLR 648. In *Kong Cheuk-kwan,* the commanding officers of both the hydrofoil ferries which were involved in the tragic collision ferrying passengers to and from Hong Kong and Macau were held liable when their navigational acts created an obvious and serious risk of causing physical injury to others. In *R v Adomako* [1995] 1 AC 171, the *mens rea* was a grossly negligent act (omission) resulting in death. In *Adomako,* an anaesthetist was held to have breached his duty when he failed to notice and reconnect a tube that had become disconnected during an operation.

Intention

In its narrow sense, intention can be said simply to mean the defendant intended the consequences of his or her prohibited act or a result is intended if it is the purpose of the doer. However, through a combination of various common law decisions, intention has taken on a much wider meaning. In order to determine intention, foresight of consequences and the extent to which the consequences might have been foreseen is important. In *R v Moloney* [1985] AC 905 and *R v Hancock & Shankland* [1986] 2 WLR 35, it was held that questions of whether death was a natural and probable consequence of the prohibited act and the degree of probability will be relevant. The defendant cannot be said to have the culpable mental state if he or she had merely foreseen the consequences of the prohibited act, although foresight of the consequences is admissible as evidence of the defendant's intention. In such cases, it is necessary to prove that the defendant is virtually certain of the probability of that consequence occurring as a result of his or her act (*R v Nedrick* [1986] 1 WLR 1025). This was so in *Nedrick* where it was the defendant's intention to burn out the woman living in the house when he poured flammable liquid through the front door letterbox of the house and set it alight. However, instead of the woman, her child was killed.

In Hong Kong, it has been accepted that if the juries are to be directed on the defendant's foresight, the 'virtual certainty' direction would be the correct direction to be given. This was so in *R v Wong Tak Shing* [1989] 2 HKC 94, where the court held that juries should be directed that they may infer that a result is intended, though not desired, when the result is a virtually certain consequence of the act and the doer knows that it is a virtually certain consequence. It should be noted, however, that whether or not a defendant intends or foresees a consequence is determined by the court or the jury by reference to all the evidence, drawing such inferences from the evidence as appear proper in the circumstances. This is provided for in section 65A of the *Criminal Procedure Ordinance* (Cap. 221) which states:

> A court or jury in determining whether a person has committed an offence
> (a) shall not be bound in law to infer that he intended or foresaw a result of his acts or omissions by reason only of its being a natural and probable consequence of those acts or omissions but
> (b) shall decide whether he did intend or foresee that result by reference to all the evidence drawing such inferences from the evidence as appear in the circumstances.

Recklessness

As far as recklessness as a mental state is concerned, a person is reckless if he or she consciously and wilfully takes on an unjustifiable risk. This is subjective recklessness: where the defendant knew there was a risk or has foreseen the risk and proceeded to take it was provided for in *R v Cunningham* [1957] 2 QB 396. Although narrow, the subjective test was adopted by the House of Lords in *R v R and G* [2003] UKHL 50. The latter case involved criminal damage by fire when the defendants, two young boys of 11 and 12 years, set fire to some newspapers in the back of the store which had spread extensively, damaging adjoining buildings. Caldwell recklessness, on the other hand, as enunciated in *R v Caldwell* [1982] AC 341, is a much broader concept, one in which a person can be liable if he or she takes on an obvious risk which no reasonable person would take (objective recklessness) and he or she did so either without giving any thought to the risk or he or she had consciously and wilfully ignored the consequences of the risk.

In Hong Kong, the opportunity to consider the application of the decision in *R v R and G* arose in *Sin Kam Wah & Anor v HKSAR* [2005] 8 HKCFAR 192. Sin, a senior police officer, was convicted of misconduct in a public office when he accepted free sexual services from prostitutes. The CFI in that case agreed that the Caldwell recklessness 'exposed the defendant who caused a risk of injury to another, of a serious crime although he did not genuinely perceive the risk'. This could lead to an unjust conviction of the defendant on the strength of not what the defendant had himself apprehended but on what another person would have apprehended. The court continued by holding that juries in Hong Kong should be directed in terms of *R v R and G*'s subjective interpretation of recklessness such that 'it had to be shown that the defendant's state of mind was culpable in that he acted recklessly in respect of a circumstance if he was aware of a risk that it would occur, and it was circumstances known to him, unreasonable to take the risk'. *Sin* was an important decision in that in addition to clarifying Hong Kong's position with respect to recklessness, the court went further to hold that the defendant must genuinely appreciate or foresee the risks involved in his actions before he can be held liable. Failure to appreciate or foresee the risks of his or her actions can be due to age or personal characteristics of the defendant. It should be noted that cases decided on Caldwell recklessness such as *R v Chau Ming Cheong* [1983] 1 HKC 6 and *R v Dung Shue Wah* [1983] HKC, were overruled in *Sin*. In *R v Chau Ming Cheong,* the defendant was convicted of manslaughter for his gross indifference to his wife's beatings of his four-year-old child, causing the child's death.

Knowledge

The defendant can also be required to prove he or she had knowledge of the circumstances. This can arise if the establishment of the offences refers to the existence of specified circumstances. For example, section 118(3) of the *Crimes Ordinance* (Cap. 200) provides 'a man commits rape if (a) he has unlawful sexual intercourse with a woman who at the time of the intercourse does not consent to it; and (b) at that time he *knows* that she does not consent to the intercourse or he is reckless as to whether she consents to it'.

In the offence of rape, knowledge can be actual knowledge that the woman does not consent to intercourse or that the defendant is reckless or indifferent as to whether she consents or not. In determining recklessness, the courts will adopt the subjective test laid down in *Sin Kam Wah & Anor* [2005] 8 HKCFAR 192 (for brief facts of *Sin,* see above).

Strict liability

Although in most cases the prosecution must prove *mens rea* in respect of any one of the elements of *actus reus,* there are offences which do not require such proof. Such offences are called strict liability offences. Strict liability offences do exist at common law. The majority, however, are created by statute. It can be said that strict liability is generally used to enforce social behaviour where minimal stigma is attached to a person upon conviction or where society is concerned with the prevention of harm and wishes to maximize the deterrence of the offender. It is thus the duty of the court to ascertain the legislative intention of the provision to determine if *mens rea* is a requirement. In so doing, the court first presumes that *mens rea* is required before a person can be convicted of any offence unless it is rebutted by necessary implication in the statute. This is particularly the case where the offence is truly criminal in nature. The only situation in which the presumption can be rebutted is where the statute is concerned with issues of social concern such as public health or safety. Even in such circumstances, the presumption of *mens rea* still applies unless the imposition of strict liability is required to effectively achieve the purpose of the statute, for example to prevent the prohibited act by promoting and ensuring greater vigilance. In *Gammon (Hong Kong) v Attorney-General of Hong Kong* [1985] 2 HKC 661, the issue was one of social concern as it was dealing with construction site safety and maintenance. Other social concerns include food safety and hygiene, public health and environment or as in the case of *AG v Demand Enterprise Ltd* [1987] HKLR 195, the employment of under-aged children.

Factors affecting liability

A person can only be held liable if he or she voluntarily carries out the elements of the offence with the necessary *mens rea*. However, there are a number of factors that can reduce or negate the person's criminal responsibility for the offence. The following are some of the factors:

Age

The criminal responsibility of a person may be affected by his or her age. Section 3 of the *Juvenile Offenders Ordinance* (Cap. 226) provides that it shall be conclusively presumed that no child under the age of 10 years can be guilty of an offence. This means the child is 'doli incapax' – incapable of committing any offence although he or she might have carried out the elements of the offence. There is, however, a rebuttable presumption if the child is over 10 years but under 14 years. In such circumstances it is necessary for the prosecution to prove beyond reasonable doubt that when committing the criminal act, the child knew that the act was 'seriously wrong' – that he or she had a 'mischievous discretion'. If mischievous discretion is proved, the child may be convicted of any offences proved by the prosecution, including murder. Children (under the age of 14) and young persons (between the ages of 14 and 16) are dealt with in the juvenile court and if found guilty of an offence will only be committed to prison if there are no other suitable methods of dealing with them.

Insanity

A factor which the court has to consider with respect to the criminal responsibility is a person's mental capacity. A defendant is not capable of forming the requisite *mens rea* for an offence if he or she is found to be insane. In determining if the defendant is insane, the courts in Hong Kong apply the *M'Naghten* test, which states:

> to establish a defence on the ground of insanity; it must be clearly proved that at the time of committing the act, the party accused was labouring under such a defect of reason, from the disease of mind as not to know the nature of the act he was doing or if he did know it, that he did not know what he was doing was wrong. (*M'Naghten Case 8* ER 718[1843] 10 CL & F 200)

As such, it must be proved that the defendant was suffering from such a disease of mind as to impair his or her reasoning, memory, and understanding powers. In considering a disease of mind, it is immaterial if the condition is curable, incurable, transitory, or permanent (*R v Kemp* [1957] 1 QB 399). Disease of the mind has been held to include sleepwalking (*R v Burgess* [1991] 2 QB 92), epilepsy (*Bratty v Attorney-General for Northern Ireland* [1963] AC 386), hyperglycaemia (*R v Hennessy* [1989] 1 WLR 287), and arteriosclerosis resulting in blackouts (*R v Kemp* [1957] 1 QB 399). The defence of insanity can only be established if the defect of reason has resulted in the defendant not knowing the physical nature of the act or, if he or she did know, he or she did not know that it was wrong. It cannot be said to be established if the defendant knew what he or she was doing and knew the act he or she was committing was wrong but he or she could not stop himself or herself from so acting, for example when the defendant was suffering from uncontrollable behaviour due to battered baby syndrome as in *Pang Bing Yee v R* [1984] HKLR 298.

The existence of insanity may have the effect of rendering the defendant unfit to stand trial. For a trial against the defendant to proceed, it is vital to prove not only that the defendant understands the charges against him or her, but that he or she is able to raise a defence to those charges (*R v Podola* [1960] 1 QB 325). Such is the importance of the issue of insanity that section 75(3) of the *Criminal Procedure Ordinance* (Cap. 221) provides that it must be determined by the jury as soon as it arises.

The defence of insanity is normally raised by the defendant, although it may be raised by the judge or the prosecution. As the court proceeds on the basis that 'everyone is presumed sane' (presumption of sanity), the burden will be on the defendant to prove insanity on the balance of probabilities. If the *M'Naghten* test is satisfied, the jury must return a verdict of not guilty by reason of insanity (see section 74 of the *Criminal Procedure Ordinance*). In such circumstances, sections 76(1) and 76(2) of the Ordinance provide that the court must make an order committing the defendant to a mental hospital or the Correctional Services Department Psychiatric Centre.

Automatism

Akin to insanity is involuntary conduct or automatism. Automatism has been described as:

> an act which is done by the muscles without any control of the mind, such as spasm, a reflex action or a convulsion; or an act done by a person who is not conscious of what he is doing such as an act done whilst suffering from concussion or whilst sleepwalking. (*Bratty v A-G for Northern Ireland* [1963] AC 386)

Thus for automatism to succeed, the defendant must prove that the commission of the act by the defendant was the result of an unconscious and a total lack of control over his or her actions; that he or she was acting in a 'trance-like' state, unaware and unable to control his or her actions. A mere declaration that he or she cannot remember what happened (amnesia) or that his or her mind just went blank or that his or her actions were the result of an 'irresistible impulse' is not sufficient. The CFI in *R v Chan Tak Kwong* [1997] HKLY 225 took the view that what was required to raise a defence of automatism is a 'total destruction of voluntary control of the defendant'. In *Chan Tak Kwong*, Chan was convicted of criminal damage when the court held that the defendant knew what he was doing when after taking some medication for a pain in his foot he proceeded to cause damage to a window and car windscreen. A reduced or partial control is insufficient to find for the defence (*AG Reference (No 2 of 1992) (1994) QB*). In this respect, one should note *HKSAR v Luk Chiu-Ki* [2005] HKEC 390 CFI where the issue of post-traumatic automatism, hysterical disassociation, and malingering was raised and discussed.

Automatism may be the cause of internal or external factors. If the automatism is caused by a disease of mind within the *M'Naghten* Rules (internal factor), it is called insane automatism and will be treated in the same way as insanity. Consequently, the considerations are the same as for insanity. Further, as in the defence of insanity the defendant who raises insane automatism bears the burden of laying the proper evidential foundation for the defence. It is only when this has been done that the court will leave the defence to be considered by the jury. For instance, in *R v Mohammed Hussain* [1993] 1 HKCLR the defendant's argument that his hypoglycaemic state was due to his large consumption of alcohol on an empty stomach failed on a charge of rape. Non-insane automatism, on the other hand, includes unconscious acts due to external causes such as a blow to the head resulting in a concussion or low blood sugar (see, for example, *R v Budd* [1962] Crim LR 49; *R v Quick & Paddison* [1973] QB 910). Automatism may also be caused by the defendant having taken drugs or alcohol. However, such automatism is regarded as 'self-induced' and is therefore a restricted defence in that it does not negate liability for a basic intent offence. In *R v Bailey* [1983] 1 WLR 760 on a charge of causing grievous bodily harm, the defence that the defendant was in a state of automatism having failed to take sufficient food after taking his insulin, was unsuccessful.

Intoxication

There are circumstances where the consumption of alcohol or drugs has impaired the mental faculties of the defendant so as to negate criminal liability. In *R v Yeung Ka Wah* [1992] HKLY 299, for example, the court held that the defendant bears a persuasive burden to show that he was so affected by the drug that he did not form the intent to rob. Intoxication can be self-induced (voluntary), where the defendant knowingly consumes alcohol, drugs, or other intoxicating substances. Voluntary intoxication is only admissible where the offence is a specific intent offence (*DPP v Majewski* [1977] AC 443 *reaffirming R v Beard* [1920] AC 479) and where the offence requires proof of intention (*MPC v Caldwell* [1982] AC 341). Accordingly, it is not a defence for an offence requiring basic intent or in circumstances where recklessness as *mens rea* of the offence suffices.

The admissibility of intoxication as a defence thus requires a determination of whether the offence is a specific intent or a basic intent offence. Specific intent offence requires the prosecution to prove that 'the purpose for the commission of the offence extends to the intent expressed or implied in the definition of the crime' per Lord Simon in *DPP v Majewski*. By comparison, 'the *mens rea* in crimes of basic intent does not go beyond the act and its consequence ... as defined in the *actus reus*' per Lord Simon in *DPP v Morgan* [1976] AC 182.

In *HKSAR v Chan Ping Kwan* [2005] 2 HKLRD 5 the defendant was charged with making a call of menacing character, an offence contrary to section 20(a) of the *Summary Offence Ordinance* (Cap. 228). The court held that the offence was completed once it was proved that it was the defendant who had sent the message of menacing character. The *mens rea* here was that the defendant was aware of the message's menacing character – the intent required for the offence was a basic intent. Other examples of crimes of basic intent include common assault, assault occasioning actual bodily harm, indecent assault, manslaughter, assault on a police officer in the execution of his duty, taking a conveyance without the owner's authority, arson or criminal damage, and rape. As for specific intent crimes, these include theft, burglary, wounding with intent to cause grievous bodily harm, handling stolen goods, and murder.

Intoxication may also be involuntary where the defendant was unaware that the drink or food he or she has consumed was laced with an intoxicating substance. It can also arise as a result of consuming a prescription drug. In such cases, it can only be raised as a defence if it negatives the *mens rea*. If it merely disinhibits the defendant, it is not a defence (*R v Kingston* [1995] 2 AC 355). The prosecution must still therefore prove beyond reasonable doubt that the defendant had the necessary *mens rea* for the offence despite the defendant asserting and proving that he or she was involuntarily intoxicated.

Duress and necessity

A person who commits an offence under an imminent threat of death or serious violence against himself or herself or another is not criminally liable. The threat or violence must be of death, personal injury, or of other dangers of similar nature or gravity (*R v Valderrama-Vega* [1985] Crim LR 220). A connection must also exist between the threat and the defendant's decision to act in the manner he did. In *R v Howe* [1987] AC 417 approving *R v Graham* [1982] 1 WLR 294, it was held that in circumstances where there is in fact no threat or violence, duress is available if the defendant has good cause to fear and honestly believes that the threat or violence would be carried out if the defendant did not commit the offence. Accordingly, the defence is not available if steps can be taken to remove the threat or if the threats are as a result of the defendant's knowledge and voluntary association with organizations which are likely to use violence such as triad societies and terrorist organizations. The defence is also not available for offences such as murder, attempted murder, and treason.

Necessity and duress of circumstances

Necessity is a defence where the defendant is asserting he or she was left with little choice to do as he or she did in view of the threatened harm. The defence can only arise if pressure is exerted on the defendant's will from wrongful threats or violence threatening the defendant, his or her family, or other persons. To assert the defence, the defendant must also be said to be acting reasonably and proportionately in order to avoid the threat of death or serious injury. Once the defence is raised, it is to be left to the jury to decide a) whether the defendant was impelled to act as he or she did because of what he or she reasonably believed to be the situation he or she had good cause to fear that otherwise death or serious physical injury would result and b) if so, would a sober person of reasonable firmness have responded to that situation by acting as the defendant did? If the answer to both questions is 'yes', the defendant will be acquitted per Simon Brown J in *R v Martin* [1989] 1 All ER 652 where a conviction for driving while disqualified was set aside by the court.

In *A-G v Chan Yuen Long* [1989] 1 HKC 470 the victim was restrained by his four limbs by metal chains and padlocks against a bed in an old people's home for his own safety and the safety of others. The court in that case held that necessity can be relied upon only if a) the conduct was done to avoid consequences which if they had not been followed would have inflicted upon the defendant or upon others upon whom he was bound to protect, inevitable or irreparable evil, b) no more was done than was reasonably necessary for the purposes, and c) the evil inflicted was not disproportionate to the evil avoided. It must be noted that Simon Brown J's summary of the factors in *R v*

Martin constituting duress of circumstances was applied successfully in a recent case of *HKSAR v Ip Chung San* [2005] HKEC 1338 where the defendants were charged with dangerous driving, failing to stop after a motor collision, and criminal damage.

Specific offences

The remaining part of this chapter deals briefly with a number of offences listed under the following sections: offences against the person, offences against property, offences against public order, offences against the public interest, and offences against morals and public policy. Offences against the person include murder, manslaughter, and assault, while offences dealt with under offences against property are primarily offences under the *Theft Ordinance*. Some of the offences considered as offences against public order are treason, terrorism, sedition, public gatherings and processions, unlawful assembly and rioting, and unlawful organizations. As for offences against the public interest, these would include corruption and bribery offences, gambling offences, and drug offences. Last but not least, the section on offences against public morals and policy deals with offences such as public nuisance, the offence of bigamy, the publication of obscene and indecent materials, and child pornography. The considerations of the above offences under the prescribed sections are not meant to be exhaustive and neither are they meant to give a full and complete account of the law.[4]

Offences against the person

Homicide is the killing of another life in being. It includes murder, manslaughter, infanticide, and child destruction. A person commits murder if he or she unlawfully kills another with the intent to kill or to cause grievous bodily harm. However, not all acts of killing are unlawful. For example, it is not murder if the unlawful act is aimed at an unborn child or a dead person. The act of killing may also be justified in certain circumstances such as where it was done in accordance with the law, for instance the execution of a prisoner or if the killing was done in self-defence. Further, the defendant may not be guilty of murder if the act was the result of provocation or if the defendant was suffering from diminished responsibility.

Murder

Murder is a very serious offence punishable by life imprisonment (section 2 of the *Offences against the Person Ordinance Cap. 212*). With the severity of the punishment imposed, it is crucial for the prosecution to prove that the act of killing be accompanied by either the intention to kill or to cause grievous bodily harm (*R v Moloney* [1985] AC 905, *R v Nedrick* [1986] 1 WLR 1025, *Lau Cheong & Anor v HKSAR* [2002] 2 HKLRD 612). Proof of forethought or premeditation is not required; rather what is necessary is that the relevant intention exists at the time of killing and it was the defendant's unlawful act or omission which is the cause of the victim's death (*R v Lo Yung-kan* [1985] 1 HKC 302, *R v Yeung Lung-fai* [1991] 2 HKC 102).[5]

Voluntary manslaughter

Voluntary manslaughter is where the defendant commits murder but circumstances exist in which the conviction for murder is reduced to manslaughter on grounds of provocation or diminished responsibility. Provocation is a statutory defence available only when a defendant is accused of murder. Section 4 of the *Homicide Ordinance* (Cap. 339) provides:

> Where on a charge of murder there is evidence on which the jury can find that the person charged was provoked (whether by things done or by things said or by both together) to lose his or her self-control, the question whether the provocation was enough to make a reasonable man do as he or she did will be left to be determined by the jury; and in determining that question the jury shall take into account everything both done and said according to the effect which in their opinion, it would have on the reasonable man.

The questions to be answered thus are i) whether the defendant was provoked to lose his or her self-control and ii) was the provocation so serious as to make a reasonable man act as he or she did? Accordingly, there must be a direct causal connection between the provoking conduct of the victim and the defendant losing his or her self-control. The time-lapse between the two must not be too long. In *R v Vu Van Thang* [1991] 2 HKC 90, the time-lag of at least one month between the alleged act of provocation and the then alleged loss of self-control was held to be too far separated in time. The court (or jury), in considering whether a reasonable man had been provoked to act as the defendant did, must take into account a person having the power of self-control expected of an ordinary person of the sex, age, and characteristics of the defendant as they would think would affect the gravity of the provocation to him or her. In *R v Camplin* [1978] AC 705, for example, a 15-year-old boy lost his self-control and killed the man who had not only just buggered him against his will but mocked him after the incident.

In fact, in *Luc Thiet Thuan v R* [1996] 2 All ER 1003 (PC) where the defendant's mental infirmity was his distinguishing characteristic as compared to an ordinary person, the Privy Council opined that it is necessary for the provocation to have been directed at the relevant characteristics of the defendant, where he was the subject of taunts by the deceased. Once the defence is raised, the prosecution bears the burden of proving that the defendant did not lose his or her self-control (*R v Tran Dihn Thannh & Anor* [1994] 2 HKC 260).

A defendant commits manslaughter if he or she kills another person while suffering from such an abnormality of mind so as to substantially impair his or her mental responsibility for his or her acts: section 3(1) of the *Homicide Ordinance*. The abnormality of mind must be the result of retarded development of the mind, inherent causes, or induced by disease or injury. Consequently, neither self-induced intoxication through drinks or drugs nor extreme emotion such as anger or jealousy can amount to abnormality of the mind (*HKSAR v Leung Wai Chung* [1999] 2 HKC 471). Thus the defendant must prove that more likely than not, his or her mental responsibility at the time of the killing was substantially impaired – the impairment being more than merely trivial (*HKSAR v Tsui Chu Tin, John* [2005] 1 HKC 518). Whether the impairment was sufficiently substantial is a question for the jury.

Involuntary manslaughter

Involuntary manslaughter is unlawful killing without the intention to kill or to cause grievous bodily harm. It can be committed either by an unlawful and dangerous act or by gross negligence. In the case of the former, what is required is the intention to do the act coupled with any fault required to make the act unlawful. It is irrelevant that the defendant was not aware of the unlawful nature of his or her act or that it was dangerous or that he or she had failed to foresee its consequences. The act, however, must be a crime, thus making it unlawful. Unfortunately, this was what happened in *R v Lamb* [1967] 2 QB 981. In *Lamb*, the defendant had pointed a loaded gun in jest at his friend. He did not intend to injure his friend. Neither he nor his friend believed there was any danger in pulling the trigger. The defendant's friend was killed when the trigger was pulled. The test to be applied must be that which was previously stated in *R v Church* that 'The unlawful act must be such as all sober and reasonable people would inevitably recognise must subject the other person to, at least, the risk of some harm resulting therefrom, albeit not serious harm' (*DPP v Newbury* [1977] AC 500 (a manslaughter case), *R v Church* [1966] 1 QB 59).

Manslaughter by gross negligence, on the other hand, requires the consideration of the ordinary principles of negligence of whether i) there is a duty of care, ii) the defendant has breached his duty of care, and iii) such breach resulted in the death of the victim. In such circumstances, the jury must consider whether the defendant's breach was so grossly negligent that it amounted to a criminal act or omission (*Re Adomako* [1995] AC 171). The jury must (in the words of Lord Mackay LC) be satisfied there is a:

> reckless disregard of danger to the health and welfare of the infirm person. Mere indifference is not enough. The defendant must be proved to have been indifferent to an obvious injury to health or actually to have foreseen the risk but to have determined nevertheless to run it.

Thus, what is required is a) the creation of an obvious and serious risk of causing injury to others by a wrongful act of the defendant and b) the defendant proceeded with his wrongful act either i) without giving consideration to the risk of injury or ii) having recognized the risk, took it (*R v Kong Cheuk-kwan* [1986] HKLR 648, *R v Chang Wai Kwan* [1994] 1 HKC 301). In the latter case, a pedestrian was killed when the defendant who had parked his heavy goods vehicle on a slope failed to engage both the vehicle's handbrake and the gears. In such circumstances, it is clear that the approach adopted, justifiably reflects the sentiments of society, in that conduct that exposes others to an obvious and serious degree of risk to injury should be penalized severely.

Assault

It is common for the word 'assault' to cover both the threat of violence (assault) and the actual unlawful use of force (battery). An important element of assault is that there must be a threat of violence calculated to cause immediate apprehension or fear in the victim. Thus, throwing a chair at a person or a shout of 'Get out the knives' would be an assault (*R v Wilson* [1955] 1 All ER 744).

Assault includes an assault occasioning actual bodily harm where the injury caused by the assault must be calculated to interfere with the health or comfort of the victim and wounding or inflicting grievous bodily harm (sections 17, 19, and 39 of the *Offences against the Person Ordinance*. In *HKSAR v Law Kwok Fai* (Unrep. Criminal Appeal No. 204 of 2003), the court held that 'grievous bodily harm' should be given its natural and ordinary meaning of really serious bodily harm. Although it is not necessary for such harm be permanent or dangerous, grievous bodily harm does extend to serious psychological or biological harm. Thus, infecting a person with HIV virus will amount to inflicting grievous bodily harm (*R v Mohammed Dica* [2004] EWCA Crim 1103). Defences in respect of assault include consent (this does not include consent to the satisfaction of sado-masochistic desires or the infliction of bodily harm), lawful correction, self-defence, defence of property, and necessity.

Offences against property

The most important offences relating to property are covered by the *Theft Ordinance*. These offences include theft, burglary, handling stolen goods, deception, and conspiracy to defraud. Theft is defined as the dishonest appropriation of property belonging to another with the intention of permanently depriving the other of it: section 2 of the *Theft Ordinance*. All the elements of theft are defined and provided for in the ordinance, as with the offences of burglary, handling stolen goods, deception, and conspiracy to defraud. For example, the *mens rea* to the offence of theft is dishonesty with the intention to permanently deprive. It is not dishonesty if the defendant believes he or she has the right in law to deprive the victim of the property; perhaps in cases where the defendant believes the item does not belong to the victim or where the defendant believes the victim will consent to the item being taken or where the owner of the property cannot be discovered by taking reasonable steps: section 3 of the Ordinance. In *Pang Hei-cheung v R* [1971] HKLR 80 the defendant 'borrowed' money belonging to his employer intending to 'repay' it the following day. The court held that despite the defendant's intention to replace the money, there was dishonesty when the defendant intentionally appropriated property without the consent of the owner. The *actus reus* of theft is the appropriation of property belonging to another. Appropriation is seen as the assumption of the rights of the owner of property and can include an assumption of rights where consent has been fraudulently obtained. Property includes money, real and personal property, things in action, and other tangible property – section 5 of the *Ordinance*. Property was held to include export quotas (*Attorney-General of Hong Kong v Chan Nai-keung* [1988] HKLR 88) and debts (*Chan Man-sin v R* [1987] 2 HKC 56). In addition to offences created by the *Theft Ordinance*, one should note section 60(1) of the *Crimes Ordinance* which provides for the offence of criminal damage to property. Under section 60(1), a person is guilty of an offence if he or she, without lawful excuse, destroys or damages any property belonging to another with the intention of so destroying and damaging the property or is reckless as to whether such property is destroyed or damaged. Examples of property damage include adulterating milk with water as in *Roper v Knott* [1898] 1 QB 868 and painting a pavement with water-soluble paint (*Hardman v Chief Constable of Avon and Somerset* [1986] Crim LR 330). It can be seen from these examples that the damage to property need not necessarily be of temporary or permanent physical harm. It is sufficient if the damage renders the property temporarily or permanently impaired of its value or usefulness.

Offences against public order

The offences that fall under this heading are those that affect the security of the state. Examples of some of these offences include treason, terrorism, sedition, unlawful assembly, riot, and membership of unlawful organizations.

Treason

The offence of treason is an offence committed against the duty of allegiance to the State. It is seen as a betrayal of trust. Treasonable offences include causing physical harm or forming the intention to cause such harm to the Central People's Government (of China) or competent authority of the People's Republic of China, levies war, or instigates or assists in any way, any foreigner to do so. Any person found guilty of treason shall be sentenced to nothing less than life imprisonment (sections 2(1) and 2(2) of the *Crimes Ordinance*).

Terrorism

As a result of the terrorist attacks in the United States of America in September 2001, the United Nations Security Council resolved that certain preventive measures be adopted to prevent terrorists' acts. Hong Kong in so implementing the UN resolutions, enacted the *United Nations (Anti-Terrorism Measures) Ordinance* (Cap. 575). Essentially, the

Ordinance empowers the Chief Executive and the CFI to specify by a notice or an order a person to be a terrorist or a terrorist associate, or property to be terrorist property. In so specifying who are terrorists and what property are terrorist property, certain prohibited acts in relation to terrorists and terrorist property are spelt out. These prohibited acts include the supply and making available of funds and weapons to terrorists and terrorist associates and the recruitment of another to be a member of a terrorist organization: sections 7–10 of the *Ordinance.* The penalty for contravening the provisions is a fine and a term of imprisonment of 14 years, if convicted on an indictment.

Sedition

Section 10 of the *Crimes Ordinance* makes it an offence to do or conspire with any person to do any act with seditious intention, to utter any seditious words, print, publish, sell, offer for sale, distribute, display, reproduce, or import any seditious publications. Seditious intention includes the intention to bring into hatred or contempt, to raise discontent and disaffection among the State's subjects, to incite persons to violence, and to counsel disobedience to lawful order: section 9 of the *Ordinance*. However, it should be noted that it is not seditious if the act, speech, or publication is to point out errors or defects in the government, constitution, legislation, or administration of justice with a view of remedying such errors or defects: section 9(2) of the *Ordinance*.

Public gatherings and processions

Part III of the *Public Order Ordinance* (Cap. 245) provides for the control of public gatherings and processions. Essentially, under the provisions, public gatherings and processions can only take place if the police have been notified in advance and have given their approval for the holding or taking place of the gathering and procession. The police in such circumstances may in the interest of national security, public safety, public order, or merely for the protection of rights and freedom of others, control and direct the conduct of such gatherings and if necessary specify the route which the public procession may take: section 6(1) of the *Ordinance*.

Unlawful assembly and rioting

Any person who takes part in a gathering of three or more persons and behaves in a disorderly, intimidating, insulting, or provocative manner likely to cause a reasonable person to fear that a breach of peace will be committed, commits an offence of unlawful assembly and can be liable on conviction to 5 years' imprisonment: section 18(1) of the *Public Order Ordinance*. It is important to prove that the assembly caused such fear amongst innocent third parties or members of the public that there would be a breach of peace. For example, a breach of peace is likely to result if the offender's disorderly conduct causes other members of the public to come forward and use violence, to seize and punish the offender as in *HKSAR v Cheng Siu Wing* [2003] 4 HKC 471. The unlawful assembly is a riot when any participant of that unlawful assembly commits a breach of peace: section 19(1) of the *Ordinance*. In considering sentencing for rioting, which is a maximum of 10 years' imprisonment on indictment, the court needs to consider the severity of the violence, the scale of the riot, and whether the riot was premeditated. In *Secretary for Justice v Cheung Chun Chin* [2002] 2 HKLRD 233, rioting in a correctional institution with the intention to inflict harm and violence on Vietnamese inmates, correctional officers, and the police attracted a sentence of 6 years' imprisonment. It should be noted that the rioting is viewed and treated very seriously, such that any acts which are incidental or arise as a result of the riot such as pulling down, destroying or unlawfully damaging any motor vehicle, tramcar, aircraft, vessel, building, railway, machinery or structure can attract a term of 14 and 10 years' imprisonment respectively: sections 20 and 21 of the *Ordinance*.

Unlawful organizations

Unlawful organizations are organizations which are prohibited by the societies' officer for reasons of national security or public safety, public order, or the protection of the rights and freedoms of others: section 8(1) of the *Societies Ordinance*. Unlawful organizations may also include triad societies. Triad societies are societies which utilize triad ritual, or adopt and make use of any triad title or name. Registering under the *Ordinance* does not make a triad society lawful. Accordingly, sections 19 and 20 of the *Ordinance* make it an offence to be a member of an unlawful society, attend its meetings, or pay money or give aid to it.

Offences against public interest

Bribery and corruption offences

The *Prevention of Bribery Ordinance* (Cap. 201) governs corruption offences in Hong Kong. The enforcement of the Ordinance is carried out by the Independent Commission against Corruption (ICAC), which was established under the *Independent Commission Against Corruption Ordinance* (Cap. 204). The ICAC is also responsible for investigating election offences under the *Elections (Corrupt and Illegal Conduct) Ordinance* (Cap. 554).

Essentially, under the *Prevention of Bribery Ordinance*, it is an offence for a public servant to solicit or accept, or a member of the public to offer an advantage as an inducement to, a reward for the public servant's performance or non-performance of his job. This includes delaying, expediting, or hindering the transaction or favouring the donor: see section 4 of the *Ordinance*. The giving of advantage includes making gifts, or giving a fee, loan, or commission whether in money terms or otherwise, including office, employment, or contract: section 2. It is a defence under the *Ordinance*, however, if permission was obtained prior to the solicitation and acceptance of the advantage: section 3.

Gambling offences

The *Gambling Ordinance* (Cap. 148) provides that all gambling (save for some exceptions) in the form of gaming, betting, and bookmaking is unlawful. Exceptions are provided for in section 3, for example, which states that gambling is lawful if it is one in which dice, dominoes, mahjong or tin kau tiles, or playing cards are used and it is played on a social occasion and not conducted as a trade, business, or for private gain. This would probably include minor hobby gambling such as those held during weekends or in celebration of festivities. In fact, in *HKSAR v Man Kwok-yau* (Unrep. Mag. App. No. 704 of 1988), the court did not excuse the clansmen of the village who habitually and regularly met at their usual meeting place for social gambling. What was necessary, the court said, was for the defendants to prove it was a social occasion, the social occasion being the essential character of the gathering. Gambling is lawful if one gambles in licensed premises, for instance in mahjong parlours, or if one participates in gambling activities authorized under the *Betting Ordinance* (Cap. 108) such as horse racing at the Hong Kong Jockey Club and the Mark Six Lotteries. It should be noted that with amendments made to the *Ordinance*, offshore and internet gambling have been outlawed. On the other hand, football gambling is now legal.

Drug offences

Drug offences are regulated under the *Dangerous Drugs Ordinance* (Cap. 134). Under the *Ordinance*, every aspect of the drug trade is covered and provided for. For instance, it is an offence to traffic, offer to traffic, supply, manufacture, have in possession, keep in the management of a divan, or have in possession a pipe or an apparatus for administering dangerous drugs. It is also an offence to cultivate cannabis: section 8 of the *Ordinance*. Dangerous drugs are those drugs listed in Part I of the First Schedule to the Ordinance. Trafficking includes the importation into Hong Kong and exportation from Hong Kong or procuring, supplying, dealing, or possessing dangerous drugs for trafficking. The *Ordinance* has been drafted widely to criminalize those found in charge and control of the premises such as the owner, tenant, or occupier where drug-related activities take place. Also, under the *Drug Trafficking (Recovery of Proceeds) Ordinance* (Cap. 405), it is now possible to trace, confiscate, seize, forfeit, and recover proceeds of drug trafficking.

Offences against public morals and policy

Public nuisance

Public nuisance is an offence at common law. However, in recent years most instances of public nuisance have been regulated by Ordinances. At common law, public nuisance is an act or an omission which when committed is likely to cause discomfort and possibly annoyance to others. This discomfort or annoyance may or may not interfere with the enjoyment of rights common to all. For example, to a non-smoker, smoking is seen as a public nuisance being an act endangering the health of others. To a smoker it is merely an exercise of his liberty to engage in the enjoyment of a chosen activity. The example of smoking is now regulated by the *Smoking (Public Health) Amendment Ordinance 2005* where it is an offence punishable by a maximum fine of $5,000 to smoke in a public place. Although most common law public nuisance has been overridden by statutes, they continue to exist for purposes of regulating intolerable conduct which affects the reasonable enjoyment of comfort to others. Most common of these instances would be the emission of fumes or creating excessive noise.

Bigamy

Polygamy is not encouraged in Hong Kong. As such, section 45 of the *Offences against the Persons Ordinance* makes it an offence for any person who is married to marry another. Any person found guilty of section 45 can be imprisoned for a maximum term of 7 years. An essential element is thus proof of a valid marriage. A marriage is valid if the person had gone through a form of marriage recognized under the *Marriage Ordinance* (Cap. 181). In most circumstances, the easiest way to prove marriage is by producing the marriage certificate issued by the Registrar of Marriages. Where this is not possible, evidence of marriage celebration is required. This can be obtained by requiring a wedding guest to provide details of the wedding ceremony. It is defence to section 45 of the *Ordinance* to prove that the spouse had been absent for 7 years.

Publication of obscene and indecent materials

The *Control of Obscene and Indecent Articles Ordinance* (Cap. 390) regulates the publication and public display of materials regarded as obscene and indecent. Obscene material include materials which has the tendency to deprave and corrupt the public or a section of the public. The materials may be repulsive, of a sexual nature, or induce violence, for example materials that advocate the benefits of drug taking such that it may tempt people to experiment. Materials are classified into three categories by the Obscene Articles Tribunal: section 29(1) of the *Ordinance*. These classes are Class I – article that is neither obscene nor indecent, Class II – indecent article, and Class III – obscene article. An article is obscene if it is not suitable to be published to any person but is indecent if considered not suitable for juveniles. The Obscene Article Tribunal has sole jurisdiction in determining what articles are indecent or obscene and in so determining will have regard to, among other factors, the standards of morality and decency of the community and the effect the article might have: section 10(1) of the *Ordinance*. Some of the defences under the *Ordinance* include having no reasonable grounds for believing the article is obscene or indecent or having inspected proof of age believing the juvenile is not a juvenile: section 27A(2)(c) and section 22(2)(b) respectively.

Child pornography

In an effort to stem the rising global tide of child pornography, Hong Kong does its part in the protection of children by criminalizing the possession, publication, and production of child pornography by enacting the *Prevention of Child Pornography Ordinance* (Cap. 579). The *Ordinance* also amended the *Crimes Ordinance* (a) to prohibit the use, procurement, or offer of persons under the age of 18 for making pornography or for live pornographic performances and (b) to extend the application of certain sexual offence provisions of the *Crimes Ordinance* to acts committed against children outside Hong Kong. This latter extension was intended to cover activities relating to child sexual tourism. Any person found guilty of producing (including making, copying, printing, importing, or exporting) child pornography can be fined HK$2,000,000 and imprisoned for a term not exceeding 8 years: sections 3(1) and (2) of the *Ordinance*. In the context of making, it should be noted that this activity includes downloading a pornographic image from the internet (*R v Bowden* [2000] 1 CR App R 438). Before the *Prevention of Child Pornography Ordinance*, possession was not an offence. The enactment of the *Ordinance* changed this. A specific offence of possession now provided for under section 3(3) of the *Ordinance*. Under the section, any person found guilty of possession of child pornography can be fined HK$1,000,000 and imprisoned for 5 years. The question thus is, 'What is child pornography?' Child pornography is a pornographic depiction of a child. It does not matter if the pornographic depiction was made electronically or otherwise, or whether the depiction is of a real person or if it was modified. In such circumstances, pseudo images of children (not real children) made electronically by using such advanced programmes such as Photo Editor or images of children in which the pictures of adult breasts and genitalia are pasted onto the body of a child will be regarded as child pornography. The court will take into account the age of the child depicted when deciding whether or not there was a pornographic depiction. There are several defences provided for under the *Ordinance*. For example, it is a defence if the defendant can prove he had taken all reasonable steps to ascertain the age of the child that was pornographically depicted or in answer to a charge of possession, that the child pornography was for the use of a genuine educational, scientific, or medical purpose.

Conclusion

Criminal law is an essential part of every society. It can be said that the basis of criminal law is to promote and to maintain a sense of security, well-being and harmony within society. It does this by regulating a great part of our daily life, activities, and relationships with others and their interests and property. Criminal law deals with something as trivial as to how we should behave in a public area (no spitting in public) to instilling respect and care for the property of others (prohibiting criminal damage) to regulating and prohibiting matters of a more serious nature such as killing, grievously wounding another, drug trafficking, or becoming a member of a terrorist organization. It matters not that criminal offences are established either by common law or by statute. What is of paramount importance is that before criminal liability can be imposed, all the elements of the offence and its requisite mental state must be proven. Even when this is sufficiently proven, the defendant might still not be convicted of the offence if a defence is successfully raised.

Notes

1 For more insight on negligence or tort law, see Deakin, Johnston, and Markesinis (2003) and Lunney and Oliphant (2003).
2 This Latin maxim dates back to prominent English jurist Edward Coke in his work *Institutes, Part II, Chapter 1, Folio 10* (1797 edition).
3 Ibid.
4 Readers are advised to refer to texts on criminal law such as Findlay, Howarth and Dobinson (1996), Jackson (2003) and Ormerod (2005).
5 Please also refer to the provisions of section 65A of the *Criminal Procedure Ordinance*.

Review questions

1 What does 'actus non facit reum nisi mens sit rea' mean?
2 Can a child aged 11 years old commit an offence? What does the prosecution need to prove?
3 Is there a difference between duress and necessity?
4 In what circumstances can a conviction of murder be reduced to manslaughter? What must be proved?
5 Name some offences relating to property and what are some of the offences that affect the moral values of society.

References

Deakin, S., Johnston, A. and Markesinis, B. (2003) *Markesinis and Deakin's Tort Law* (5th edn). Oxford: Clarendon Press.
Findlay, M., Howarth, C. and Dobinson, I. (1996) *Criminal Law in Hong Kong: Cases and Commentary* (2nd edn). Hong Kong: Butterworths Asia.
Jackson, M. (2003) *Criminal Law in Hong Kong*. Hong Kong: Hong Kong University Press.
Lunney, M. and Oliphant, K. (2003) *Tort Law: Texts and Materials* (2nd edn). Oxford: Oxford University Press.

Ormerod, D. (2005) *Smith and Hogan Criminal Law* (10th edn). London: LexisNexis.

Legislation cited

Betting Ordinance (Cap. 108)
Control of Obscene and Indecent Articles Ordinance (Cap. 390)
Crimes Ordinance (Cap. 200)
Criminal Procedure Ordinance (Cap. 221)
Dangerous Drugs Ordinance (Cap. 134)
Drug Trafficking (Recovery of Proceeds) Ordinance (Cap. 405)
Elections (Corrupt and Illegal Conduct) Ordinance (Cap. 554)
Gambling Ordinance (Cap. 148)
Homicide Ordinance (Cap. 339)
Independent Commission Against Corruption Ordinance (Cap. 204)
Inland Revenue Ordinance (Cap. 112)
Juvenile Offenders Ordinance (Cap. 226)
Marriage Ordinance (Cap. 181)
Offences against the Person Ordinance (Cap. 212)
Prevention of Child Pornography Ordinance (Cap. 579)
Prevention of Bribery Ordinance (Cap. 201)
Public Order Ordinance (Cap. 245)
Registration of Persons Ordinance (Cap. 177)
Road Traffic Ordinance (Cap. 374)
Smoking (Public Health) Amendment 2005
Societies Ordinance (Cap. 151)
Summary Offence Ordinance (Cap. 228)
Theft Ordinance (Cap. 210)
United Nations (Anti-Terrorism Measures) Ordinance (Cap. 575)

Cases cited

Hong Kong cases

A-G v Chan Yuen Long [1989] 1 HKC 470
A-G v Demand Enterprise Ltd [1987] HKLR 195
A-G of Hong Kong v Chan Nai-keung [1988] HKLR 88
Chan Man-sin v R [1987] 2 HKC 56
Gammon (Hong Kong) v Attorney-General of Hong Kong [1985] 2 HKC 661
HKSAR v Chan Ping Kwan [2005] 2 HKLRD 5
HKSAR v Cheng Siu Wing [2003] 4 HKC 471
HKSAR v Ip Chung San [2005] HKEC 1338
HKSAR v Law Kwok Fai (Unrep. Criminal Appeal No. 204 of 2003)

HKSAR v Leung Wai Chung [1999] 2 HKC 471
HKSAR v Luk Chiu-Ki [2005] HKEC 390 CFI
HKSAR v Man Kwok-yau (Unrep. Mag. App. No. 704 of 1988)
HKSAR v Tsui Chu Tin, John [2005] 1 HKC 518
Lau Cheong & Anor v HKSAR [2002] 2 HKLRD 612
Kong Cheuk-kwan v R [1986] HKLR 648
Kwan Ping Bong v R (1979) HKLR 1
Pang Bing Yee v R [1984] HKLR 298
Pang Hei Cheung v R [1971] HKLR 80
R v Chan Tak Kwong [1997] HKLY 225
R v Chang Wai Kwan [1994] 1 HKC 301
R v Chau Ming Cheong [1983] 1 HKC 6
R v Dung Shue Wah [1983] HKC
R v Kong Cheuk-Kwan [1986] HKLR 648
R v Lo Yung-kan [1985] 1 HKC 302
R v Mohammed Hussain [1993] 1 HKCLR
R v Tran Dihn Thannh & Anor [1994] 2 HKC 260
R v Vu Van Thang [1991] 2 HKC 90
R v Wong Tak Shing [1989] 2 HKC 94
R v Yeung Ka Wah [1992] HKLY 299
R v Yeung Lung-fai [1991] 2 HKC 102
Secretary of Justice v Cheung Chun Chin [2002] 2 HKLRD 233
Sin Kam Wah & Anor v HKSAR [2005] 8 HKCFAR 192

English cases

A-G Reference (No. 2 of 1992) (1994) QB
Bratty v Attorney-General for Northern Ireland [1963] AC 386
Donaghue v Stevenson [1932] All ER Rep 1
DPP v Majewski [1977] AC
DPP v Morgan [1976] AC 182
DPP v Newbury [1977] AC 500
Hardman v Chief Constable of Avon & Somerset [1986] Crim LR 330
Luc Thiet Thuan v R [1996] 2 All ER 1003 PC
M'Naghten Case 8 ER 718 [1843] 10 CL & F 200
MPC v Caldwell [1982] AC 34
R v Adomako [1995] 1 AC 171
R v Bailey [1983] 1 WLR 760
R v Beard [1920] AC 479
R v Blaue [1975] 3 All ER 446
R v Bowden [2000] 1 Cr App R 438
R v Budd [1962] Crim LR 49
R v Burgess [1991] 2 QB 92
R v Caldwell [1982] AC 341
R v Camplin [1978] AC 705
R v Church [1966] 1 QB 59

R v Cunningham [1957] 2 QB 396
R v Graham [1982] 1 WLR 294
R v Hancock & Shankland [1986] 2 WLR 35
R v Hennessy [1989] 1 WLR 287
R v Howe [1987] AC 417
R v Kemp [1957] 1 QB 39
R v Kingston [1995] 2 AC 355
R v Lamb [1967] 2 QB 981
R v Martin [1989] 1 All ER 652
R v Miller [1983] 2 AC 161
R v Mohammed Dica [2004] EWCA Crim 1103
R v Moloney [1985] AC 905
R v Nedrick [1986] 1 WLR 1025
R v Pagett [1983] 76 Cr App R 279
R v Podola [1960] 1 QB 325
R v Quick & Paddison [1973] QB 910
R v R & G [2003] UKHL 50
R v Smith [1959] 2 All ER 193
R v Stone & Dobinson [1977] QB 354
R v Valderrama-Vega [1985] Crim LR 220
R v White [1910] 1 KB 124
R v Wilson [1955] 1 All ER 744
Roper v Knott [1898] 1 QB 868

Useful websites

The Basic Law of the Hong Kong Special Administrative Region	http://ww.info.gov.hk/basic_law/flash.html
Bilingual Laws Information System (BLIS) (Hong Kong)	http://www.legislation.gov.hk/eng/index.htm

Chapter 3

Crime trends

Roderic Broadhurst, King Wa Lee and Ching Yee Chan

Introduction

This chapter examines crime trends in Hong Kong (HK) over the past 30 years and discusses factors that may have impacted on the prevalence and nature of crime. Frequently cited factors include age, economy, social malaise, abortion, guns, gangs, drug use, media, anticrime measures, and crime opportunities (Siegel and Senna 2007). Levels of crimes in HK are usually measured by official statistics and victim surveys but occasionally involve self-report youth delinquency surveys (Wong 1992; Vagg, Bacon-Shone, Gray, and Lam 1995). Official crime statistics underestimate crime because of under-reporting and recording practices. This so-called 'dark figure' is addressed by victim surveys that estimate the 'true' victimization rate, but are also subject to sampling and non-sampling errors. In this chapter, our discussion is limited to the role of age, reporting behaviour, economic change, and policy on crime trends. First we provide an overview of the crime situation in HK.

An overview of the crime situation

As one of the safest cities in the twenty-first century, HK ranked low in overall recorded crime per capita among industrialized countries surveyed in the *Seventh United Nations Survey on Crime Trends and the Operations of Criminal Justice Systems* (7th UNSCTOCJ 1998–2000).[1] According to the 7th UNSCTOCJ, the HK overall recorded crime rate per 100,000 populations in year 2000 was 1185.7, lower than Singapore (1,202.6), Japan (1,924.0), South Korea (3,262.6), Italy (3,822.8), France (6,403.8), Canada (8,040.6), and England & Wales (9,766.7), but higher than the Philippines (106.0), China (288.7), Malaysia (717.5), and Thailand (931.0). Perceptions of corruption, however, are higher in the Philippines, China, Malaysia, and Thailand, according to the 2006 Transparency International's Corruption Perceptions Index (CPI),[2] and suggests official crime rates may be under-reported or recorded. HK ranked 15th among 163 countries participating in the 2006 CPI and along with Singapore (ranked 5th) was perceived as one of the least corrupt in Asia.

The United Nations International Crime Victim Survey (UN ICVS) provides an alternative source to official crime figures in HK. The UN HK ICVS[3] surveyed a sample of 2,083 households about their crime victimization experience[4] during 2001–5 and showed that 7.9 per cent of HK citizens experienced at least one crime in year 2005.[5] Thefts from households were low, while no respondent encountered car theft, and 0.5 per cent experienced theft from a car and 0.1 per cent motorcycle theft.[6] Crimes outside the household setting were more common at 1.3 per cent for bicycle theft and 3.6 per cent for personal theft. Robbery was relatively rare (0.4 per cent) but 1.2 per cent were sexually victimized and 1.2 per cent assaulted or threatened. Most (92.7 per cent) HK residents reported feeling 'fairly safe' or 'very safe' walking alone in their own neighbourhood after dark. Compared to other industrialized countries surveyed in the year 2000,[7] crime victimisation in HK is lower than western countries but similar to other Asian countries such as Japan. Compared to Japan, HK has lower household crime, such as vehicle theft and burglary, but a higher personal victimization for theft, assault, and robbery (see Table 3.1). The low rate of crime is thus supported by data from periodic crime victim surveys. Crime trends, however, have fluctuated over the past 50 years and we next examine police statistics compared with crime victim surveys.

Official crime trends

HK was not always a safe place, and in the early days of the colony it was considered a place full of 'vagabonds', 'thugs', and 'villains' (Fortune 1847 cited in Faure 1997: 19). Even by the 1950s and 1960s the safe image of HK had not been established. Although the recorded crime rates of that time were low in comparison with

Table 3.1 Hong Kong UNICVS 2006 compared with industrialized countries in the 4th UN ICVS

	Surveyed year**	Car theft	Theft from car	Motor-cycle theft	Bicycle theft	Burglary	Attempted burglary	Robbery	Personal property theft	Sexual victimization	Assaults and threats
Australia	1999	1.9	6.8	0.1	2.0	3.9	3.3	1.2	6.5	4.0	6.4
Canada	1999	1.4	5.4	0.1	3.5	2.3	2.3	0.9	4.7	2.1	5.3
England & Wales	1999	2.1	6.4	0.4	2.4	2.8	2.8	1.2	4.6	2.7	6.1
France	1999	1.7	5.5	0.3	1.8	1.0	1.3	1.1	3.0	1.1	4.2
Japan	1999	0.1	1.6	1.0	6.6	1.1	0.8	0.1	0.5	1.2	0.4
Sweden	1999	1.3	5.3	0.4	7.2	1.7	0.7	0.9	5.8	2.6	3.8
USA	1999	0.5	6.4	0.3	2.1	1.8	2.7	0.6	4.9	1.5	3.4
All 17 Countries*	1999	1.0	4.6	0.3	3.2	1.8	1.8	0.8	3.9	1.7	3.5
Hong Kong	2005	0	0.5	0.1	1.3	0.6	0.4	0.4	3.6	1.2	1.2

*17 industrialized countries: Australia, Belgium, Canada, Catalonia, Denmark, England & Wales, Finland, France, Japan, Netherlands, Northern Ireland, Poland, Portugal, Scotland, Sweden, Switzerland, USA
**Comparison refers to the 2000 survey

Source: van Kesteren, Mayhew, and Nieuwbeerta (2000)

later years, they were not lower than other major jurisdictions. For instance, the HK homicide rate in 1950 was 1.31 per 100,000 persons, compared with 0.78 in the UK, and 1.1 in Australia. In 1980 the HK robbery rate was 184 compared with the world average of about 40 per 100,000 (Shaw, Dijk and Rhomberg 2003). However, a less lethal picture emerges for HK homicide rates in 2000 and 2005 at 0.6 and 0.5 per 100,000 respectively, compared with 1.6 for the UK and 2 per 100,000 for Australia in 2001. Similarly, in 2000 the robbery rate for HK also dropped to 51 compared with the world average of over 60 per 100,000 (Shaw, Djik and Rhomberg 2003).

HK has experienced several crime waves and three major civil disturbances in the last half-century (Scott 1989). After the riots in 1967, HK recorded a continuous increase in crime but also the then Royal Hong Kong Police (now HKP) and the government embarked on a new era of crime prevention. The official overall *police recorded crime* in HK featured a rapid rise during the early 1970s but this stabilized between 1974 (1,294 per 100,000) and 1995 (1,493 per 100,000). The overall crime rate rose from 407 per 100,000 in 1963 to a peak of 1,610 in 1983. The violent crime rate rose tenfold from 48 in 1963 to peak at 477 per 100,000 in 1976 and thereafter declined but increased again from 1986 (259) to 1991 (340). The year of the handover, 1997, documented a comparatively low overall (1,038) and violent (212) crime rate. The overall drop in crime also matched the declining population group aged 15–29 – the part of the population with the highest risk of offending. The 15–29 age group declined from 1,643,400 in 1980 to 1,396,700 in 2005 (see Figure 3.1).

Definitions of crime used by police have also changed over time. For example, in 1987 the number of violent crimes was reduced from 21,215 to 14,303 (–32 per cent) due to re-categorization; in 1990 'throwing objects from a height' was reclassified from 'serious assault' to 'other crimes', producing a 6.4 per cent decline in serious assault and 2 per cent decline in total violent crime; and in 2003 the minimum age of criminal responsibility was increased to 10 years from 7. Thus, trends in crime may be significantly influenced by recording practices.

Serious offences such as homicide, rape, and robbery (with firearms) exhibited periodic 'waves' between 1961 and 2005 (see Figure 3.2). Homicide is regarded as a robust temporal measure of violent crime because it is much less subject to the vagaries of reporting, recording, and definitional changes. Homicide rates increased 3.5 times from 0.79 (n=17) in 1961 to 2.79 (n=115) in 1972. The spike in 1967 was a direct consequence of the civil disturbances that occurred in the

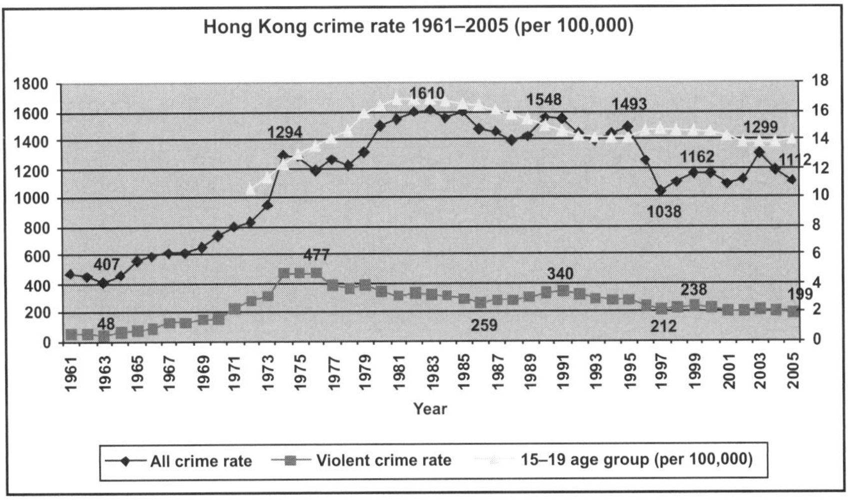

Figure 3.1 All Crime and Violent Crime Rates in Hong Kong, 1961–2005
Source: Hong Kong Police (1961–8, 1998–2005), Royal Hong Kong Police (1969–97), Crime Wing, Statistics Office (1978–2001, 2002–5)

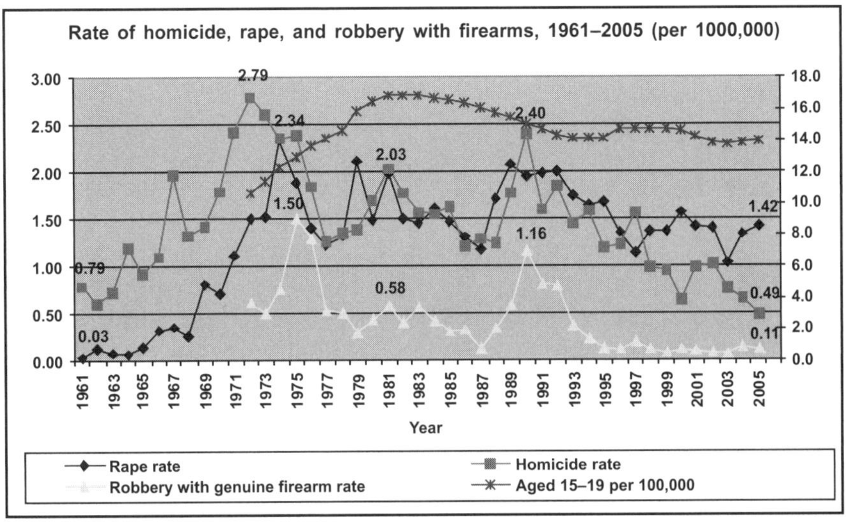

Figure 3.2 Rate of Homicide, Rape, and Robbery with Firearms in Hong Kong, 1961–2005
Source: Hong Kong Police (1961–8, 1998–2005), Royal Hong Kong Police (1969–97), Crime Wing, Statistics Office (1978–2001, 2002–5)

same year. The homicide rate then dropped quickly between 1972 and 1977 before turning upward again to 2.03 in 1981 reaching a second peak of 2.4 in 1990 (n=137) before gradually decreasing to 0.49 (n=34) in 2005. Rates for firearm robbery experienced a similar trend and reached a peak of 1.5 per 100,000 in 1975 (n=66), thereafter declining but spiked to 1.16 in 1990 (n=66) before declining tenfold to 0.11 per 100,000 in 2005 (n=8).

The trend for rape, however, illustrates the systematic under-reporting of early police statistics. Changes in recorded rape often reflect the shifting patterns of victim reporting behaviour and/or improving police administrative procedures, rather than the 'real' fluctuations in this offence. In 1961 there was only one police recorded rape incident (0.03) in a population of 3,168,100, while over the next few years (1962–65) the incident number was around five cases per annum. From 1968 onward the reported rape rate rose quickly reaching a peak rate in 1974 of 2.34 (n=101) and thereafter fluctuating between 1 and 2 per 100,000 with a second peak of 2.08 in 1989 (n=120).

Victim surveys: an alternative measure of crime

Addressing the systematic under-reporting problem, six sweeps of the HK Crime Victim Surveys (HKCVS) were officially conducted in 1978, 1981, 1986, 1989, 1994, and 1998 to estimate the actual risk of criminal victimization. The survey, conducted in January 1999, contacted 17,602 households and interviewed 49,942 persons 12 years and over from an eligible population of 5,674,600 persons and 2 million households (or 0.88 per cent of persons). The survey scope is confined to crimes against the person or household crimes and excludes some serious crimes (such as corruption and commercial crime). The HKCVS, like other victim surveys, is subject to non-sampling error because it depends on the respondent's memory, honesty, and willingness to co-operate, but face-to-face interviews can help to reduce ambiguous and inconsistent responses about victimization over the past year. Large samples tend to produce more reliable estimates and the HKCVS sample is large, but even so, for some rare crimes the sample may be too small for reliable estimation. Repeated surveys thus provide valuable guidance on trends and the impact of crime policies.[8]

The most recent HKCVS was conducted in 2006 and results were not available at the time of writing. Only detailed findings for 1998, the sixth survey,[9] are reported although summary findings for 2005 are included in Table 3.2 FN 9. Overall, 352,200 crimes were estimated for 1998 and 175,400 persons experienced 192,700 criminal events at a rate of 3.4 per cent of persons for personal crime or 4.1 per cent if minor offences excluded in the 1998 count are included.[10] A further 137,900 'households' experienced 159,500 crimes at a rate of 8.0 per cent of households (see Table 3.2), a rate higher than found for the first UN ICVS conducted in 2006 (see Table 3.1). Nevertheless, this is one of the lowest rates of victimization among the industrialized nations participating in the UN ICVS (van Dijk and van Kesteren 1996; Newman 1999). About 5 per cent (9,100 persons) of the victims of personal crime experienced more than five victimization events in 1998, showing that some segments of the population are at very high risk. Overall, 14.8 per cent (52,300) of the crimes reported to the survey involved crimes of violence, 39.9 per cent (140,400) theft from persons, and 45.3 per cent (159,500) crimes affecting households such as burglary and theft of cars. The general trends of personal crime victimization show decreases in risks compared to previous sweeps in most age groups, except for a significant rise in 1998 reported by the youngest respondents. Overall, older women (40–49 age group) are more at risk of personal theft and violence, but younger males have higher risks of violent offences (12–19 years age group). Violent

Table 3.2 Trends in HKCVS estimates of crime, 1978–2005

	1978	1981	1986	1989	1994	1998	2005
All personal							
% population	2.19	3.92	4.02	2.43	3.32	3.40	3.53
% report to police	18.0	37.7	39.1	42.2	38.9	36.3	20.9
Crimes of violence							
% population	0.98	0.98	0.95	0.67	1.05	0.92	1.07
% report to police	28.4	41.2	38.4	44.6	34.5	31.3	17.6
Personal crimes of theft							
% population	1.20	2.94	3.01	1.75	2.27	2.47	2.46
% report to police	9.5	36.6	39.4	41.3	40.9	38.2	22.4
All household crimes							
% population	4.65	8.64	7.37	6.12	9.34	7.98	6.57
% report to police	18.7	15.0	19.6	24.2	22.2	20.7	16.5

Source: Fight Crime Committee and Census and Statistics Department (1979, 1982, 1987, 1990, 1995, 1999, 2007)

and personal crime victimization peaks for either sex in the younger 12–19 age group.

Some of the select offences compared in Table 3.3 show contradictory trends and different periods of high and low rates depending on the source. Except for robbery, the data shows relatively low rates in 1978 that increase substantially in the 1980s and then decline or remain below peak levels, but higher than those found in 1978. Generally both measures indicate increases in wounding and assault, criminal damage, and burglary, and declines in robbery. Trends in victim data show steep increases in sexual assaults, criminal intimidation, theft from vehicles, snatching, and pickpocketing, whereas rates based on police figures show slight increases for sexual assault, stable rates for intimidation and theft from vehicles but declines in pickpocketing. Blackmail and fraud victim rates indicate increases since 1978, but police rates indicate significant declines.

Impact factors

The first crime wave occurred between 1963 and 1971, with steady increases in reported crime through this period. The second wave showed further increases from 1979 and reached the peak in 1982. The next crime wave noted in 1989–90 ended in 1995. The latest crime wave appeared in 2003 as a temporary rise after the sharp falls observed between 1996 and 1998. Overall, the 'crime waves' from 1979 onwards form a plateau of relatively stable levels of reported crime that has lasted 30 years. These fluctuations in crime have often been attributed to the impact of various social, economic, personal, and demographic factors, as well as reporting behaviour and law-enforcement policies and practices. We now turn to discuss these issues to account for the changes in crime in HK.

Reporting behaviour

Traver (1991) argued that the first crime wave was the result of the combined effect of an increased willingness to report crime and the curtailment of a widespread corruption within the police and other agencies. He argued that the first crime wave accelerated when the anti-corruption campaigns within the police were followed by the establishment of the Independent Commission Against Corruption (ICAC) in 1974. This dealt with every aspect of corruption in HK society. Active promotion of anti-corruption measures along with

Table 3.3 HKCVS and Hong Kong Police trends for select offences

	1978	1981	1986	1989	1994	1998
Rape and indecent assault						
HKCVS rate	58	32	127	126	165	376
Police rate	34	33	33	41	39	39
Wounding and assault						
HKCVS rate	48	83	225	121	162	181
Police rate	13	99	103	123	107	129
Robbery						
HKCVS rate	661	633	284	229	295	200
Police rate	123	160	122	114	103	48
Blackmail						
HKCVS rate	17	17	71	33	99	25
Police rate	58	22	12	10	14	7
Criminal intimidation						
HKCVS rate	48	35	145	102	233	251
Police rate	14	10	9	10	14	15
Snatching						
HKCVS rate	78	146	172	111	198	129
Police rate	16	39	33	26	27	14
Pickpocketing						
HKCVS rate	683	1795	1635	784	947	1142
Police rate	23	44	56	17	14	10
Deception/Fraud						
HKCVS rate	26	18	96	128	116	112
Police rate	60	85	33	31	53	41
Burglary						
HKCVS rate	361	698	659	545	630	576
Police rate	118	206	216	192	223	146
Theft from vehicle						
HKCVS rate	196	322	291	220	431	312
Police rate	45	93	94	91	63	42
Criminal damage						
HKCVS rate	35	74	94	141	408	320
Police rate	40	59	82	96	96	100

Note: Rates per 100,000 total population are rounded to the nearest whole number.
Source: Fight Crime Committee and Census and Statistics Department (1979, 1982, 1987, 1990, 1995, 1999)

consensus-style policing led to the dissolution of the symbiotic relationship between police and triads (organized criminals) observed during the 1940s through the 1960s. The breakdown of 'informal policing' by the triads resulted in a rapid surge in street crimes. Simultaneously the decolonization and relegitimization of the HK police force was achieved by implementing the community policing model, one that also led to positive increases in the public's willingness to report crime (Lethbridge 1985; Traver and Vagg 1991; Lo 1993; Gaylord and Traver 1995; Leung 1996).

Nevertheless, the proportion of respondents who claim to have reported offences to the HKP appears to have peaked in the 1989 HKCVS sweep, thereafter declining, especially for crimes of violence (see Table 3.2). The extent that decreases in crime after 1990 are accounted for by decreased willingness to report crime is unknown. The reporting rates for personal crimes of theft remain fairly stable at around two in five cases since the mandatory requirement to carry a universal identification card for all those over 15 was introduced in 1980. Household crime is not often reported, despite the incentive of insurance, but this crime includes a large number of criminal damage offences, attempted burglary, and other minor thefts where the victim suffered little or no loss. Generally in 1998, about 20 per cent of victims suffered no loss and 33.5 per cent losses of $150 or less, but for household crimes the proportion resulting in losses of $150 or less was higher at 42.2 per cent. Although 80 per cent of victims of crimes of violence sustained no injuries, the majority of those (63 per cent) who did report to the police had sustained an injury, suggesting the importance of evidence of an offence (for example, injury) in reporting behaviour.

The victim-reporting rate for HK also differs across different types of offences, as is typical in all jurisdictions. Compared to victims in Japan, those in HK reported less sexual victimization, personal property theft, attempted burglary, bicycle theft, motorcycle theft, and theft from cars but were more likely to report assaults/threats, robbery, and burglary (see Table 3.4).

People fail to report victimization for many reasons: about half (49.4 per cent) reflect a 'no need to report' attitude and about one-third did not report because they suffered little or no loss; over a quarter (28.1 per cent) believed that 'nothing could be done' due to lack of evidence and that police could not or would not help (15.3 per cent); a further 14.6 per cent attributed not reporting to difficult procedures or they were 'too busy';[11] and a further 7.4 per cent gave other reasons including reporting to someone else or fear of reprisal

Table 3.4 Reporting rate (%) by Crime UN ICVS*

	Surveyed year	Car theft	Theft from car	Motor-cycle theft	Bicycle theft	Burglary	Attempted burglary	Robbery	Personal property theft	Sexual victimization	Assaults and threats
Australia	1995–9	92	53	70	63	81	41	60	38	15	43
Canada	1995–9	99	58	34	50	80	46	41	28	19	35
England & Wales	1995–9	89	71	94	69	90	62	59	49	14	41
France	1995–9	91	64	78	35	73	37	32	51	26	34
Japan	1995–9	61	42	70	36	60	35	31	39	11	21
Sweden	1995–9	98	76	85	61	71	37	71	47	12	36
USA	1995–9	95	61	71	54	71	45	69	31	15	53
All 17 Countries	1995–9	91	62	79	56	78	40	55	42	15	36
Hong Kong	2001–5	n/a	28	59	56	77	29	39	29	10	36

*Estimates based on the last incident reported in the past five years: HK 2001–5, for other countries 1995–9.
Source: van Kesteren, Mayhew and Nieuwbeerta (2000); HK UNICVS cited in van Dijk, van Kesteren and Smit (2007).

(Fight Crime Committee and Census and Statistics Department 1999). Analysis of victim surveys shows that the better-educated and higher-income groups are more likely to report to the police. There is also considerable variation in the levels of reporting depending on the gravity of the offence and the relationship of the victim to the offender. Respondents also may tend to over-report that they or a friend had contacted police or assume the victimization was only a private matter (van Dijk and van Kesteren 1996). The importance of reporting behaviour in understanding the nature and prevalence of crime is borne out in Table 3.3, which compares police-recorded crime rates with estimates from the HKCVS that reflect the experience (and perception) of criminal victimization for selected offences.

Economy

Poverty and income inequality are often thought to influence crime trends because theft is usually about material gain. Gaylord and Lang (1997) examined the correlation between real wages and the robbery rate from 1970 to 1980, and they argued that in the case of robbery:

> the absence of a social safety net and when most of the population live close to the margin of survival relative to local standards of consumption, an economic downturn that substantially reduces average real wages will be reflected quickly in an increase in crimes involving little prior knowledge of criminal methods, planning and personal risk. (1997: 17)

Also an improved economy and rising wages could reduce the motivation to commit robbery and this may account for the continual decline of certain violent crimes since 1976 (see Figure 3.1).

Traver (1991) asserted that observed increases in crime during the second crime wave (1978–82) are largely a result of increased illegal opportunities combined with a lessening of social constraints in a modernizing and urbanizing society. Rejecting the view that HK had a crime and disorder problem due to the invasion of capitalist investment, he argued crime trends would eventually decline or level off as the effects of rapid social and economic change begin to lessen and prosperity and opportunities are more evenly distributed in society. The data supports such a contention as the overall crime rate since 1982 was in decline, albeit slowly, but more significantly from the mid-1990s onwards (see Figure 3.1). This was a period when the social security system was also expanding quickly, but the Gini coefficient (which signifies the gap between the poor and the rich) worsened in the 2000s.

Expanding business opportunities during the 1980s provoked keen competition, particularly in some sectors, and enabled triad gangs to expand protection markets by franchising their different brands of violence (Chu 2000; Lee, Broadhurst and Beh 2006). After the dissolution of the police–triads symbiosis in the 1970s, triads soon found new footholds in various legitimate or semi-legitimate businesses such as the management of entertainment premises or acting as 'arbitrators' in debt disputes. Triad gang-related blackmail or wounding became rare during the later crime wave. The open market economy in China during the 1980s and 1990s also extended the effect of income inequality, and cross-border crimes, such as firearm robbery, illegal immigration, and smuggling, increased rapidly throughout this period (Vagg 1991).

The reasons for the abrupt decline in the overall crime rate between 1995 and 1997 and thereafter a significant reduction in rates is less clear. Although the economic development of HK was stable, we note the decline observed is far less evident in the data from crime victim surveys. The enactment of the *Organized and Serious Crimes Ordinance* (Cap. 455) in 1994 also impacted on triad activities but had a minor influence on the overall crime rate.

HK has gone through several crises after the People's Republic of China (PRC) resumed sovereignty in July 1997. Shortly after the transfer of sovereignty HK's economy suffered as a result of the collapse of the Thai stock market and the subsequent Asian financial crisis, which triggered the 1998 recession in the HK property market. An epidemic of severe acute respiratory syndrome (SARS) in 2003 further depressed the already weakened HK economy. These events intensified social instability and may have been reflected in the small increase in the overall crime rate in 1999 and 2003 (see Figure 3.1), but the effect was temporary because the overall crime rate soon returned to the previous lower level in the following years. Formal and informal responses to these problems (such as tax relief and social security) appear to have had a dampening effect on prolonged social instability.

Indeed, the 2006 Heritage Foundation/*The Wall Street Journal* ranked HK first out of 157 countries in their 'Index of Economic Freedom' – for the 11th consecutive occasion. The gross domestic product at purchasing power parity per capita (GDP [PPP] per capita)[12] of HK reached $346,710 in 2006.[13] HK also ranked 8th in GDP (PPP) $ per capita among 181 members of the International Monetary Fund in

2005, which was the highest among all the Asian members.[14] The percentage of the population in higher education increased from 43 per cent in 1991 to 52 per cent in 2001. Nonetheless, HK's economic success is not shared by all sectors and the Gini coefficient[15] as noted increased from 0.476 to 0.525 between 1991 and 2001 (Table 3.5), reflecting greater income inequality. Yet the crime trends for two key instrumental offences – burglary and robbery – as well as all violent crime declined during the same period (see Table 3.5). This does not disprove Gaylord and Lang's (1997) hypothesis, but an aging HK population may counter growing income inequality.

Criminal justice policy

Considering crime control and 'punitiveness',[17] the 7th UNSCTOCJ survey showed HK ranked among the largest police forces per capita with 487 police per 100,000 persons. Only Portugal (491.2)

Table 3.5 Key social index and crime rate in Hong Kong

	1991	1996	2001
Median monthly domestic household income (HK$)	9,964	17,500	18,705
Gini coefficient*[16]	0.476	0.518	0.525
Population aged 15 and over by educational attainment (Highest level attended)			
Upper secondary and Matriculation (% by population =>15)	1,383,848 (31.7%)	1,712,019 (33.8%)	2,001,771 (35.8%)
Tertiary (% by population =>15)	490,891 (11.2%)	768,520 (15.2%)	918,500 (16.4%)
All crime (rate per 100,000 populations)	1,541	1,253	1,086
All violent crime (rate per 100,000 populations)	340	241	202
All burglary (rate per 100,000 populations)	794	617	570
All robbery (rate per 100,000 populations)	158	62	47

Source: Crime Wing, Statistics Office (1978–2001; 2002–5); Hong Kong Census and Statistics Department (2001)

and Italy (559.4) exceeded HK, while most other Asian jurisdictions had proportionally smaller forces (e.g. Philippines 147.8, Japan 181.7, South Korea 190.7, Singapore 324.2, Malaysia 353.6, and Thailand 354.9). HK's large police force exceeds that of most industrialized countries such as Canada (181.9), France (211.0), Australia (219.0), and England and Wales (233.9). According to the 7th UNSCTOCJ survey, HK also has a moderately high incarceration rate per 100,000 of 176.8 in 2000, higher than Japan (48.2), France (87.3), Italy (93.7), Australia (113.1), England & Wales (123.1), and South Korea (134.2), but notably lower than Malaysia (339.9), Thailand (368.0), Singapore (411.5), and the United States of America (638.1).

Since the 1980s, HK has sent more people to custodial sentences, and substantial 'net widening' in the 1970s and 1980s in the juvenile justice system was noted by Gray (1991) and has continued. The admission rate of correctional centres has increased from 222 in 1994 to 418 per 100,000 in 2004. From 1982 to 2004, there was a three-fold increase in the admission rate (excluding remands, recalls, and those sentenced to drug treatment centres) from 141 to 418, despite a general decline in overall crimes since the 1990s (see Figure 3.3). This punitive sentiment might partially contribute to the decrease in crime rate by incapacitating at risk persons.

HK's relative freedom from large-scale public disorder partly reflects the success of a proactive strategy of crime prevention and control. Partnerships between the private sector, government, and the community are strongly encouraged. The police are actively engaged in youth work and sponsoring youth clubs – notably *Junior Police Call* with over 130,000 children regularly involved. Following the British model of crime control that focuses on offender rehabilitation, HK has developed its own integrated welfare-control correctional model. For instance, in 2006 more than one-fifth of the HK government budget was spent on human security[18] (10 per cent, HK$27,050 million) and social welfare[19] (13.7 per cent, HK$36,231 million).[20] Social welfare policies have also received increasing attention reflected by the rising proportion of the Government's budget devoted to this area from 2001 (11.0 per cent) to 2006 (13.7 per cent) (see Table 3.6).

The low crime rate in HK may also reflect the relative effectiveness of law enforcement, as indicated by the relatively high incarceration rate, large police force, and the significant public resources allocated. Nevertheless, state action accounts for only part of the reason for the stability and low crime levels experienced and the roles of socio-cultural and other factors are relevant. The successful transition from a once suppressive colonial quasi-military police force into the

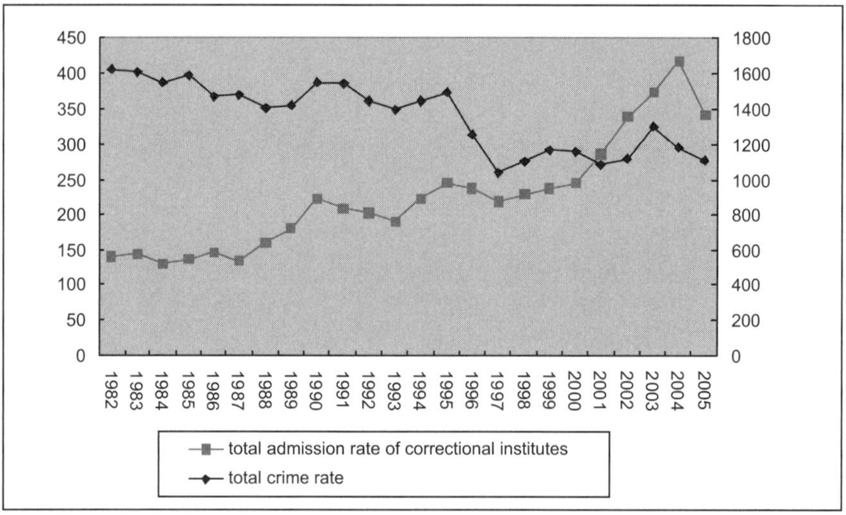

Figure 3.3 Correctional Admissions (excluding Drug Addiction Treatment Centres)
Source: Crime Wing, Statistics Office (1978–2001; 2002–5); Hong Kong Correctional Services Department (1982–97a; 1997b –2005)

Table 3.6 Total public expenditure by policy area 2001–2 to 2006–7

Policy area groups	Actual				Revised estimate	Estimate
	2001–2 %	2002–3 %	2003–4 %	2004–5 %	2005–6 % ($M)	2006–7 % ($M)
Social welfare	11.0	12.1	12.3	12.9	13.5 (33,826)	13.7 (36,231)
Security	10.2	10.3	9.9	9.9	10.0 (25,111)	10.2 (27,050)
Total public expenditure, $M	269,359	263,520	271,098	257,137	250,255	264,889

Source: Hong Kong Special Administrative Region Government (2001–7)

service-based, client-oriented community policing practice of the modern period contributed to effective crime prevention (Gaylord and Traver 1995; Lo and Cheuk 2004). Local pro-social traditions, such as utilitarian familism (Lau 1982), also serve informal social control and crime prevention.

Age cohort and arrest rate

We argue that age is a crucial factor in shaping crime trends, as illustrated in Table 3.7. Between 1990 and 2005 the number of arrested persons declined for all age groups but the proportions in the younger 16–30 age group dropped from 51 per cent to 36 per cent (–15 per cent), while the older (31+) group increased from 34 per cent to 53 per cent (+19 per cent). The proportion of the HK population in the age group 15–29 decreased from 26 per cent to 20 per cent (–6 per cent), while the 30 or above age group increased from 52 per cent to 66 per cent (+14 per cent). The proportion of violent crime as a percentage of all reported crime also declined from 21 per cent to 18 per cent. These figures suggest the proportion of higher-risk juveniles and youths in HK is an influential factor in crime. The significant contribution of juveniles has merited additional government attention in the form of various interventions, sanctions and social policies that led to the promotion of partnerships between the government and the HK community.

In the past four decades, many jurisdictions, including HK, had experienced rising crime until the mid- and late 1990s. Nevertheless, how HK has emerged as a 'safe' city is complex and can only be generally addressed in this chapter. On average the HK Government spends one-tenth of its public expenditure on security. The HKP has long been equipped with extensive powers of 'stop and search' and it is one of the largest police forces deployed. Having striven to improve its image and relations with the public, the HKP has in general obtained the support of the HK people, and successfully transformed from the 'rough and corrupted bullies' of the colonial past into a professional and modern police service. This high level of legitimacy despite sporadic criticism about police misbehaviour and corruption reflects these efforts. According to the 2006 UN ICVS, 94 per cent of respondents reported that police in their areas had done a 'fairly good job' or a 'very good job' in controlling crime.

Why Hong Kong has a lower than expected level of crime despite its dense urban environment is an important question. The protective value of cultural and ethnic homogeneity combined with the preservation of traditional Confucian values and extended kinship structures are crucial, but the resultant compliant pro-social society could also be a reflection of the 'collective apathy' associated with utilitarian familism (Lau 1982). Familism also amplifies the shaming effect of crime because the shame is shared by the entire family and this combined with a government hostile to crime reinforces conservatism. Also, strict gun laws have effectively reduced firearm

Table 3.7 Age and arrest rate

	1990	1995	2000	2005
Overall crime (no.)	88,300	91,886	77,245	77,437
Overall crime rate (per 100,000)	1,547.9	1,492.6	1,159.0	1,111.7
Violent crime (no.)	18,820	17,087	14,812	13,890
Violent crime (rate per 100,000)	329.9	277.6	222.2	199.4
Violent crime (% of all crime)	21	19	19	18
Total arrest (no.)	43,713	53,098	40,930	40,804
Total arrest (rate per 100,000)	766.3	862.5	614.1	585.8
Arrested aged 16–30 (no.)	22,312	23,950	17,442	14,737
Arrested aged 16–30 (% of all)	51	45	43	36
Population aged 15–29 (no.)	1,503,400	1,410,600	1,458,300	1,396,700
Population aged 15–29 (% of all)	26	23	22	20
Arrested aged 31 or above (no.)	14,818	22,425	17,259	21,536
Arrested aged 31 or above (% of all)	34	42	42	53
Population aged 30 or above (no.)	2,974,800	3,550,400	4,138,400	4,587,500
Population aged 30 or above (% of all)	52	58	62	66

Note: Juveniles are those aged 7–15 prior to July 2003, thereafter those aged 10–15 due to the change in the minimum age of criminal liability.
Source: Crime Wing, Statistics Office (1978–2001; 2002–5)

robbery to fewer than five events per year and not a single incident of domestic violence was perpetrated with a firearm in the past five years. The successful suppression of cross-border crime by way of mandatory Identity Cards and co-ordinated efforts with the Public Security Bureau PRC has had a significant impact on a small, enclosed jurisdiction like HK (Broadhurst 2005). Punishment is also generally severe on either side of the border, as reflected by the high incarceration rate in HK and the death penalty in PRC.

The densely populated nature of urban high-rise living also provides higher levels of natural or informal surveillance by facilitating the presence of capable guardians and reduces the opportunity for crime. The availability of attractive wealthy targets within the city has a limited stimulus on crime opportunity due to the large numbers of private security officers employed.[21] In addition, advanced crime prevention technologies including closed-circuit televisions are installed in public housing, public recreational, areas and crime hot spots, and these serve to reduce potential offenders' willingness to commit crime.

Various measures that attempted to bring the public and state together in fighting crime have been successfully implemented since the late 1960s. The continual localization and professionalization of the HK Police Force also overcame the challenge caused by the rising proportion of at-risk youths during the 1970s and the cross-border crime waves in the late 1980s and early 1990s. The Fight Crime Committee and the HKP work closely with the public to develop programmes that aim at reducing youth offending and recidivism. District Fight Crime Committees proactively co-ordinate the local community's effort in fighting against crime and retain their potency as a means for mobilizing public responses to crime (see also Chapter 12 of this volume on crime prevention).

Conclusion

There are limitations to this chapter. We focus mainly on street crimes but omit crimes of the powerful, such as corruption and other white-collar crimes. We only touch on some crimes and we did not discuss the impact of drug use, media, or technology on crime trends. Nonetheless, age, economic factors, policy, and changes in the willingness to report have impacted on crime trends at different times. Compared to other nations, the low crime rate observed in HK is the outcome of a complex mixture of cultural traditions, proactive crime prevention, and the emergence of a legitimate 'consensus' style of law enforcement. Thus family-oriented Confucian values, a large professionalized and localized police *service*, strict gun laws, effective suppression of cross-border crime, high levels of formal or informal surveillance, ethnic homogeneity, proactive efforts against organized crime and corruption, and severe punishment of the convicted all serve to reduce opportunity for crime. However, with an aging population more attention will be needed to curb the growing incidence of crime against the elderly. HK's service-oriented policing, however, faces new challenges. The challenges are not only about the threat of transnational crime and traditional crime and its evolution in cyberspace, but in the demand for proactive action on domestic violence such as the increasing number of homicide-suicide incidents (Chan, Beh and Broadhurst 2003), where the would-be guardians may be the perpetrators themselves. This requires balancing the role of state intervention in family disputes with heightened respect for civil rights, while at the same time ensuring social services and police collaborate in crime prevention.

Notes

1 This questionnaire provides statistical data about the criminal justice system for 1998–2000. Please refer to http://www.unodc.org/unodc/en/crime_cicp_survey_seventh.html

2 The 2006 CPI (163 countries) for Asia (rank): Japan (17), Macao (26), Taiwan (34), South Korea (42), Malaysia (44), Thailand (63), China (70), India (70), Vietnam (111), Philippines (121), and Indonesia (130). Source: http://www.transparency.org

3 The survey was conducted by the Centre for Criminology and Social Science Research, University of Hong Kong.

4 Included in the survey: car theft, theft from car, motorcycle theft, bicycle theft, burglary and attempts, personal property theft, sexual victimization, and assault/threat.

5 Percentages are adjusted by age, gender, and district to reflect the actual population distribution of HK.

6 If only owners of vehicles were counted, the percentage victimized at least once was for car theft (0 per cent), theft from car (2.2 per cent), motorcycle theft (2.9 per cent), and bicycle theft (4.2 per cent).

7 The 2005 UN ICVS results were not available at the time of writing.

8 The text of this section is drawn from Broadhurst (2005).

9 The smaller UN HKICVS also undertaken in 2006 and discussed below involved 2,283 respondents over the age of 18 years interviewed on the telephone. The 2005 HKCVS showed rates of crime remained largely similar to 1998 levels. Small increases were found for all personal crime (3.53% in 2005 compared to 3.4% in 1998) and crimes of violence (1.07% in 2005 compared to 0.92% in 1998). A significant decrease was observed for household crimes (6.57% in 2005 compared to 7.98% in 1998) while personal crimes of theft remained about the same (2.46% in 2005 compared to 2.47% in 1998). However, a substantial decline in the proportion of respondents who stated that they reported the crime to police was observed. The reduction in the willingness to report to police appears to be a consequence of the decline in the severity of the offences reported by victims.

10 Note 39,000 'minor offences' comprising: 1,400 attempted assault; 15,600 attempted pick-pocketing, 4,300 common assault with no injury and; 17,700 involving objects dropped from a height without injury were excluded from the 1998 data and thus the overall rate compared to previous years is artificially reduced.

11 A small number of respondents (2.5 per cent) said they did not report because they were 'too busy', with as many as 10 per cent of snatching victims giving this as the reason for not reporting.

12 The value of all final goods and services produced within a nation in a given year divided by the average population for the same year.
13 Source: http://www.yearbook.gov.hk/2005/
14 GDP (PPP) $US per capita calculations as prepared by the International Monetary Fund in 2005: Hong Kong ($33,479), Japan ($30,615), Singapore ($28,368), Republic of China (Taiwan) ($27,721), South Korea ($20,590), Malaysia ($11,201), Thailand ($8,368), PRC ($7,198), Philippines ($4,923), Indonesia ($4,459), India ($3,320), Vietnam ($3,025).
15 A Gini index of 0 represents perfect equality, while an index of 100 implies perfect inequality.
16 According to the data compiled by the World Bank, the Gini Index for HK (2001), 52.5, was higher than most western countries: Canada (2000): 32.6; Germany (2000): 28.3; Netherlands (1999): 30.9; Sweden (2000): 25; UK (1999): 36; US (2000): 40.8; but closer to Asian countries: Philippines (2000): 46.1; Singapore (1998): 42.5; China (2001): 44.7. Source: Table 2.8 Distribution of income or consumption, from World Bank (2006) http://devdata.worldbank.org/wdi2006/contents/Section2.htm.
17 Although the death penalty was abolished in 1992, HK had been a *de facto* abolitionist jurisdiction since the 1960s. Nevertheless, many offences, such as firearm-related offences, often result in lengthy sentences when compared to sentences given in western countries for like offences (Tonry and Frase 2001).
18 The security budget includes the Administration of Justice, Anti-Corruption, Immigration Control, Internal Security, Legal Administration, and Legal Aid.
19 The social welfare budget covers Social Welfare and Women's Interests.
20 The estimated total public expenditure is HK$264,889 million. The remaining allocations: education (21.3 per cent), health (12.2 per cent), infrastructure (9.2 per cent), housing (6.0 per cent), economic (5.8 per cent), environment and food (4.4 per cent), community and external affairs (3.2 per cent), support (14.0 per cent). Source: http://www.budget.gov.hk/2006/
21 Approximately 130,000 people are registered security providers, mostly employed in guarding services.

Review questions

1 To what extent have changes in the youth population contributed to declines in HK's crime rate?
2 Discuss why strict gun laws may have made robbery less commonplace in HK.
3 Crime victim surveys show that reporting behaviour can be a crucial determinant in changes in crime rates, but why do they vary so much for different offences?

4 Is the criminal justice system in HK becoming more punitive? Does the use of custodial sentences reflect community attitudes to social control?
5 What will the crime trend in HK be like in the next five–ten years?

References

Broadhurst, R.G. (2005) 'Crime trends in Hong Kong', in R. Estes (ed.) *Social Development in Hong Kong: The Unfinished Agenda* (pp. 185–92). New York: Oxford University Press.

Chan, C.Y., Beh, S.L. and Broadhurst, R.G. (2003) 'Homicide-suicide in Hong Kong, 1989–1998', *Forensic Science International*, 137 (2/3), 165–71.

Chu, Y.K. (2000) *The Triads as Business*. London: Routledge.

Crime Wing, Statistics Office (1978–2001, various issues) *Crime and Enforcement Report*. Hong Kong: Government Printer.

Crime Wing, Statistics Office (2002–5, various issues) *Crime in Hong Kong*. Hong Kong: Government Printer.

Faure, D. (ed.) (1997) *A Documentary History of Hong Kong: Society*. Hong Kong: Hong Kong University Press.

Fight Crime Committee and Census and Statistics Department (1979) *Crime and its Victims in Hong Kong in 1977*. Hong Kong: Government Printer.

Fight Crime Committee and Census and Statistics Department (1982) *Crime and its Victims in Hong Kong in 1981*. Hong Kong: Government Printer.

Fight Crime Committee and Census and Statistics Department (1987) *Crime and its Victims in Hong Kong in 1986*. Hong Kong: Government Printer.

Fight Crime Committee and Census and Statistics Department (1990) *Crime and its Victims in Hong Kong in 1989*. Hong Kong: Government Printer.

Fight Crime Committee and Census and Statistics Department (1995) *Crime and its Victims in Hong Kong in 1994*. Hong Kong: Government Printer.

Fight Crime Committee and Census and Statistics Department (1999) *Crime and its Victims in Hong Kong in 1998*. Hong Kong: Government Printer.

Fight Crime Committee and Census and Statistics Department (2007) *Crime and its Victims in Hong Kong 2005*. Hong Kong: Government Printer.

Gaylord, M.S. and Traver, H. (eds) (1994) *Introduction to the Hong Kong Criminal Justice System*. Hong Kong: Hong Kong University Press.

Gaylord, M.S. and Traver, H. (1995) 'Colonial policing and the demise of British rule in Hong Kong', *International Journal of the Sociology of Law*, 23 (1): 23–43.

Gaylord, M.S. and Lang, G. (1997) 'Robbery, recession and real wages in Hong Kong', *Crime, Law & Social Change*, 27 (1): 49–71.

Gray, P. (1991) 'Juvenile crime and disciplinary welfare', in H. Traver and J. Vagg (eds) *Crime and Justice in Hong Kong* (pp. 25–41). Hong Kong: Oxford University Press.

Hong Kong Census and Statistics Department (2001) *Population Census 2001: Summary Results*. Hong Kong: Government Printer.

Hong Kong Correctional Services Department (1982–97a, various issues) *Annual Review*, Hong Kong: Government Printer.
Hong Kong Correctional Services Department (1997b–2005, various issues) *Annual Report*. Hong Kong: Government Printer.
Hong Kong Police (1961–8, 1998–2005, various issues) *Annual Report*. Hong Kong: Government Printer.
Hong Kong Special Administrative Region (2001–7, various issues) *The Budget, Hong Kong Special Administrative Region Government*. Hong Kong: Government Printer.
Lau, R.W.K. (2004) 'Community policing in Hong Kong: Transplanting a questionable model', *Criminal Justice: The International Journal of Policy and Practice*, 4 (1): 61–80.
Lau, S.K. (1982) *Society and Politics in Hong Kong*. Hong Kong: Chinese University Press.
Lee, K.W., Broadhurst, R.G. and Beh, S.L. (2006) 'Triad-related homicides in Hong Kong', *Forensic Science International*, 62 (1/3): 183–90.
Lethbridge, H.J. (1985) *Hard Graft in Hong Kong: Scandal, Corruption and the ICAC*. Hong Kong: Oxford University Press.
Leung, B.K.P. (1996) *Perspectives of Hong Kong Society*. Hong Kong: Oxford University Press.
Lo, T.W. (1993) *Corruption and Politics in Hong Kong and China*. Milton Keyes: Open University Press.
Lo, W.H.C. and Cheuk, C.Y.A. (2004) 'Community policing in Hong Kong: Development, performance and constraints', *Policing: An International Journal of Police Strategies & Management*, 27 (1): 97–127.
Newman, G. (ed.) (1999) *Global Report on Crime and Justice*. New York: Oxford University Press.
Royal Hong Kong Police (1969–97, various issues) *Annual Report*. Hong Kong: Government Printer.
Scott, I. (1989) *Political Change and The Crisis of Legitimacy in Hong Kong*. Hong Kong: Oxford University Press.
Shaw, M., Dijk, J.V. and Rhomberg, W. (2003) 'Determining trends in global crime and justice: An overview of results from the United Nations Surveys of Crime Trends and Operations of Criminal Justice Systems', *Forum on Crime and Society*, 3 (1/2): 35–63.
Siegel, L.J. and Senna, J.J. (2007) *Introduction to Criminal Justice* (11th edn). Belmont, CA: Wadsworth.
Tonry, M. and Frase, R.S. (eds) (2001) *Sentencing and Sanctions in Western Countries*. New York: Oxford University Press.
Traver, H. (1991) 'Crime trends', in H. Traver and J. Vagg (eds) *Crime and Justice in Hong Kong* (pp. 10–24). Hong Kong: Oxford University Press.
Vagg, J. (1991) 'Illegal immigration and cross-border crime', in H. Traver and J. Vagg (eds) *Crime and Justice in Hong Kong* (pp. 83–97). Hong Kong: Oxford University Press.

Vagg, J., Bacon-Shone, J., Gray, P. and Lam, D. (1995) *Research on the Social Causes of Juvenile Crime*. Hong Kong: Government Printer.

van Dijk, J.M. and van Kesteren, J.N. (1996) 'The prevalence and perceived risk seriousness of victimisation by crime; some results of the international crime victim survey', *European Journal of Crime, Criminal Law and Criminal Justice*, 4 (1): 48–71.

Van Dijk, J., van Kesteren, J. and Smit, P. (2007) *Criminal Victimisation in International Perspective: Key Findings from the 2004–2005 ICVS and EU ICS*. Tilburg: University of Tilburg and UNODCP.

van Kesteren, J.N., Mayhew, P. and Nieuwbeerta, P. (2000) *Criminal Victimisation in Seventeen Industrialized Countries: Key-findings from the 2000 International Crime Victims Survey*. The Hague: Ministry of Justice.

Wong, S.W. (1992) *Youth Problems in North District: An Integrated Study on Unruly and Delinquent Behaviours*. Hong Kong: Working Group on Youth Problem, North District Board (in Chinese).

World Bank (2006) *World Development Indicators 2006*. Washington, DC: World Bank.

Legislation cited

Organized and Serious Crimes Ordinance (Cap. 455)

Useful websites

Census and Statistics Department	http://www.censtatd.gov.hk/home/index.jsp
Centre for Criminology, University of Hong Kong	www.crime.hku.hk
Hong Kong Police	http://www.police.gov.hk/hkp-home/english/index.htm
Hong Kong Security Bureau	http://www.sb.gov.hk/eng/about/welcome.htm
Hong Kong Yearbook (2006)	http://www.yearbook.gov.hk/
The Budget (2006–7)	http://www.budget.gov.hk/2006/eng/speech.htm
United Nations	http://un.org
United Nations Surveys on Crime Trends and the Operations of Criminal Justice Systems	http://www.unodc.org/unodc/en/crime_cicp_surveys.html

Chapter 4

Crime victims

Wai To Chan

Introduction

Victims of crime play various roles in the criminal justice process. For instance, they report offences to law enforcement agencies, provide evidence, make statements, attend identification parades in police stations, and attend court as a witness. However, in contemporary society, considerable attention has been paid to the defendant. Those persons at the receiving end of the crime (notably the crime victims) have not been given corresponding equal attention. Quite often, both the rights and interest of crime victims are neglected. In the criminal sciences literature, crime victims are rightfully called 'forgotten persons' (United Nations 1999a: 1; see also United Nations 1999b).

In view of the above, it seems that the victims of crime are left to fend for themselves from statutory resources or assistance from family and/or community groups or non-government organizations. This chapter attempts to review the present provision of various victim programmes and to discuss the drawbacks as well as the absence of a sound philosophical basis for action.

Who are 'crime victims'?

The definition of 'crime victims' is controversial. Generally, the term refers to those persons being at the receiving end of a crime. According to a legal definition, crime victims are those persons who, individually or collectively, have suffered harm, loss, or damage through acts or omission which are in violation of criminal laws (Sutherland 1949: 31). A human rights definition implies that crime victims are those persons who have been deprived of basic human rights (Schwendinger and Schwendinger 1970: 148). A social process definition widens the category of crime victims by considering all those who have suffered pain as a consequence of social interaction (Cohen 1973: 624). In other words, they are the ones being victimized by the process of social perception and reaction as applied and interpreted by agents of the state authorities.

The above definitions throw light on the meaning of the crime victims from different angles. Yet, upon closer scrutiny, it is very difficult for all academics, professionals, practitioners, or clients to reach unanimous agreement on the exact category of both 'direct' and 'indirect' or 'primary' and 'secondary' victims of crime. For instance, victimization surveys in Hong Kong (Census and Statistics Department 1979, 1982, 1987, 1990, 1995, 1999) distinguish between household crimes and personal crimes. On typical household crimes questions such as 'burglary does not cause serious problems of interpretation' are common. However, with personal crimes like theft of a vehicle, the circle of victims may be defined differently by various groups of respondents. Parents may see themselves as victims when their child's vehicle is stolen. Yet, others may not. Equally, no conclusion can be arrived at on the question of whether family members of victims of crimes of violence must be considered as crime victims.

In any case, the definition of crime victims remains quite controversial. Even international bodies such as the United Nations and the European Committee on Crime Problems have different emphases on the conception of crime victims. The United Nations, on the occasion of its Seventh Congress on the Prevention of Crime and the Treatment of Offenders, defined crime victims as 'persons who, individually or collectively, have suffered harm … through acts or omissions which are in violation of criminal laws operative within Member States, including those laws which proscribe criminal abuse of power' (Colvin 1988: 57); whereas the European countries, at their Sixteenth Criminological Research Conference, defined crime victims as 'persons who stand a reasonable chance of winning a civil law suit against the perpetrator of an act which is defined by positive law as a crime' (European Committee on Crime Problems 1984: 11). Seen in the above definitions, the United Nations, in a much more restrictive sense, considers crime victims to be those within the legal framework or criminal justice system; while in western Europe, the term refers to the broader civil law concept of the damaged person. This covers all persons who have suffered any form of damage such as pain arising from the consequence of offence under consideration in legal terms.

In short, there is no unanimous agreement on the concept of 'crime victims' as the notion can be principally examined from legal, human rights, and social process perspectives. The situation is further complicated by the fact that the exact category of 'crime victims' can be quite arguable (as in the case of personal crimes according to the legal definition). The lack of a unified formal definition of 'crime victims', indeed, poses considerable problems within the criminal jurisprudence in general and in the field of victimology in particular.

In reality, the number of victims always being a 'dark figure' could be explained by the following:

- Those involved may know that an offence has been committed, but are willing parties to it (e.g. illegal abortion, under-age sexual relations, or drinking under-age).
- The offender may know that he or she has committed a crime, but the victim may not be aware of it (e.g. shoplifting or sexual assaults on children).
- The non-reporting of offences is due to (a) victims' fear, (b) feelings of helplessness and the perceived powerlessness of police, and (c) the threat of further retaliation by offender(s) and further victimization from authorities (Kidd and Chayet 1984).
- The police, with their discretionary power at hand, may fail to record crimes simply because of lack of resources and power, and at times they might have the view of not wanting to antagonize the general public by pursuing every single incident.

The costs of victimization may include such things as damaged property, pain and suffering, time lost from work, and so forth. The explanation of victimization depends on how the problem is being conceptualized (Siegel 2007: 75): (a) victimization participation theory asserts that victims provoke criminals either through active or passive participation; (b) lifestyle theory suggests that victims put themselves in danger by going out late at night or associating with peers of dubious character; (c) deviant place theory argues that victimization is related to the neighbourhood crime rate; and (d) the routine activities theory maintains that a pool of motivated offenders exists and that these offenders will take advantage of unguarded or suitable targets.

Indeed, the treatment of victims depends on different victimological schools of thoughts. Some programmes help victims by providing court services, economic compensation, crisis intervention, public education, and so forth. Some countries have even created a victim's Bill of Rights or Victim's Charter. Nevertheless, rather than relying on the justice system, victims are often left to fend for themselves in the community or through support from community groups for self-protection or rehabilitation. The relationship of both community care and crime victim is not distant at all, to say the least.

Relationship between community care and crime victim

At first sight, the terms 'community care' and 'crime victim' appear to be totally unrelated. While the former refers to health and social services being provided for those who require more care and support from others because they are elderly, mentally ill, mentally challenged, or physically disabled (notably not the crime victim), the latter refers to those persons who are at the receiving end of a crime as defined in the contemporary criminal justice system.

The concept of 'community care' (in the sector of health and welfare) generally aims to provide sufficient support to allow the individual to lead as normal a life as possible and to develop his or her ability to the maximum, hopefully resulting in complete independence for the individual. However, the 'crime victim' (in the sector of criminal justice) is not placed at the centre since the system of justice is primarily concerned with the maintenance of rules of law, and not much with victims' interest or needs.

However, allowing the differences in aims, the two terms are not totally unrelated, particularly before the emergence of the modern criminal justice system (Harding 1982). Victims in the past used to have greater involvement and to exert considerable influence throughout the conflict resolution in their own communities. Nowadays, community care is important, particularly to crime victims, not only because they are marginal members of the criminal justice system, but also because they are often the forgotten people in the field of social services or welfare provision. More crucially, in view of the government's current philosophy of welfare provision which aims to minimize its obligation, crime victims cannot expect much from the government's intervention on the basis of a collective well-being.

Rather, individual crime victims have to solicit assistance from statutory programmes in the community and from non-government services rendered by those community groups or organizations entirely outside the criminal justice system.

In this respect, the terms 'community care' and 'crime victim' become closely connected, particularly with the core problem of crime victims being their loss of social trust and their feelings of alienation from their community (Smale 1984). This urgently calls for a redevelopment of 'community' which can be achieved through the mobilization and integration of a diverse range of organized social resources, including both voluntary and state-financed (Clarke 1982: 465–9). Indeed, the statutory victim programmes in the community and those voluntary efforts sustained by community groups or local volunteers have significant and complementary roles to play to help the crime victim.

Provision of victim programmes in Hong Kong

The major provision of victim programmes can be categorized: statutory provisions of both Compensation Order and Criminal and Law Enforcement Injuries Compensation, and voluntary efforts sustained by non-government organizations such as Harmony House for Battered Wives and Services for Sexually Assaulted Victims (see, for example, Tsun and Lui-Tsang 2005; Chui and Fu 2007).

Compensation order

Since 1972, the use of court-ordered compensation has been the most direct way for offenders to recompense their victims. The courts can require the offender to pay compensation to the victim for any injury or loss or damage resulting from the offence of which he or she has been convicted and any other offence taken into consideration. The court has the power to ensure that the offender pays what he or she can afford, even if it is not what the victim is fully entitled to.

Both the *Criminal Procedure Ordinance* (Cap. 221) and the *Magistrates Ordinance* (Cap. 227) provide the court full power to compensate the victims of crime through the offenders. Section 73 of the *Criminal Procedure Ordinance* provides:

> Where a person is convicted of an offence, the court may, in addition to passing such sentence as may otherwise by law be

passed or making an order under section 107(1), order the person so convicted to pay any aggrieved person such compensation for personal injury; loss of or damage to property; or both such injury and loss or damage; as it thinks reasonable.

The amount ordered as compensation under subsection (1) shall be deemed a judgement debt due to the person entitled to receive the same from the person so convicted, and the order for payment of compensation may be enforced in such and the same manner as in the case of any costs or expenses ordered by the court to be paid under section 72.

Section 98 of the *Magistrates Ordinance* provides:

> Where a magistrate makes an order under section 36(1) or convicts a person of an offence and passes such sentence (if any) as may otherwise by law be passed, he may in addition to the order or sentence, order the offender to pay to any aggrieved person such compensation for personal injury; loss of or damage to property; or both such injury and loss or damage; not exceeding HK$100,000 as he thinks reasonable.

Unfortunately, figures related to the use of the orders are not systematically kept and are quite often difficult to obtain from the Judiciary for in-depth analysis. The inherent constraints of this programme are obvious in at least three areas. First, compensation order can only be imposed after the defendant has been convicted. Second, the offender's means to pay must be considered by the court. It is often difficult to make impoverished offenders comply with regulations, especially if payment extends over a long period of time. Finally, compensation orders are not awarded equitably. Victims of violent crimes are more frequently awarded compensation orders than victims of personal crimes of theft or crimes against households (e.g. burglary, theft from vehicle, criminal damage to property). Perhaps the core problem is that crime victims do not regularly file for compensation claims because they are not aware of their legal right to do so.

Criminal and Law Enforcement Injuries Compensation Scheme

The scheme was first introduced in May 1973. The scheme is operated by the Criminal and Law Enforcement Injuries Compensation Boards (the Boards) appointed by the then Governor for decision making and administratively serviced by the Social Welfare Department. The scheme aims to assume government responsibility for compensating victims sustaining personal injuries in crimes of violence and law enforcement exercises. The objective is to provide ex-gratia compensation to all qualifying victims or their dependants without an age-limit, residential qualification, or test of means and on a non-contributory basis.

Specifically, the scheme administered by respective Boards provides monetary compensation to victims suffering personal injury arising out of the following: a crime of violence (including arson and poisoning); an arrest or attempted arrest of an offender or suspected offender; the prevention or attempted prevention of an offence; and the giving of help to any police officer or other person who is engaged in arresting or attempting to arrest an offender or suspected offender, or preventing or attempting to prevent an offence.

During the initial phase of implementation, only 282 applications (within the first 10 months) were received in 1973. In the following three decades, the number of cases reached its climax (consistently around 1,000) throughout the 1980s. In the 1990s, it reduced slightly to between 650 and 950, and the total number of new cases paid each year was between 500 and 700. Notably, in the last three years the number of applications has gradually decreased from 637 (2003–4) to 563 (2004–5) and further to 436 (2005–6), which is the second-lowest since the launch of the scheme.

If victim compensation is an adequate gauge, the scheme appears to be a success. Yet, a number of its shortcomings are apparent. Firstly, compensation is paid only to claims of personal injury caused by crime. Property loss caused by property crimes, which constitutes a significant proportion of reported crime, is not compensated. Secondly, the victim should not contribute to their own injury, or help to cause the crime of which he or she is the victim. Thus, members of the Boards may be inclined to be more biased against those victims with criminal records or dubious character. Thirdly, effective from December 1982, the scheme has extended to victims of family violence, provided they follow strict prosecuting procedures before receiving compensation. Thus, the chance of family reunion would be discouraged. Fourthly, victims are only eligible for compensation if they satisfy the Boards' requirement to report crimes to the police without reasonable delay. This practice is thought to be a government safeguard against fraudulent claims because it is assumed that the longer a victim waits to report a crime, the more complicated and, perhaps, dishonest the claim may be. Although members of the Boards cannot check the validity of claims or the circumstances surrounding the alleged offence, failure to report to and co-operate with the police could deter compensation or may even result in the amount being eventually reduced. Finally, the scheme has been criticized because only those crime victims with 'serious' injuries, as defined by medical examiners, have a real incentive to apply. 'Serious' injuries justifies a minimum of three days' sick leave from work. Although this rule does not apply to cases where the victim is killed or has sustained permanent disability, or where the victim sustained injury while trying to prevent crime, the effect is that the scheme does not encourage victims suffering 'less grievous' harm from applying for the compensation they deserve. This scheme's major shortfall could be related to the methodology employed by members of the Boards to award compensation. Rather than focusing on victims' needs, the Boards tend to support the notion that only those 'deserving' or 'innocent' victims warrant the government's sympathy. The end result is that the scheme is more of a symbolic gesture of pity for selected crime victims, rather than a panel which awards remuneration to all those who may be deserving. From the official statistics, the number of victims awarded compensation, in general, has been very limited as compared to those who are eligible to apply (see Tables 4.1 and 4.2).

House for battered spouses

The voluntary welfare sector has been more responsive to the growing incidence of broken homes and those problems experienced by victims of family violence who are mostly the battered wives and/or their children. In early 1985, Harmony House with its capacity of 40 was established to provide a retreat for women, with or without children, who are in immediate danger of violence. Its primary task is to provide for the safety of victims of violence and to give them necessary financial and practical support, while the ultimate goal is to help battered spouses find the strength, self-confidence, and resources to lead a life free from the threat of violence.

In late 1986, the government also began to assume its responsibility by running a similar place of refuge for victims, known as Wai On Home for Women, under the administration of the Social Welfare Department. The admission criteria, apart from battered spouses, are extended to girls aged 13 and over who are ill-treated or sexually molested, or in an emotional crisis resulting from serious conflict with their parents or unexpected hospitalization of parents or guardians.

Table 4.1 Application for criminal and law enforcement injuries compensation and total number of new paid cases

Year	Applications for criminal injury (a)	Applications for law enforcement injury (b)	Total applications (a)+(b)=(c)	Total no. of new cases paid
1973/1974	280	2	282	193
1974/1975	719	3	722	362
1975/1976	853	3	856	514
1976/1977	623	–	623	475
1977/1978	582	–	582	412
1978/1979	546	–	546	325
1979/1980	710	1	711	317
1980/1981	900	1	901	410
1981/1982	996	1	997	450
1982/1983	1,300	–	1,300	545
1983/1984	1,325	3	1,328	585
1984/1985	1,192	3	1,195	656
1985/1986	1,329	–	1,329	690
1986/1987	1,117	–	1,117	931
1987/1988	1,206	–	1,206	824
1988/1989	1,138	1	1,139	887
1989/1990	1,025	3	1,028	680
1990/1991	1,094	3	1,097	801
1991/1992	930	2	932	696
1992/1993	766	3	769	686
1993/1994	867	2	869	601
1994/1995	979	–	979	707
1995/1996	760	1	761	555
1996/1997	800	–	800	568
1997/1998	663	–	663	604
1998/1999	760	–	760	557
1999/2000	756	–	756	447
2000/2001	679	–	679	351
2001/2002	589	–	589	388
2002/2003	759	–	759	370
2003/2004	637	–	637	325
2004/2005	563	–	563	314
2005/2006	436	–	436	305

Source: Compiled from the Annual Reports of Criminal and Law Enforcement Injuries Compensation Boards (various issues)

Table 4.2 Breakdown of applications for criminal injuries compensation

Year	1991/ 1992	1992/ 1993	1993/ 1994	1994/ 1995	1995/ 1996	1996/ 1997	1997/ 1998	1998/ 1999	1999/ 2000	2000/ 2001	2001/ 2002	2002/ 2003	2003/ 2004	2004/ 2005	2005/ 2006
Application No.	930	766	867	979	760	800	663	760	756	679	589	759	637	563	436
Types of Violence															
Homicide, Murder and Manslaughter	45 (91)	59 (125)	45 (95)	33 (90)	32 (81)	46 (95)	33 (92)	38 (57)	37 (76)	31 (52)	20 (69)	42 (78)	23 (61)	16 (41)	14 (39)
Robbery, Theft and Burglary	198 (1,760)	157 (1,628)	132 (1,449)	130 (1,520)	89 (1,403)	92 (1,039)	81 (782)	91 (866)	156 (946)	107 (791)	93 (802)	121 (939)	100 (673)	78 (495)	4 6 (382)
Assault and Wounding	670 (7,032)	537 (6,765)	656 (6,854)	799 (7,316)	622 (7,879)	624 (7,500)	517 (7,507)	558 (7,574)	535 (7,832)	503 (7,016)	457 (6,906)	581 (7,211)	492 (6,761)	458 (7,441)	370 (7,798)
Rape and Sexual Assault	3 (100)	4 (88)	3 (95)	3 (119)	4 (113)	6 (27)	5 (25)	6 (22)	7 (28)	9 (14)	8 (16)	8 (60)	4 (53)	4 (61)	2 (68)
Arson	4	1	17	5	8	23	12	55	7	26	5	1	9	0	2
Falling Object	10	8	14	7	5	5	10	10	12	3	5	4	7	5	2
Others	0 (92)	0 (96)	0 (126)	2 (68)	0 (95)	4 (137)	5 (109)	2 (128)	2 (139)	0 (119)	1 (113)	2 (120)	2 (87)	2 (113)	0 (95)
Remark of Family Violence	9	3	13	15	10	3	16	19	31	11	8	6	9	15	10

Note: (1) Figures shown in brackets ( ) represent the number of cases reported to the police.
(2) In police records, 'Arson' and 'Falling Object' are grouped under 'Others'.

Source: Compiled from the *Annual Reports* of Criminal and Law Enforcement Injuries Compensation Boards (various issues).

The designed capacity is 40, broadly categorized into the family section for spouses and children, and a single-person section for girls at risk. In 1996, a very similar establishment known as Serene Court (run by another non-government organization, Christian Family Service Centre) began its service for battered wives and abused children. The accommodation capacity is also 40.

All the above houses operate round the clock. While the accommodation is offered free of charge, residents may be required to pay for their own meals and daily necessities. Battered women coming to stay with or without children and/or girls at risk or abused are rendered individual counselling and supportive group services. Essentially, this kind of victim programme is a crisis service, and the victims are anticipated to be reintegrated into their own families rather than creating a dependency role for the clients. The period of stay varies from victim to victim. However, as an emergency service, the maximum period of residence is 3 months.

This victim programme fails to reach the vast majority of victims. The number of admissions to Harmony House in the first three years was quite steady: 166 in 1987–8, 105 in 1988–9 and 141 in 1989–90; and the cases known to the Social Welfare Department were 685 in 1987–8, 433 in 1988–9 and 252 in 1989–90 (Shin 1990). However, starting from the early 1990s, rapid social changes have begun to have a great impact on families and marriages. Domestic violence has become more serious than ever. From 1993 to 1997, the annual number of battered spouse cases soared from 198 to 491, representing a five-fold increase over five years on police records (Harmony House 2005: 3). The number of battered-spouse cases, as reported by the Social Welfare Department, further rose from 1,171 in 1998 to 1,292 in 1999 (the first 10 months), with 5 per cent of cases involving wives attacking their husbands. The figures are alarming and believed to be just the tip of the iceberg, particularly starting from the turn of the century.

One sample survey conducted by the University of Hong Kong in 2006 (as part of the United Nations International Violence Against Women Survey) revealed that about 20 per cent of Hong Kong women suffer at least one violent incident in their lifetime; 14 per cent experience physical attacks, while 16 per cent experience sexual violence (Faculty of Social Sciences 2006). The survey further revealed that the city's annual physical and sexual violence victimization rates (at 1.7 per cent and 2.1 per cent) were much higher than in the police and official crime reports.

Indeed, it is very difficult to know the full extent of violence against spouses, since it is probable that many incidents go unrecorded. This may occur because women and men feel ashamed or guilty about confessing that their marriage has gone wrong. Alternatively, they may fear that self-disclosure would probably lead to further attacks or that nothing can be done to help them. In short, the official statistics provide no more than an indication of the extent of the problem. The vast majority of victims could hardly be contacted or even helped. Such a programme could only be regarded as a humanitarian response to people in trouble, the fulfilment of the psycho-social need of the victims, and an indispensable crisis service provided by groups of welfare personnel. This programme falls along the conservative lines of inquiry, focusing more on the psycho-social dimension, rather then seeing the more diffuse and subtle relationships of power and oppression between both sexes in society. From the official statistics, many victims rarely ask for assistance or compensation, and in fact the number of cases involving family violence in the Criminal and Law Enforcement Compensation Scheme has been surprisingly low for many years (see Table 4.2).

Services for sexually assaulted victim

Services for victims of rape were initiated by the Family Planning Association in 1977. The service was started for adolescents and young adults with problems concerning general sexual development as well as a victim programme specifically related to rape or sexual assault. Clients include victims of rape, indecent assault, incest, child abuse, and so forth, who are referred by police, school, parents, social workers, friends, or client themselves. The Association recorded 1,114 clients, with the average figure of about 80 per year from 1977 to 1989 (Kwan 1990). From the early 1990s, the Association was able to maintain more or less 100 cases every year up to the turn of the century (see Table 4.3). Yet the Association eventually ceased this special service in July 2003 with the opening of a 24-hour one-stop Rape Crisis Centre operated by another service provider, Rainlily. However, the Association, since 1979, has been well-appreciated in catering for the sexual and reproductive health needs of the mentally challenged, physically handicapped, or persons with impaired hearing, who could be potential victims of abuse. From the service statistics, around 300 to 500 clients have been served annually in the last 10 years (see Table 4.4).

The service statistics indicate the extent of the seriousness of the problem of abuse in the community, and yet the services fail to reach the vast majority of victims who feel too guilty or embarrassed to

Table 4.3 Sexually assaulted victim service

	1991/ 1992	1992/ 1993	1993/ 1994	1994/ 1995	1995/ 1996	1996/ 1997	1997/ 1998	1998/ 1999	1999/ 2000	2000/ 2001	2001/ 2002	2002/ 2003	2003/ 2004 (Apr–Jul)
Case Reporting													
Reported Cases (known to police)	68	56	67	62	57	34	40	43	28	43	27	23	4
Unreported Cases (not known to police)	37	56	48	29	47	45	54	65	71	77	59	44	16
	(105)	(112)	(115)	(91)	(104)	(79)	(94)	(108)	(99)	(120)	(86)	(67)	(20)
Types of Sexual Assault													
Acquaintance Rape	36	42	31	44	45	18	34	46	37	54	41	39	10
Victim Under Drug/ Alcohol Influence	–	–	–	–	12	23	27	16	13	32	16	13	4
Blitz Rape	18	22	27	20	19	20	6	14	18	11	9	4	0
Suspected Rape	14	12	16	7	9	6	13	11	5	10	6	3	2
Gang Rape	9	8	5	3	4	3	4	7	4	2	1	1	0
Indecent Assault	4	5	5	2	6	1	5	5	18	5	6	6	2
Drug Rape	5	6	11	4	7	6	3	5	2	3	6	0	2
Incest	2	7	4	4	2	1	1	4	2	3	1	1	0
Buggery	9	2	1	4	–	1	1	–	–	–	–	–	–
Unspecified	8	8	15	3	–	–	–	–	–	–	–	–	–
Current Age of Victims													
Under 16	35	39	39	26	38	30	25	21	18	57	24	22	4
16–20	31	43	40	25	25	25	45	44	34	11	27	24	11
Over 20	39	30	36	40	41	24	24	43	37	47	34	17	5
	(105)	(112)	(115)	(91)	(104)	(79)	(94)	(108)	(89)	(115)	(85)	(63)	(20)

*As some victims reported more than one incident of assault, the number of victims does not equal to the number of cases.
Source: Compiled from the *Annual Reports* of The Family Planning Association of Hong Kong (various issues)

Table 4.4 Special sexual and reproductive health service for the disabled

Year	1996/ 1997	1997/ 1998	1998/ 1999	1999/ 2000	2000/ 2001	2001/ 2002	2002/ 2003	2003/ 2004	2004/ 2005	2005/ 2006
No. of Clients	374	476	500	501	291	303	505	378	367	348

Note: The services specially caters for the sexual/reproductive health needs of people who are mentally challenged, physically handicapped, or have impaired hearing. Contraceptive advice, counselling and health services are rendered by counsellors, sign-language interpreters, and medical staff.
Source: Compiled from the Annual Reports of the Family Planning Association of Hong Kong (various issues).

report the incidents to external bodies. Moreover, victims of sexual abuse or domestic violence can hardly be detected by others since a large number of cases may occur in the victims' own homes and victims may be familiar with their abusers. Also, victims may feel stigmatized while they receive practical help or counselling. It is particularly true that, in the present ethical and cultural context, rape or serious sexual assaults and indecent assaults would bring disgrace, misfortune, or guilt to the family and/or community.

In brief, this victim programme is generally considered to be a humanitarian response to people who are in trouble. It separates the problem from the psycho-social dimension of the individual, rather than being a re-examination of the inadequacy of the justice system and structural or societal forces which constitute the social problem of sexual assault or abuse.

Examination of current ideologies of crime victim programmes

As a matter of fact, our crime victim programmes vary significantly in their objectives, structure, forms of help, targets of victims, and so forth. Generally speaking, the underlying ideological currents can be discerned as 'care' or 'welfare' ideology, 'retributive' ideology, and the 'right-based' model.

'Care' or 'welfare' ideology

The first conceptual approach, known as the 'care' or 'welfare' model, is mainly based on the principle that the community should, as far as possible, absorb the burden of severe hardship suffered by individual citizens as a consequence of misfortunes such as illness, accidents, or unemployment. Emphasis is placed on providing victims rather than on the criminal nature of the offence. The problems of crime victims are perceived to be a manifestation of stress, psychological trauma, or economic needs. No specific reference is made to the moral aspect of crime or to the punishment of the offender, providing that the victim's injuries or traumas are treated professionally and hardship is alleviated. The Criminal and Law Enforcement Injuries Compensation Scheme, refuges for battered spouses, services for sexually assaulted victims, and other related social welfare services are typical examples.

The conceptual framework of the 'care' and 'welfare' model can be challenged on a number of grounds:

- Should the needs of crime victims be viewed as problems of a more general psychological or economic nature?
- Would these services avoid such an unintended side-effect of generating expectations among victims which cannot be satisfied?
- Would these services be free from the stigmatizing features of the established welfare institutions as victims might often be unduly labelled as persons in need of treatment?
- Indeed, victim programmes characterized by the 'care' ideology bear moralistic overtones and represent a form of charity act or a humanitarian response to people in trouble, and in no way will this model promote social justice for victims.

'Retributive' ideology

The second model is based on the principle that the offender should be punished in proportion to the seriousness of the offence. This approach advocates a punitive penal measure according to the damage inflicted on both victim and society and considers compensation of the victim as one of the primary aims of sentencing. The use of compensation orders in court is a typical example.

While this kind of ideology seems to gain the support from the public, it does not necessarily imply that victims share the same view of imposing punishment on the offenders. This model of practice does not answer the most pressing questions related to victims' desire for greater participatory rights within the criminal justice process.

'Right-based' model

The 'right-based' model has taken hold in Hong Kong for the past decade. The *Victims of Crime Charter* (Department of Justice 1996) was first publicized through concerted efforts from various government departments such as the Hong Kong Police Force, Social Welfare Department, Judiciary, Department of Justice, Legal Aid Department, Independent Commission Against Corruption, Hospital Authority, and Security Branch.

As defined by the Charter, a victim is a person 'who suffers physical or emotional harm, or loss or damage to property, as a direct result of a criminal offence'. The definition covers 'anyone who has suffered directly from the commission of the offence [which] may include, for example, the parent of a child who has been sexually abused or the immediate family of a murder victim'. The Charter sets out both the duties and rights of victims. Victims have a duty to help maintain law and order, such as abiding by the law, taking proper precaution, reporting crime, giving assistance to the police, and attending court as witnesses. On the other hand, victims have the right (a) to be treated with courtesy and respect, (b) to have a proper response to complaints of crime, (c) to information including reporting the crime, investigation, and prosecution, (d) to access proper court facilities, (e) to be heard in court, (f) to seek protection, (g) to privacy and confidentiality, (h) to property, (i) to access support and aftercare, and (j) to seek compensation. In this model, the ideal would be that victims could have the opportunity to influence the key decision in dealing with the victimization experience, not simply as witnesses in law courts against the offender.

Regrettably, the definition of victim is largely confined to the legal framework or criminal justice system. The Charter (despite the last revisions by the Department of Justice in early 2000 and 2003) seems to be simply a workplace moral guideline for personnel within the criminal justice process. No legal jurisdiction has been made to safeguard those who are not fully exercising their power. The Charter has no legal status at all, and courts in this jurisdiction cannot be compelled to accept any impact statement from the victim.

Could the criminal justice personnel involved be more humanized so as to address victims' needs and rights? Public education and wide publicity of the Charter are indispensable. The latest crime victimization survey (Census and Statistics Department 1999: 20) revealed that only 8 per cent of persons aged 12 or above had heard of the Charter, and the major channel was through the mass media, such as television (66 per cent), newspapers (20 per cent), and radio (17 per cent). Notably, the channels had rarely been made known to victims from the professionals within the system or related community organizations at the time of the survey.

By contrast, much less attention is paid to victims despite their making a major contribution such as reporting crime to the police, detecting unlawful acts, providing evidence, and so forth. Quite often, they need a great deal of support from family and friends after their traumatic experiences, with particular regard to crimes of violence. The costs of victimization are not simply time lost from work, property loss or damage, physical injury, and the like. Some victims may begin to suffer depression and low self-esteem. It is probable that they may shy away from and lose confidence in the justice system.

In short, the victim's needs and feelings are ignored by professionals at various criminal justice stages. The victim, in general, has no accepted role to play other than being functionally and legally 'just another witness in court' (Shapland 1982: 21–3), despite the fact that the place of victims within the system has been addressed through the introduction of a *Victim's Charter* in England and Wales (Home Office 1986, 1988, 1990, 2001).

It is noticeable that the provision of victim programmes in Hong Kong is characterized by their diversity in theoretical assumptions, objectives, selection criteria of victims, forms of help, sources of referral, year of establishment and organizational bases, financial sources, and so forth. For instance, the Criminal and Law Enforcement Injuries Compensation Scheme aims to compensate victims for personal injuries resulting from violent crimes; the Compensation Order aims to compensate victims for injury, loss, or damage by the offender through the monetary payment from offenders; the refuges for battered spouses endeavour to provide voluntary short-term practical assistance and psycho-social help to victims; the services to victims of rape aim to reduce clients' anxieties and fears. However, the current major provision of victim programmes seems to be hampered by the absence of a sound philosophical basis for action. Given the current practice models, namely (a) 'care' or 'welfare' model: being typified by refuges for battered spouses, services to victims of rape, and Criminal and Law Enforcement Injuries Compensation Scheme, (b) 'retributive' model: being demonstrated by the Compensation Order, and (c) 'right-based' model: being seen in the *Victims of Crime Charter*. None of the above can be considered entirely satisfactory.

The first model symbolizes an act of charity or a humanitarian response to people in trouble, and in no way can this promote social justice. The second model focuses on punishing the offender without genuine consideration of victims' needs and participatory rights within the criminal justice process. The third model has no legal status or jurisdiction throughout the entire criminal justice process.

Perhaps what is needed is a comprehensive review of victims programmes and a debate or discussion on the underlying philosophical framework prior to action. A combination of a humanized criminal justice system and a network of outreaching victim support with a strong input from the local community could only be the starting point (van Dijk 1998) and research findings tend to support 'a guiding principle for working with victims of crime is inter-agency partnership, and this at least will provide some grounds for optimism in the search for more effective public policy for crime victims in the next decade' (Davis 2003: 119).

Finally, attention should be paid to the fact that crime victims have their rights to both remedial and restorative services aimed at addressing the difficulties and inconveniences caused by crime. It would be worthwhile considering some kinds of mediation or reparation practices as well as innovative services for both the victim and offender, with the ultimate goal of achieving restoration in society (Braithwaite 1998; Fattah and Peters 1998).

The way ahead

The 'right-based' model which has taken hold in Hong Kong and as evidenced by the *Victims of Crime Charter* is the starting point of victim protection. Hopefully, the Charter will be given the legal status in due course. On the other hand, the court and the general public may wish to consider that, instead of simply imposing punishment on the wrong-doers, there is a growing concern on restorative justice which emphasizes restitution as a means of restoring both parties; and reconciliation of both parties is considered an important goal (Umbreit 1995, 1999, 2001; Wright 1999; Morris and Maxwell 2001; Weitekamp and Kerner 2003).

Victims of crime, despite their unforgettable victimization experiences, are human beings in need of love, respect, and care throughout the justice process. They would no longer be the forgotten people in society if we all strive for the well-being of victims through co-operation among professionals and volunteers heading for the goal of restoration. I believe that this is highly desirable in the course of reconstructing a caring, harmonious, and civilized community.

From the victim's perspective, there is a great need for the paradigm shift from the current retributive justice to restorative justice. The basic differences between these two models, as Zehr (1995) and Zehr and Harry (1998) have respectively pointed out, are summarized below:

Retributive justice	**Restorative justice**
• Wrong as a violation of rules	• Wrong as a violation of people, relationships
• Wrongs create guilt	• Wrongs create liabilities and obligations
• Crime seen as categorically different from other harms	• Crime recognized as related to other harms and conflicts
• Debt paid by taking punishment	
• Focus on past	• Focus on future
	• Restitution as a means of restoring both parties
• Imposition of pain to punish and deter	• Harm by offender balanced by making right
• Harm by offender balanced by harm to offender	• Harm by offender balanced by making right
• Offender denounced	• Harmful act denounced
• Justice serves to divide	• Justice aims to bring together
• Victim's needs and rights ignored	• Victim's needs and rights central
• Ignores social, economic, and moral contest of behaviour	• Total context relevant
• Process alienates	• Process aims at reconciliation
• State monopoly on response to wrongdoing	• Victim, offender, and community roles acknowledged
• Community on sideline, represented abstractly by state	• Community as facilitator in restorative process

The proposed shift of paradigm (from retributive justice to restorative justice) puts a great emphasis on the process whereby all parties with a stake in a particular offence come together to resolve collectively how to deal with the aftermath of the offence and its implications for the future (Marshall 1998: 32).

Put simply, restorative justice programmes encourage the voluntary efforts brought forward by the victims, offender, their families, and community representatives. They are arranged to meet one another so as to bring about reconciliation between the two sides of the offence or victimization. In some countries like Australia, both the police and the court, as a form of youth justice models, can even refer cases to a community or youth justice conference for young people (aged 10 to 16 inclusive) when they break the law (Chui, Kidd and Preston 2005). The outcome of conferencing based on extensive literature review has been quite encouraging (Hayes and Daly 2003), and the general impression is that getting both parties of an offence involved in the reconciliation process would enable them to face the consequences of victimization or assume active responsibility for their offending behaviour (Hayes and Daly 2003).

The above suggested use of offender–victim mediation and reparation schemes is the initial step in the course of advocating restorative justice and might be considered at different stages of the justice process. The suggestion could be justified on two grounds: victims have a greater involvement in the process and offenders have the chance to appreciate the impact of their crime and to provide reparation in a much wider sense, such as restoring stolen property to the victim, repairing damage inflicted on the victim's property, performing services for a victim, a group of crime victims generally, or the community at large, and giving an apology (oral and/or written) to the victim of the offence. Theoretically speaking, the model could be beneficial to both parties from the rehabilitative perspective.

From the victim's perspective, he or she may gain material compensation for the loss incurred, other than the monetary payment. In addition, the victim may benefit in psychological terms, from meeting the offender. Fear or feelings of insecurity may fade away upon visualizing that the 'offender' was recognizably human after all, with sympathetic problems and emotions. It would also give the victim a chance to feel a certain reintegration into the community after understanding the circumstances leading to the offence, the psycho-social make-up of the criminal, and the way of helping the criminal to reform.

From the offender's viewpoint, reparation may encourage the criminal to accept responsibility for the misdeed or harm inflicted on the victim, to face the reality of the crime which has been committed without resorting to such self-defence as neutralization techniques (Siegel 2007), to understand the impact of victimization and have a positive attitude or behaviour change accordingly, and so forth.

Furthermore, the use of victim–offender encounter groups could be considered as mediation initiatives in the post-sentence stage. Distinctive from normal 'own offender' and 'own victim' methods of mediation or reparation, this encounter group model involves the meeting of offenders (particularly of burglary) with unrelated victims through the creative use of therapeutic group processes and dynamics. The main purpose is to provide adequate opportunities for two parties to challenge each other's prejudices, stereotypes, and rationalization related to the offence. This model has two merits: in terms of group composition, it involves 'voluntary' offenders and a variety of victims of solved, unsolved and unreported crimes; and in terms of optimal timing of the group encounter, both parties are able to decide when they feel ready to meet each other, because there are great individual differences in recovery from victimization; thus, an honest exchange is seen.

The above proposals are simply some suggested innovative programmes for consideration. In full recognition of various thought-provoking practice models of restorative justice (particularly in youth justice) as documented and submitted to the Security Bureau (Lo, Wong and Maxwell 2003, 2005), it is the right time to place 'victims of crime' at the centre for further thoughts. It is an important step believed to be in the right direction of the victim protection or restoration movement in Hong Kong.

The development of victim programmes in Hong Kong seems to be much affected by the absence of a sound philosophical basis for action. Frustrated by the criminal justice policy in contemporary society (which is essentially retributive), an alternative model, which protects the community and makes sure that the offender is held responsible in a constructive way, is therefore suggested. This model, broadly known as 'restorative justice', could be the guiding philosophical framework in the future. Hopefully, this chapter will lead to further discussion on the use of restorative justice while working with victims of crime who are equally important participants in the justice process. Whether or not it is a myth or reality depends much on our perception, our attitude, and our devotion to make it possible.

Review questions

1 Why is the definition of 'crime victim' so controversial in the field of criminology or victimology?
2 What is the relationship between community care and crime victim?

3 Compare and contrast the strengths and weaknesses of various victim programmes in Hong Kong.
4 Should the *Victims of Crime Charter* be improved along the line of restorative justice?

References

Braithwaite, J. (1998) *Restorative Justice: Assessing an Immodest Theory and a Pessimistic Theory*. Canberra: Australian National University.

Census and Statistics Department (1979, 1982, 1987, 1990, 1995, 1999) *Crime and Its Victim in Hong Kong*. Hong Kong: Government Printer.

Chui, W.H. and Fu, X. (2007) 'Victims' rights and protection in the Hong Kong criminal justice system', in H. Zhang (ed.) *Studies on Victim Protections* (pp. 267–97). Beijing: Court Press (in Chinese).

Chui, W.H., Kidd, J. and Preston, C. (2005) 'Treatment of child and juvenile offenders in Queensland, Australia', in T.W. Lo, D.S.W. Wong and G. Maxwell (eds) *Alternatives to Prosecution: Rehabilitative and Restorative Models of Youth Justice* (pp. 171–205). Singapore: Marshall Cavendish Academic.

Clarke, M. (1982) 'Where is the community which cares?', *British Journal of Social Work*, 20 (2):, 459–69.

Cohen, S. (1973) 'The failures of criminology', *The Listener*, 8 November, 622–25.

Colvin, G. (1988) 'Report on the 7th United Nation Congress on the Prevention of Crime and the Treatment of Offenders', *Crime and Social Justice*, 25: 55–61.

Davis, P. (2003) 'Crime victims and public policy', in P. Davis, P. Francis and V. Jupp (eds) *Victimization: Theory, Research and Policy* (pp. 101–20). London: Palgrave Macmillan.

European Committee on Crime Problems (1984) *Research on Victimization* (Collected Studies in Criminological Research). Strasbourg: Council of Europe.

Faculty of Social Sciences (2006) *Press Release – United Nations International Violence Against Women Survey: The Hong Kong Part*. Hong Kong: Faculty of Social Sciences, The University of Hong Kong. Available at: http://www.hku.hk/socsc/univaws/IVAWS_Press_Release.pdf

Family Planning Association of Hong Kong (various issues) *Annual Reports*. Hong Kong: Family Planning Association of Hong Kong.

Fattah, E. and Peters, T. (1998) *Support for Victims of Crime in a Comparative Perspective*. Leuver: Leuver University Press.

Harding, J. (1982) *Victims and Offenders: Needs and Responsibilities* (NCVO Occasional Paper No. 2). London: Bedford Square.

Harmony House (2005) *Annual Report of 2004/2005*. Hong Kong: Harmony House.

Haynes, H. and Daly, K. (2003) 'Youth justice conference and re-offending', *Justice Quarterly*, 20(4): 725–64.
Home Office (1986) *Criminal Justice: A Working Paper*. London: Home Office.
Home Office (1988) *Victims of Crime* (Home Office Circular 20). London: Home Office.
Home Office (1990) *Victim's Charter: A Statement of the Rights of Victim*. London: Home Office.
Home Office (2001) *A Review of the Victim's Charter*. London: Home Office.
Department of Justice (1996, 2000, 2003) *The Victims of Crime Charter*. Hong Kong: Government Printer.
Kidd, R.F. and Chayet, E.F. (1984) 'Why do victims fail to report? The psychology of criminal victimisation', *Journal of Social Issues*, 40 (1): 39–50.
Kwan, M. (1990) 'Service rendered by the Family Planning Association of Hong Kong to sexually assaulted victims', in F. Cheung, R. Andry and R. Tam (eds) *Research on Rape and Sexual Crime in Hong Kong* (pp. 47–51). Hong Kong: Institute of Asia-Pacific Studies, The Chinese University of Hong Kong.
Lo, T.W., Wong D.S.W. and Maxwell, G. (2003) *Measures Alternative to Prosecution for Handling Unruly Children and Youth Persons: Overseas Experiences and Options for Hong Kong* (Report submitted to the Security Bureau of Hong Kong SAR Government). Hong Kong: Youth Studies Net, City University of Hong Kong.
Lo, T.W., Wong D.S.W. and Maxwell, G. (eds) (2005) *Alternatives to Prosecution: Rehabilitative and Restorative Models of Youth Justice*. Singapore: Marshall Cavendish Academic.
Marshall, T. (1998) *Restorative Justice: An Overview*. St. Paul, MN: Centre for Restorative Justice and Mediation, University of Minnesota.
Morris, A. and Maxwell, G. (eds) (2001) *Restorative Justice for Juveniles: Conferencing, Mediation and Circles*. Oxford: Hart Publishing.
Schwendinger, H. and Schwendinger, J. (1970) 'Defenders of order or guardian of human right?', *Issues in Criminologist*, 5 (2): 148–52.
Shapland, J. (1982) 'The victim in the criminal justice system', *Home Office Research Bulletin*, 14: 21–3.
Shin, K. (1990) 'Battered spouse: A community responsibility?', Address at Annual General Meeting of Harmony House on 28 September 1990, Hong Kong.
Siegel, L.J. (2007) *Criminology: Theories, Patterns, and Typologies* (9th edn). Belmont, CA: Wadsworth/Thomson Learning.
Smale, G.J.A. (1984) 'Psychological effects of behavioural changes in the cases of victims of serious crime', in R. Block (ed.) *Victimization and Fear of Crime: World Perspectives* (pp. 87–92). Washington, DC: US Department of Justice.
Sutherland, E. (1949) *White Collar Crime*, New York: Dryden Press.
Tsun, A.O-K. and Lui-Tsang, P.S-K. (2005) 'Violence against wives and children in Hong Kong', *Journal of Family and Economic Issues*, 26 (4), 465-86.

Umbreit, M. (1995) 'The development and impact of victim offender mediation in the United States', *Mediation Quarterly*, 12 (3): 263–76.
Umbreit, M. (1999) *The Handbook on Justice for Victims*. New York: United Nations.
Umbreit, M. (2001) *The Handbook of Victim/Offender Mediation: An Essential Guide to Practice and Research*. San Francisco, CA: Josey Boss.
United Nations (1999a) *Guide for Policy Makers on the Implementation of the United Nations Declaration of Basic Principles of Justice for Victims of Crime and Abuse of Power*. New York: United Nations. Available at: http://www.unodc.org/unodc/crime_cicp_publications.html
United Nations (1999b) *Handbook on Justice for Victims: On the Use and Application of the Declaration of Basic Principles of Justice for Victims of Crime and Abuse of Power*. New York: United Nations. Available at: http://www.unodc.org/unodc/crime_cicp_publications.html
Weitekamp, E.G.M. and Kerner, H-J. (eds) (2003) *Restorative Justice in Context: International Practice and Directions*. Cullompton, Devon: Willan.
van Dijk, J. (1988) 'Ideological trends within the victims movement: An international perspective', in M. Maguire and J. Pointing (eds) *Victims of Crime: A New Deal* (pp. 115–26). Milton Keynes: Open University Press.
Wright, M. (1999) *Restoring Respect for Justice: A Symposium*. Winchester: Waterside Press.
Zehr, H. (1995) *Changing Lenses*. Scottdale, PA: Herald Press.
Zehr, H. and Harry, M. (1998) 'Fundamental concepts of restorative justice', *Contemporary Justice Review*, 1 (1): 47–55.

Legislation cited

Criminal Procedure Ordinance (Cap. 221)
Magistrates Ordinance (Cap. 227)

Chapter 5

The police force

Raymond W.K. Lau

Introduction

In many ways, the Hong Kong Police Force (HKPF) can be regarded as one of the world's finest police organizations. Surveys show that the public generally regard the HKPF as free of serious corruption, professional, and efficient and effective in maintaining law and order in Hong Kong (HKPF 2000, 2001a, 2001b). However, this has not always been the case. In the past, the HKPF was once a target of public hatred (Grant 1992: 70). The HKPF does not become complacent with its present achievements, but strives to move forward in order to keep abreast of the changing demands of Hong Kong society. How has the HKPF developed into what it is today, and what are the prospects of it moving further ahead? This chapter attempts to address these questions.

I begin by explaining how the HKPF, formed soon after Hong Kong became a British colony in 1841, was established along the lines of the classic colonial paramilitary model. Just as the character of the colonial regime remained essentially unchanged up to the early 1970s, the HKPF retained its colonial paramilitary nature throughout the entire period. In the early 1970s, Britain changed the style of colonial governance, as a result of which policing reform was implemented in the mid-1970s. The law enforcement or anti-crime policing function, previously neglected, began to acquire increasing prominence. However, the establishment of the Independent Commission Against Corruption (ICAC) in 1974, as part and parcel of the overall reforming of the HKPF, undermined the HKPF organizationally, as well as damaging police morale. In 1977 a police 'mutiny' against the ICAC erupted, in the aftermath of which corruption offences prior to 1977, with rare exceptions, were generally pardoned. Despite the pardon, corruption as a way of life in the HKPF was gone forever. The pardon allowed the HKPF to recuperate and continue to reorient itself to becoming, by the mid-1980s, a professional force employing coercive tactics in maintaining law and order. Political developments in the late 1980s and since, however, have impelled the HKPF to abandon its previous strong-arm public order maintenance tactics. In the mid-1990s, under the impact of the last colonial governor, Chris Patten's radical reforms, the HKPF launched its strategy of transforming itself into a 'service of quality'. This strategy has been maintained up to the present, despite Patten's departure, in the context of political and socio-political developments since Hong Kong's return to Chinese sovereignty in 1997. Throughout the period of almost continuous reorientation of the HKPF from the mid-1970s until today, the HKPF has emphasized the importance of maintaining its paramilitary capabilities and hard anti-crime tactics. I argue that the maintenance of these capabilities and tactics, generally supported by all and sundry in Hong Kong, is conducive to the retention of a traditional police culture, which does not serve to facilitate the HKPF's attempt to reorient itself into a 'service of quality'. On the other hand, however, in the context of the above-mentioned political and socio-political developments, in terms of daily street patrolling and the policing of public order events, the HKPF's approach has indeed become service-oriented. Furthermore, as a result of what I call the 'governability' crisis in Hong Kong since 1997, police authority at street level has been significantly eroded. Thus, the HKPF today and its future developmental trajectory are pulled by contradictory forces. It is still highly effective in maintaining law and order. However, whereas the top brass is committed to the service strategy, there is evidence that a significant number of experienced frontline police still steeped in traditional values are demoralized due to the erosion of street-level police authority, while under these circumstances, the development of a strong sense of organizational and professional commitment among new recruits appears to be encountering some difficulties.

The HKPF up to the early 1970s: a classic colonial paramilitary force

Hong Kong became a British colony in 1841. With regard to the policing of colonies, Jeffries (1952) opined that colonial police forces go through three phases: improvised arrangements to secure basic law and order in the initial period of colonization; establishment of a paramilitary force; and development into a civilian force as colonial rule relaxes and developments towards democratization and/or decolonization occur. As a descriptive thesis, Jeffries' view is useful for gaining an overview of the HKPF's development from 1841 to the present day.

The paramilitary model is based upon the recognition of a hostile (usually indigenous) population ruled (usually by an alien colonial power) primarily by coercion with the threat of armed force. The main purpose of the armed police is to suppress disorder without having to resort to the military. The principle of policing strangers (the indigenous population) by strangers (the police staffed and/or controlled by aliens) is practised. Police lived mainly in barracks, and police stations were heavily fortified. Among the three general functions of the police,[1] public order maintenance was given primacy, law enforcement being secondary, while civilian police work was regarded as a nuisance. Special units were established to gather political intelligence and engage in political policing against political activists considered unfriendly to the government (Tobias 1972; Andrade 1985; Anderson and Killingray 1992). All these features could be found in the HKPF right up to the mid-1970s.

Policing arrangements in Hong Kong began haphazardly upon colonization with the recruitment of British and (in a well-established practice of British colonialism at that time) Indian rejects from the local garrison. In 1944 the HKPF was formally established and subsequently developed on the lines of the classic colonial paramilitary model (Crisswell and Watson 1982). Table 6.1 shows its ethnic composition (the years 1941–2 and 1946–7 are selected for illustrative purposes).

It can be observed that all gazetted officers were recruited from the British Isles, with only a very small number of inspectors recruited locally. Though locals were recruited to rank and file positions, mostly for linguistic reasons, the classic tactic of policing strangers (locals) by strangers (aliens) was adopted in the rank and file by the use of South Asians and Shandong natives. The departure of the South Asians in 1946–47 was due to the independence of India and Pakistan

Table 6.1 Ethnic composition of the HKPF in the 1940s

	1941–2		1946–7	
Officers*	% of total	Number	% of total	Number
Gazetted officers (overseas)**	0.8	16	1.0	25
Gazetted officers (local)	0.0	0	0.0	0
Inspectorate (overseas)	12.9	265	10.2	244
Inspectorate (local)	2.5	52	3.7	88
Rank and file*				
Cantonese (i.e. local)	39.0	797	72.9	1,749
Northern Chinese (from Shandong)	8.0	164	8.0	193
Indians/Pakistanis	36.8	752	0.1	3
Portuguese	0.0	0	4.1	99

Source: Adapted from Gaylord and Traver (1995: 34).
*Officers refers to inspectors and above; rank and file to their subordinates (constables, sergeants, and station sergeants). The latter are now known as Junior Police Officers (JPO).
**Gazetted officers refers to officers at superintendent rank and above; overseas officers refers to those recruited from the British Isles.

in 1947. The HKPF wished to replace them by recruiting Portuguese, but the exercise was unsuccessful and thenceforth it was forced to man the rank and file mostly with locals. For decades, only European officers carried firearms. Unmarried European officers as well as the alien rank and file were housed in fortified barracks. Police stations were built like fortresses with high walls and barbed wire.

In 1925–26 an anti-imperialist general strike erupted in Hong Kong led by communist agitators. In its aftermath, the HKPF formed the Emergency Unit (EU) and the Anti-Communist Squad. The latter was a political police unit which subsequently became the Special Branch (SB, *zhengzhibu*) in 1938. The EU's function was to deal with civil disturbances, and to take control at the scene of major incidents. In addition to the EU, the Police Training Contingent (PTC) was later created to provide anti-riot training. All new recruits underwent PTC training early in their career, and refresher training was provided periodically. PTC graduates returned to serve at the local level, but in what is called an Internal Security (IS) situation, i.e. in case of serious civil disorder, local police formations could instantly mobilize PTC graduates of the formation into an anti-riot squad. Police stations underwent regular 'station attack' dry runs.

In 1966, serious anti-colonial protests occurred; the following year, riots led by local communist activists erupted; the HKPF mobilized into IS Structure. After these incidents, the Police Tactical Unit (PTU) replaced the PTC. The titles of PTU units (company, platoon, etc.) were all military in origin. Instead of immediately returning to local formations after training, PTU graduates were deployed to a PTU company for a period of time. Thus, PTU became a permanent anti-riot formation, with the EU as a further backup. 'Station attack' dry runs continued. Local police formations continued to have the ability to instantly mobilize into IS Structure. Training at both the Police Training School (PTS, for new recruits) and at the PTC/PTU was militarized. Trainees were bare-chested and subject to physical punishment. Discipline, loyalty, and group solidarity were emphasized.

Up until the early 1970s, crime was only a secondary concern (Munn 1995). This is strikingly evidenced in the tolerance of the police–triad symbiosis by the HKPF's top brass (Sinclair 1983; Gaylord and Traver 1995), in which police kept crime 'under control' by protecting triad-operated vice trade and establishments in return for bribes paid in an organized manner and shared by locals and Europeans alike, a practice that began from the very first days of the HKPF's founding and reached its peak in the 1950s to 1960s.

Over the decades, some changes to the above did occur, such as the replacement of barracks after the departure of the South Asian rank and file, and the gradual increase in the local ratio of the officers' ranks (mostly at the inspectorate level). But all the other paramilitary features remained, such as in structure and organization (EU, PTC/PTU, SB), processes (e.g. militarized training), and practices (e.g. 'station attack' dry runs).

Mid-1970s: first step towards policing reform

Up until the early 1970s, the local administration was a typical colonial regime in the worst sense of the term. Although the 1967 riots were closely related to the Cultural Revolution raging on the mainland during that period, the 1966 disturbances were a spontaneous indigenous anti-colonial incident, while the 1967 disturbances also began as an indigenous labour dispute (Cheung 2000).

The 1966–7 events were a watershed, both for Hong Kong as a whole and for the HKPF. The colonial regime had always been doubtful of the loyalty of local police. Perhaps to its surprise, local police by and large were prepared to defend the colonial regime against both indigenous anti-colonial and local pro-Beijing activists and protesters. For instance, in my discussions with police informants from that period, I was informed of only one high-profile resignation by a local inspectorate officer in protest against the HKPF during the course of the 1967 events. In the later stages, the 1967 riots developed into indiscriminate bombing, which alienated most of the local population, and hence local police's willingness to suppress at this stage was easier to understand. The HKPF were prepared to go into suppression mode right from the beginning in 1966 and again in the initial stages of the disturbances in 1967.

Up to the early 1970s, in the same way as the colonial regime was seriously degenerate, the HKPF was thoroughly corrupt and abusive. At that time there were several common local sayings that aptly summed up how the public viewed the police: 'the good boy does not join the police'; police were dubbed 'rascals with a license'. Official enquiries into the 1966–7 events revealed that many protesters in 1966 were anti-police as much as anti-colonial (Scott 1989). In short, the police, including local police, were a beneficiary and accomplice of the degenerate colonial regime. This probably played a significant part in local police's spontaneous preparedness to defend the regime under challenge. From a social-psychological perspective, once the initial preparedness was there, as officers engaged in ongoing conflict with protesters, the conflict itself served to strengthen the *esprit de corps*, as a result of which local police's antipathy towards the protesters became battle-hardened.

Local police's readiness to defend the colonial regime surprised and greatly gratified Britain. As a reward, the HKPF was conferred the title of 'Royal' and became the Royal Hong Kong Police Force, a name retained until 1997. In practical terms, with the previous distrust of local recruits considerably reduced, the local ratio of the officers' ranks increased (Gaylord and Traver 1995).

The 1966–7 events, nonetheless, showed Britain that modifications to the style of colonial governance in Hong Kong were necessary in order to shore up the colonial regime's legitimacy. In 1971 Murray MacLehose was appointed governor. His appointment denoted a sharp break from past practices, as it demonstrated that, unlike previous governors, he did not come from the Colonial Service, and he was known to have socialist sympathies (being pro-Labour in Britain). Clearly, Britain wanted to begin a new era of colonial rule in Hong Kong in which social reforms would be implemented to bridge the gap between the rulers and the ruled – which MacLehose did indeed do soon after his assumption of governorship by introducing massive social reforms such as the ten-year public housing programme (Lo 1993).

The official enquiry into the 1966–7 events also revealed that official corruption (with the HKPF being most publicly visible) was a social time bomb. Hence, a change in governance style would require tackling official, especially police, corruption head-on. Up until then, corruption was investigated by the Anti-Corruption Branch (ACB) of the HKPF, which was a unit within the CID. Such an arrangement was obviously problematic, not only because it meant police investigating police corruption, but also because of the low ranking of the ACB. In 1971 the colonial government raised the issue of setting up an independent anti-corruption body, to which the HKPF objected. Nonetheless, under pressure, the HKPF agreed to take corruption investigation away from the CID, and upgraded the ACB by establishing the Anti-Corruption Office (ACO), headed by an Assistant Commissioner of Police. The ACO's performance was to be reviewed after three years, as a result of which it showed much greater investigative determination than its predecessor. In 1973 the ACO launched an investigation into Chief Superintendent Peter Godber, then Deputy District Commander of Kowloon. However, Godber managed to flee Hong Kong, sparking massive public outcry and street protests (Lo 1993).

Meanwhile, in 1972, the management consultants McKinsey & Co., commissioned to look into civil service reform, reported that a sizable portion of the community hated the police (Grant 1992: 70). Reform of the HKPF was clearly overdue. MacLehose proceeded on two fronts; first, as a result of the Godber scandal, he set up the ICAC in 1974 despite the HKPF's objection (Lo 1993); second, several major reform schemes (borrowed from London) were implemented by the HKPF in 1974.

The objective of the HKPF's 1974 reforms was to improve its relations with the public. I have examined these reforms in detail elsewhere (Lau 2004a); here I shall simply mention one for illustration. The Police Community Relations Officer (PCRO) at the Division (now called District) level was established in 1974 to liaise with the community and improve police–public relations by taking into consideration 'public opinion', and to 'advise, assist and guide' the community. Under the PCRO, there were officers responsible for liaising with schools, local organizations, and so on. This setup has continued to the present day.

At the same time, the function of law enforcement also began to acquire increasing importance. Initially, this was triggered by the beginning of the end of organized police corruption. With the ACO taking a more determined effort to investigate police corruption in the early 1970s, the police–triad symbiosis began to break up, a process further accelerated with the creation of the ICAC in 1974. For this reason, among others, the violent crime rate soared (Traver 1991). In 1973 the government set up the Fight Violent Crime Committee, which became the Fight Crime Committee (FCC) in 1975. In 1976 District Fight Crime Committees (DFCC) were formed. Both the FCC and DFCC remain functioning today with representation from the HKPF.

The police 'Mutiny' in 1977 and the HKPF's reorientation towards professionalism

The creation of the ICAC had a serious impact on the HKPF. This is because organized corruption syndicates existed in all police formations, with each syndicate having a 'treasurer'. An arrested treasurer who co-operated with the ICAC often led to the arrest of dozens of officers from the same formation. This not only disrupted police work, it also seriously undermined police morale. In October 1977, police hostility towards the ICAC boiled over. Hundreds of off-duty police gathered at a mass rally held at Police Headquarters. Many subsequently marched to the ICAC headquarters, with some physically breaking into its offices. MacLehose defused the 'mutiny' by announcing a general pardon of all corruption offences committed before 1 January 1977, except for the most heinous cases (Miners 1995: 97).

In retrospect, the pardon turned out to be instrumental in reorienting the HKPF towards professionalism. While individual corrupt acts did continue after the pardon, it was also clear that corruption as a way of life in the police was gone forever. Those unprepared to accept this would over time leave, either through retirement or resignation; new recruits and those opting to remain would from now on have to focus on doing proper police work. Large-scale arrests of previously existing corruption syndicates ceased completely, allowing the HKPF to recuperate and reorient itself under the changed circumstances.

As a matter of fact, reorientation had begun even before the general pardon. As said, the break-up of the police–triad symbiosis and the government's emphasis placed on fighting crime in the mid-1970s raised the importance of the function of law enforcement. In July 1977 the beat radio was introduced, which greatly enhanced police efficiency at the street level. The breathing space given to the HKPF by the general pardon, and the demise of corruption as a way of life among police, enabled the HKPF to press ahead with its reorientation. In the early 1980s the organizational structure was overhauled. The previous territorial structure comprising District (of which there were four), Division, and Sub-Division was changed to the new structure (which has lasted up till the present day) comprising Region (of which there are now six), District (equivalent to previous Division), and Division (equivalent to previous Sub-Division). This overhaul effectively upgraded the rank of the local command. For instance, previously the Divisional Commander was of Superintendent rank; now the equivalent post (District Commander) is of Chief Superintendent rank. With this upgrading of the local command, considerable decision-making authority has since been decentralized to the local command, with the objective of enhancing efficiency. At the same time, great efforts were put into upgrading the HKPF's equipment and crime-fighting capacity (personal communication to the author from senior police commanders).

As a result, by the mid-1980s, the HKPF had more or less completed a first round of reorientation, namely, the change from a thoroughly corrupt and abusive colonial paramilitary force that focused on public order maintenance into a force which, though still steeped in paramilitary traditions and equipped with paramilitary capabilities, had been much professionalized and was generally free of organized corruption, with law enforcement now being accorded equal priority to public order maintenance. For convenience, we can call this reorientation a reorientation towards professionalism, meaning that proper police work (in contrast to the previous corruption as a way of life) now occupied centre stage, with the HKPF's capabilities in carrying out proper police work being much upgraded.

However, it should be noted that the HKPF remained very much a coercive force, always ready to use the strong arm of the law against the public. A good illustration of this is its strict enforcement of the then very stringent *Public Order Ordinance* (Cap. 245) (POO), as a result of which protesters were often barred from using loudhailers or from marching in groups exceeding 20 in number.

The HKPF's reorientation towards service from the mid-1990s onwards

No sooner had the HKPF more or less completed its reorientation towards professionalism, than it was compelled to engage in a second round of reorientation, this time towards service (Lau 2004a). In policing parlance, a service is contrasted to a force, for which civilian police work is accorded equal priority. Under the impact of neo-liberal ideology since the early 1990s (see below), service also denotes a customer-service culture in the performance of all policing functions, and not only civilian work. For example, in maintaining public order, a force would emphasize strict enforcement of the relevant laws if necessary by coercion, whereas a service would aim at facilitating demonstrations as far as is consistent with minimizing disruption to the public. In law enforcement, a force would emphasize the coercive power of control, whereas a service would pay more respect to the rights of individuals. This round of reorientation (hereinafter referred to as service reorientation) occurred due to two intervening events.

The first was the mass rallies and marches in 1989. Because of the sheer size of these events, the POO was unenforceable. Even after the mass events had died down, local political activists continued to defy the POO, usually with impunity – the political atmosphere after 1989 made a return to the previous strict enforcement socially unacceptable. In short, the coercive approach that the HKPF retained prior to 1989 was, in its aftermath, starting to crumble with regard to public order maintenance.

Secondly, in October 1992 Chris Patten was appointed as the last colonial governor. For reasons best known to himself and Britain, he introduced a number of drastic reforms, of which I shall discuss only one, namely, to turn public service into 'customer service'. The background to the 'customer service' idea was that in the late 1970s the neo-liberal right wing ascended to power in Britain and America. It drastically reduced the role of government and introduced market principles into the public service. In 1991, British Prime Minister John Major put forward the Citizens' Charter, which demanded that civil servants serve the public like serving customers. Upon his arrival, Patten, a close political ally of John Major, pushed the same agenda in Hong Kong.

Shortly before Patten's arrival, the HKPF hired a British management consultancy to review its command structure. As usual, these British consultants simply recommended Hong Kong to follow the latest developments in Britain, and hence, inspired by John Major's Citizens' Charter, recommended the HKPF adopt a more customer-oriented approach. Whether or not this recommendation would have been implemented had it not been for Patten's arrival and demand to adopt this approach for the entire civil service is a moot point. In any case, it was after Patten's programmatic declaration that in May 1994, the HKPF established the Service Quality Wing (SQW), with the mission to develop a customer-service culture among police and transform the HKPF into a 'service of quality'.

In March 1995 the SQW launched the Force Strategy on Quality of Service (Hui 1995). In December 1996 two documents, *Force Vision* and *Statement of Common Purpose and Values* (Royal Hong Kong Police Force 1996), collectively known in the Force as 'the Values', were promulgated. Several rounds of 'Living-the-Values' workshops were held on a Force-wide basis (Hui 2001). In early 2001, the slogan-cum-motto of 'We Serve with Pride and Care' was adopted, implying that what the HKPF is providing is a service, which is delivered with care to (in contrast to coercive imposition upon) the public. To instil 'the Values' in new recruits, new subjects on 'the Values' and the 'Bill of Human Rights' (a new ordinance enacted in the early 1990s) were added to the recruit training syllabus. In December 2001, a new uniform was designed; after consultation and trial, it was adopted in December 2004. It should be noted that this new uniform is very similar to the uniform of most private security guards. Apparently, this similarity was intentional, with the purpose of 'civilianizing' the police in appearance – the old uniform was too paramilitary-like, hence projecting an image of being separate from, and above, the public, whereas the new uniform would supposedly eliminate this gap.

If the main impetus for the HKPF's service reorientation was initially externally driven by Patten's edict, there can be little doubt that the HKPF's top management was intent on pressing on with the reorientation even after Patten's departure. To understand why and how this came about, it is necessary to examine a third intervening event, namely, the reign of Chee-wah Tung.

Tung became the Chief Executive (CE) of the Hong Kong Special Administrative Region (HKSAR) under Chinese sovereignty on 1 July 1997. For several months he enjoyed widespread endorsement among the public, probably because Hong Kong's economy was then riding on the crest of a boom. At the end of 1997, however, the Asian Financial Crisis struck, and Hong Kong began a long period of economic decline which was to last for some six years or so, with unemployment reaching prolonged record levels. At the same time, a series of unfortunate incidents and Tung's political ineptness[2] landed his regime in a legitimacy crisis. This was not helped by the fact that the local media, from being generally pro-establishment prior to 1997, had post-1997 become one of the world's most fierce critics of, even hostile to, governments. This applied not only to media organizations such as *Apple Daily* (a local Chinese newspaper), but also to media which are generally regarded as taking a friendly stand towards the Chinese and the HKSAR governments. For instance, *Oriental Daily* (another local Chinese newspaper) might be comparatively friendly towards Beijing or the CE, but when it comes to fault-finding with the civil service and civil servants, it is no less critical.

The legitimacy crisis of Tung's regime affected not only Tung and his principal officials, but the entire civil service (and other public bodies). Prior to 1997 Hong Kong's civil service was highly praised for its efficiency. Soon after 1997 the same civil service, functioning on the same systems and processes, staffed by mostly the same people, suddenly came to be seen as being grossly inept and inefficient. What changed was not the system or the people, but the public and the media's attitude towards government and civil servants and the high demands placed upon them, in a radically changed social and socio-political environment to be discussed as we proceed.

With regard to the police, previously most members of the public tended to defer to police authority (Lau 2004b); now, police authority at the street level is often challenged. Defiance of police authority, resistance, and even assault against officers[3] occur regularly. To cite just a few cases, on 28 September 1999 police responding to a complaint against noise nuisance caused by mahjong playing were injured when the individuals concerned defied the police and resisted (*Singpao Daily*, 29 September 1999); on 23 October 2005 two officers trying to issue a fixed-penalty ticket to a car were confronted by three people and suffered injury during the resistance (*MingPao*, 24 October 2005); on 26 February 2006 freelance musicians performing in Tuen Mun Park and their fans angrily confronted and hurled verbal abuse at police and Leisure and Cultural Services Department officers who tried to stop the performance on receiving a complaint of noise disturbance (*Apple Daily*, 27 February 2006). The most dramatic case is an incident occurring on the night of 11 February 2003 (*Oriental Daily*, 12/02/2003). A squad of officers stopped a group of suspected triad members for identity checks in Yau Ma Tei[4] after midnight. The group told the officers that after midnight the area was under their, and not police, control. Calling the media, they defied and humiliated the officers in front of reporters.

The challenge against street-level police authority is not hard to understand. Because of the legitimate crisis of the Tung regime, principal officials found themselves in a very weak position. As a result, when they appeared on radio talk-shows, they were often grilled and humiliated at will.[5] If even the CE and his top officials were indiscriminately humiliated in public on a regular basis, why should members of the public pay any respect to minor civil servants such as a beat police officer? An indication of how bad the situation had become can be gained from the following incident. In May 2001, a protester was arrested in a demonstration and brought back to a police station. Legislator-cum-solicitor Cheng Ka Fu gained access to the arrested protester as his legal representative (*MingPao*, 10 May 2001). When they were conferring alone, Cheng let his mobile phone be used by the arrestee to carry out a live radio interview. This would appear to constitute a breach of a lawyer's professional code of conduct, and incensed police staff associations wanted to lodge a complaint with the Law Society of Hong Kong against Cheng. However, after the intervention of the Police Commissioner, the staff associations dropped their intention.

This erosion of authority not only affects the police, but the entire civil service, such that we can properly speak of a governability crisis consequent upon the Tung regime's legitimacy crisis. Even with the departure of Tung, this governability crisis continues, as it has already acquired its own momentum.

In addition to the governability crisis, the 'customer service' campaign has also produced significant effects. By transforming citizens into consumers, the double emphasis of rights and responsibilities in the concept of citizenship has given way to the one-sided emphasis of rights in the concept of consumerism (Lau forthcoming). Citizens-as-consumers are entitled to lodge whatever complaints they see fit. Add the governability crisis and the 'customer service' campaign together, and we have as a result a public that does not respect police authority and feels it to be their right to complain against the police at will.

In letters to newspapers' readers' columns and through other channels, frontline police have voiced their concern about the situation. In my own informal exchanges with various frontline police, it is clear that the feeling of eroded authority at the street level is significant and prevalent, and as a result of this, as well as the desire to avoid being made the subject of complaint, many frontline officers are not prepared to carry out their duties with a firm attitude – in some cases, even avoiding carrying out their duties altogether.

There is, however, one area in which current policing practice largely retains the former coercive style, namely, in some anti-crime tactics such as the regular use of 'carpet-searches' of nightspots, which in some cases involve hundreds of police.

In these operations, police enter nightspots for inspection during which the venue's normal activities are suspended for a considerable time. As a result, many hundreds (even thousands) of ordinary patrons are, at the least, being inconvenienced; at worst, they are being treated as though they are suspects, e.g. police sometimes command males to stand on one side, females on the other, and then proceed to check everybody's identity. It is interesting to note that in public order events, any hint of police strong-arm tactics would incur the wrath of human rights activists; in contrast, these strong-arm law enforcement tactics rarely raise an eyebrow, even among the same activists. One possible explanation of this is that Hong Kong has one of the lowest crime rates in the world, and the police receive credit for it from the public (though research worldwide generally provides no support for any correlation between police strength or tactics and crime). Thus, long-established anti-crime tactics have become taken for granted by the public as serving society well. And because of this, even if some human rights activists were aware of the implications of these tactics (which I doubt), it would be politically unwise to question them.

Despite what is being said, however, even in anti-crime operations, police are sometimes challenged due to the erosion of police street-level authority. For instance, on 21 October 2003 a group of 7 Special Duty Squad officers carrying out an anti-illegal gambling in a public place operation, found themselves surrounded by 200 onlookers and had to call for reinforcement. On 12 November 2005, in an anti-crime operation in Mongkok, a team of 12 officers carrying out a liquor license check were physically confronted by alleged triads who refused to co-operate (*MingPao*, 22 October 2003; 13 November 2005).

To sum up, as a result of social and socio-political changes since 1989, the HKPF's public order maintenance has now become very much a service – facilitating demonstrations – though it must be emphasized that this change notwithstanding, the HKPF's paramilitary capabilities remain intact, as demonstrated in the policing of the protests at the World Trade Organization's conference in December 2005. This ministerial-level conference was held in Hong Kong in mid-December 2005. In similar conferences in various parts of the world in previous years, violent confrontations between police and anti-globalization activists invariably occurred. On this occasion, several thousand anti-globalization activists from around the world came to Hong Kong, including the famously (or infamously, depending on one's political standpoint) militant Korean farmer activists. To cope with the challenge, the HKPF mobilized some 9,000 officers, almost a third of the disciplined manpower of the Force, to police the protests (*WenWeiPo*, 18 December 2005). Negotiations were held with the protest organizers well ahead of time. Several barricaded protest zones in the vicinity of the conference venue as well as various routes for protest marches were designated. This demonstrated the service role played by the HKPF in the maintenance of public order.

On the first few days of the week-long conference, the protests proceeded in a generally orderly manner. Violent clashes between some protesters (mostly Korean farmer activists) and police did occur at the barricades, in which pepper spray was used by the police. Nevertheless, the incidents were relatively minor, almost ritualistic in character, and the police was able to cope with them with little trouble.

On the evening of 17 December 2005, the night before the final day of the conference, the Korean farmer activists were determined to make a serious attempt to break through police cordons to reach the conference venue. Marching along the pre-agreed route, some protesters suddenly broke away from the main protest contingent. Perhaps lulled by the orderly manner in which the previous marches had proceeded, the first line of police defence which guarded the march was breached, as a result of which hundreds of protesters were able to come to within a hundred metres or so of the conference venue. The second line of police defence was, however, able to hold the line, and violent street battles between police and marauding protesters occurred. Teargas was fired and eventually the police rounded up around 1,000 protesters in Gloucester Road, the main thoroughfare 200 metres away from the conference venue. The protesters were detained there until the next morning when they were taken to the police station. Despite breaching the first line of defence, the police generally rose to the challenge, thereby illustrating its paramilitary capabilities when called upon to make use of them.

With regard to ordinary street-level policing, the HKPF's previous coercive presence (in the above-mentioned sense that the majority of the population dispositionally deferred to the police) has largely disappeared. It is in this context – of the changes in the HKPF's environment in terms of public order maintenance and street-level policing – that the HKPF's continuation to press on with the service reorientation, even after Patten's departure, should be appreciated.

Despite this change on the part of the police, in a social climate in which the public remains ever dissatisfied (see Lau forthcoming), complaints against police have remained high. Thus, reducing complaints is a top HKPF priority. The HKPF top brass believe that the means to do this is to push ahead with the service reorientation. In 2005–6, the HKPF took two significant steps in this direction. In January 2006, the Police Training School was upgraded to become the Hong Kong Police College (HKPC), for which the HKPF contracted a local university to teach two modules to new police recruits, namely Social Studies in Policing (aiming to prepare new recruits to face Hong Kong's changed social and socio-political environments for policing) and Psychology in Policing (aiming to enhance police's ability to handle cases such as domestic violence so as to avoid complaint). In 2005, a comprehensive plan for providing 'psychological competency' training to serving officers was drawn up and began to be implemented (in phases) with the help of local academia, one major objective of which was the same as the teaching of Psychology in Policing at the HKPC.

It is clear that the HKPF has changed radically from the pre-1989 era. The HKPF top brass are aware of this change and are committed to following through with the service reorientation to suit Hong Kong's changed social and socio-political environments. The remaining questions are: what is the deeper reality of the HKPF's change since 1989, and what are the future prospects of its service reorientation?

Conclusion: future prospects of the HKPF's service reorientation

As explained, transformation into a service involves two aspects: giving equal priority to civilian police work; and adopting a customer-service culture and ethos in all police work. To what extent have these aspects been realized?[6]

Concerning the first aspect, it will be recalled that a paramilitary force gives first priority to public order maintenance; a professional police gives equal priority to public order maintenance and law enforcement (hereinafter, these two types of police work will be referred to as frontline operational work) through reliance on coercive tactics; ideally, a police service values civilian police work as highly as frontline operational work. In this respect, the HKPF is apparently still under the influence of its historical roots and retains an emphasis on frontline operational work.

Firstly, all of the HKPF's paramilitary structures (e.g. EU, PTU), processes (e.g. ready mobilization into IS Structure), and so on have been retained. This is partly due to the general emphasis placed by the government and the public on the need to maintain Hong Kong's political stability, but it is also partly determined by the HKPF's historical roots. Secondly, priority is apparently still given to frontline operational work, informally regarded as 'core' duties in the HKPF. 'Core' duties are informally given greater weight in comparison to non-'core' duties (e.g. training, community work) in terms of career advancement. Thus, of the two Deputy Commissioners of Police (DCP), namely DCP (Operations) and DCP (Management), when the Commissioner retires it is always DCP (Operations) who succeeds to the post. It should, however, be underlined that the retention of the HKPF's historically entrenched values, such as the above-mentioned, is not the conscious intention of the HKPF's top management. The impression that I have gained from my own contact with some members of the top management and other senior commanders is that the wish to follow through with the service reorientation is a genuine one. My argument is that such retention occurs on the subconscious level.

As to the second aspect, the impression gained from my informal exchanges with various veteran frontline police can nicely be summed up in this comment: 'We are now polite towards ordinary citizens, that's mainly to avoid complaint. But that's on the surface. Deep down, there's no concept of service at all. That's very hard to acquire.' There is general scepticism among experienced frontline officers towards the concept of consumerism (public service as customer service) in policing. Thus, the generally known nickname given to SQW is 'idiotic wing' (in Cantonese 'Shaw Q wing'). This is not peculiar to Hong Kong. Research elsewhere also finds that ingrained police attitudes inimical to the service ethos are hard to change (Guyot 1991; Dixon and Stanko 1993; Bennett 1994; Lurigio and Rosenbaum 1994). Whereas I believe that the above is the case with many experienced frontline officers, whether or not with the establishment of the HKPC a stronger service culture can be cultivated among the new breed of recruits is an issue that awaits future research.

Today the HKPF and its future developmental trajectory are in some ways pulled by contradictory forces. On the one hand, the top management sincerely wishes to follow through with the service reorientation. However, on the other hand, the maintenance of its paramilitary capabilities and hard law enforcement tactics provide fertile soil for the persistence of a professional but hard law-enforcer culture among police. In contradiction to this, the erosion of police authority in ordinary street-level policing has been significant. Among experienced officers still largely steeped in traditionalist values, this has considerably affected morale. In the pre-1989 era, when such a contradictory situation did not exist, new recruits quickly became 'police-ified', i.e. initiated into the prevalent police culture and developed a strong sense of organizational-professional belonging. In the past few years the top management have come to notice that this sense of organizational-professional belonging among new recruits is weak. Why is this so?

While in-depth research is required to fully answer the above question, I believe it has a lot to do with the diminished morale of many experienced frontline police, through whom new recruits' initiation into the organization and its culture occurs, and the erosion of street-level police authority (new recruits begin their career on beat patrol). As various frontline officers have remarked to me, many (both the experienced and the new) now regard the job simply as a job, and the previous sense of organizational-professional *esprit de corps* has become comparatively weakened.

Despite this, the HKPF is still able to function effectively – a testimony to its well-established capabilities and professionalism. But it is clear from the above that the only viable position to take in public under Hong Kong's current social and socio-political climate (which is unlikely to change in the foreseeable future), namely, to press on with the service reorientation is creating tension with the determination (ironically, also supported by the public) to maintain its paramilitary capabilities and hard law enforcement tactics, which serves to reproduce traditionalist police culture. With street-level police authority eroded, this tension has so far been 'resolved' in the engendering of low morale among many experienced officers and a relatively low sense of organizational-professional belonging and commitment among new recruits.

To conclude, despite the sub-conscious retention of the priority given to frontline operational work, civilian police work is now given much greater weight than previously. The HKPF's history in terms of certain anti-crime tactics and ingrained police values is still exerting an influence, at least among some members of the Force; but in terms of ordinary street-level policing and the policing of public order events, the approach now taken by the HKPF is service-oriented. This juxtaposition reflects the above-explained underlying tension facing the HKPF today. It will be interesting to see how the resolution of this tension will unfold in the coming years.

Notes

1 The three general functions of the police are: (1) maintaining public order (e.g. dealing with riots, policing demonstrations, etc.); (2) law enforcement (i.e. dealing with crime); and (3) the provision of miscellaneous service (e.g. regulating traffic). Maintaining public order can further be divided into two sub-categories. One is of a political nature (e.g. policing riots and protests), and the other is of a non-political nature (e.g. dealing with drunkards causing disturbance in a public place, settling disputes between neighbours). In order to distinguish between these two sub-categories, in this chapter I shall confine maintaining public order to the first sub-category, i.e. in relation to incidents of a political nature, while the latter sub-category will be referred to as peacekeeping. I shall also on occasion refer to peacekeeping and service provision collectively as civilian police work.

2 In 1998, the bird flu epidemic struck Hong Kong; in the same year the new airport's computer system collapsed on the very first day of operation. While the government's handling of the bird flu crisis won praise internationally, and the removal of the entire airport operation from Kai Tak to Chep Lap Kok literally overnight was no mean feat at all, the media and public opinion focused solely on the negative effects of these incidents. In January 1999, the Wu Sin incident occurred. Whether it was a case of partiality or political stupidity, it reflected very badly upon Tung's administration. Before becoming CE of HKSAR, Tung announced the '85,000 policy'. It was a well-intentioned policy enjoying widespread support. However, the property market collapsed with the onset of the Asian Financial Crisis. Lacking political wisdom, Tung abandoned the policy without announcing it. In mid-2000, property developers demanded the policy's abandonment in a high-profile manner. Tung decided to make it public that the policy no longer existed, but fearing that such an announcement might be taken as giving in to the developers' demand, he also announced that the policy had in fact been secretly abandoned prior to the developers raising their demand. For a politician to say that he had secretly abandoned a policy was, of course, political stupidity of the first degree. These are just some of the coincidences and examples of Tung's political ineptitude for illustration.

3 'Assault' in such cases usually means physical resistance resulting in police being injured, as opposed to deliberate attack intended to wound.

4 One of the busiest districts in Kowloon, Hong Kong.

5 In the sociology of the media, it is well-known that the very nature and format of talk-shows favour simplistic criticism and attack, and make detailed all-round explanation difficult. Besides the weak legitimacy position of top officials of Tung's regime, this is another reason why they were often humiliated at will by hosts.

6 Lau (2004b) provides a more detailed and theoretical analysis of the following discussion.

Review questions

1 In what ways was the HKPF a classic colonial paramilitary force up to the early 1970s?
2 In this chapter, an implicit theme is that the main impetuses to the HKPF's almost continuous reorientation since the mid-1970s have been externally derived. Explain this with reference to the reforms of the mid-1970s; the service strategy begun in the mid-1990s; and the continued commitment to the service reorientation after Patten's departure up to today.
3 How would you describe the character of the HKPF today?

References

Anderson, D.M. and Killingray, D. (1992) *Policing and Decolonization: Politics, Nationalism and the Police 1917–65*. Manchester: Manchester University Press.

Andrade, J. (1985) *World Police and Paramilitary Forces*. Basingstoke: Macmillan.

Bennett, T. (1994) 'Community policing on the ground: Developments in Britain', in D.P. Rosenbaum (ed.) *The Challenge of Community Policing: Testing the Promises* (pp. 224–46). Thousand Oaks, CA: Sage.

Cheung, K.W. (2000) *Inside Story of 1967 Riot in Hong Kong*. Hong Kong: The Pacific Century Press Ltd (in Chinese).

Crisswell, C. and Watson, M. (1982) *The Royal Hong Kong Police (1841–1945)*. Hong Kong: Macmillan.

Dixon, B. and Stanko, E. (1993) *Serving the People: Sector Policing and Public Accountability*. Uxbridge: Brunel University.

Gaylord, M. and Traver, H. (1995) 'Colonial policing and the demise of British rule in Hong Kong', *International Journal of the Sociology of Law*, 23 (1): 23–43.

Grant, I. (1992) *1997: The Implications for Community Policing in Hong Kong* (unpublished MA thesis). Exeter: University of Exeter.

Guyot, D. (1991) *Policing as Though People Matter*. Philadelphia: Temple University Press.

Hong Kong Police Force (2000) Press release of 23 February 2000 by Police Public Relations Branch on public opinion survey carried out in 1999.

Hong Kong Police Force (2001a) Press release of 21 February 2001 by Police Public Relations Branch on customer satisfaction survey carried out in 2000.

Hong Kong Police Force (2001b) 'Key findings 2001 public opinion survey' (Unpublished internal management information materials of the Hong Kong Police Force).

Hui, K.-O. (1995) *A Service of Quality: Speech to the Australian Chamber of Commerce in Hong Kong*. Hong Kong: Government Printer.

Hui, K.-O. (2001) 'Management reforms in the Police Force', in A.B.L. Leung and J.C.Y. Lee (eds) *Public Sector Reform in Hong Kong: Into the 21st Century* (pp. 167–99). Hong Kong: The Chinese University Press.

Jeffries, C. (1952) *The Colonial Police*. London: Max Parrish.

Lau, R.W.K. (2004a) 'Community policing in Hong Kong: Transplanting a questionable model', *Criminal Justice*, 4 (1): 61–80.

Lau, R.W.K. (2004b) 'History as obstacle to change: A neo-institutionalist analysis of police reform in Hong Kong', *International Journal of the Sociology of Law*, 32 (1): 1–15.

Lau, R.W.K. (forthcoming) 'The contemporary culture of blame and the fetishization of the modernist mentality', *Current Sociology*.

Lo, T.W. (1993) *Corruption and Politics in Hong Kong and China*, Buckingham: Open University Press.

Lurigio, A.J. and Rosenbaum, D.P. (1994) 'The impact of community policing on police personnel: A review of the literature', in D.P. Rosenbaum (ed.) *The Challenge of Community Policing: Testing the Promises* (pp. 147–63). Thousand Oaks, CA: Sage.

Miners, N.J. (1995) *The Government and Politics of Hong Kong* (5th edn). Hong Kong: Oxford University Press.

Munn, C. (1995) '"Scratching with a rattan": William Caine and the Hong Kong magistracy', *Hong Kong Law Journal*, 25 (2): 213–38.

Royal Hong Kong Police Force (1996) *Force Vision* and *Statement of Common Purpose and Values*. Hong Kong: Royal Hong Kong Police Force.

Scott, I. (1989) *Political Change and the Crisis of Legitimacy in Hong Kong*. Hong Kong: Oxford University Press.

Sinclair, K. (1983) *Asia's Finest: An Illustrated Account of the Royal Hong Kong Police*. Hong Kong: Unicorn.

Tobias, J.J. (1972) 'Police and the public in the UK', *Journal of Contemporary History*, 7: 201–20.

Traver, H (1991) 'Crime trends', in H. Traver and J. Vagg (eds) *Crime and Justice in Hong Kong* (pp. 10–24). Hong Kong: Oxford University Press.

Newspaper articles cited (in Chinese)

「惡男女竹戰擾人清夢 狂毆投訴鄰居 反抗傷兩警員」, *Singpao Daily*, 29 September 1999.

「警搶手機阻拘留者電臺控訴」, *MingPao*, 10 May 2001.

「不滿查證六漢圍警挑釁」, *Oriental Daily*, 12 February 2003.

「警廟街掃賭遭 200 人包圍」, *MingPao*, 22 October 2003.

「兩漢小故襲警 胡椒噴霧降服」, *MingPao*, 24 October 2005.

「酒吧查牌 6 煞推撞 12 警員報稱受傷」, *MingPao*, 13 November 2005.

「強調警方有能力平亂 無需求助駐軍 一哥：街頭圍困 900示威者 , *WenWeiPo*, 18 December 2005.

「康文署出動保安員 人鏈護送離開　公園表演受阻百人圍兩警」, *Apple Daily*, 27 February 2006.

Legislation cited

Public Order Ordinance (Cap. 245)

Useful websites

Hong Kong Police Force (HKPF)	http://www.info.gov.hk/police/hkp-home/english/index.htm
The Independent Police Complaints Council	http://www.ipcc.gov.hk/en/aboutus_01.htm
The Metropolitan Police Service (London) – HKPF's early model of police service	http://www.met.police.uk/
Wikipedia's entry for paramilitary police	http://en.wikipedia.org/wiki/Paramilitary#Paramilitary_police

Chapter 6

Prosecuting crime

I. Grenville Cross

Introduction

The decision of whether or not to prosecute a suspect is a vital one, from all perspectives. It is vital for the suspect. It is also vital for the victim. Viewed broadly, it is likewise vital for the community. Great care must be taken by those who determine these issues, always remembering that wrong decisions may undermine confidence in the criminal justice system as a whole. The prosecutor must act at all times within the parameters of an established and announced prosecution policy. Those who prosecute discharge a heavy responsibility on behalf of society. They must be fair, independent, and just.

Article 63 of the *Basic Law*

The Basic Law of the Hong Kong Special Administrative Region (the *Basic Law*) came into effect on 1 July 1997. Article 63 provides that the Department of Justice shall control criminal prosecutions, free from any interference. It is reassuring that this principle, long recognized in colonial times as a convention, has finally achieved an entrenched status. This means, in practice, that prosecutors are able to discharge their duties to the public from a secure base. At times of controversy, the prosecutor can take refuge within a constitutionally guaranteed position.

Prosecutors and investigators

In the Mainland of China and the Macao Special Administrative Region, the prosecutor not only prosecutes cases but also investigates them. In those jurisdictions, the prosecutor is closely involved in the investigation of cases of corruption and of misconduct in public office. In Hong Kong, the prosecutor has no such investigative function. Whereas general crime is investigated by the Hong Kong Police Force, offences of corruption are investigated by the Independent Commission Against Corruption, and customs crime is investigated by the Customs and Excise Department. Of course, the prosecutor can advise the investigator upon lines of inquiry which can profitably be pursued and upon the admissibility of evidence, but the investigation of crime is, ultimately, a matter for the law enforcement agencies themselves.

The Department of Justice has the responsibility for the conduct of prosecutions, without the power to control or direct the investigation (Department of Justice 2002). In Scotland, by contrast, the Procurator Fiscal has the power to direct the police and to tell them what to investigate (Crown Office and Procurator Fiscal Service 2005). But the lack of any such power in Hong Kong by no means undermines effective law enforcement. Were the police to ignore legal advice to conduct the investigation in a particular way, the prosecutor holds the trump card. He or she can decline to prosecute. Alternatively, he or she can discontinue a prosecution which is in progress, if the investigator does not pursue the enquiries which he deems to be necessary. This separation of the prosecutorial and investigatory functions works well in practice, and facilitates the application of an independent and dedicated perspective to each function. In practice, the prosecutor and the investigator invariably co-operate harmoniously in pursuit of shared objectives.

When the investigator prepares his or her case, he or she will, if necessary, consult the prosecutor, on legal and evidential issues, actual or potential. He or she may also require advice on undercover operations and the legitimacy of particular areas of investigation. It is in the interest of the investigator to prepare a case which satisfies the threshold test for prosecution, and which will not collapse at court when tested by the defence. This means that while the investigator is not strictly required to accept the advice of the prosecutor, he or she will, in practice, usually do so. The interests of the prosecutor and the investigator invariably converge in a shared desire to assemble a case which is watertight and will withstand close forensic scrutiny.

The Prosecutions Division is the largest legal division in the Department of Justice. Headed by the Director of Public Prosecutions, who in turn is superintended by the Secretary for Justice, it comprises about 120 Government Counsel and about 102 Court Prosecutors (Department of Justice 2007). The role of the Division is to prosecute trials and appeals at all levels, to provide legal advice to law enforcement agencies and others in government, and to review the operation of the criminal law. The Division itself is divided into four Sub-divisions, concerned, respectively, with management and case preparation, trial advocacy, appellate advocacy, and commercial crime and corruption. In recent years, the Division has developed its capacity to prosecute transnational and organized crime, as well as to handle specific types of offences, such as copyright piracy, technology crime, and money laundering. In addition, a dedicated unit advises on and conducts criminal cases which engage *Basic Law* and human rights issues.

Qualities of the prosecutor

The prosecutor occupies a formidable position in the criminal justice system. His or her responsibilities are awesome. The decisions he or she takes can profoundly affect the lives of others. In each case, the prosecutor must carefully evaluate the evidence and apply the law and decide if a prosecution is appropriate. A decision to prosecute must be taken with the keenest appreciation of the ordeal involved in a trial, as well as with a full awareness of the trauma and stigma that can be caused to the accused and his family, even if, ultimately, there is an acquittal. At the same time, difficult decisions cannot be sidestepped. The prosecutor must possess judgement and good sense in abundance, and have the courage of his convictions.

Of the many qualities which the prosecutor needs to possess, fearlessness is perhaps the most important. Occasionally he or she will be criticized for prosecuting, but more often for not prosecuting. The decisions he or she has to reach are inherently controversial. Provided the prosecutor has acted conscientiously and correctly, he or she must have the courage of his or her convictions. This requires him or her to have the strength of character to resist criticism from whatever quarter, no matter how strident or painful. Never must he or she allow the judgement to be overborne by political, media, or public censure. The profession of prosecutor is certainly not one for the faint-hearted.

Protection of the suspect

It is often far easier for the prosecutor to decide to prosecute than it is to decide not to prosecute. Once criminal proceedings have begun, the issues move from the domain of the prosecutor to that of the court. Questions about the case can be avoided on the basis of the sub judice rule, which, quite simply, means that since the case is before the courts for trial there cannot be any public discussion of the issues, as this might prejudice the fairness of the trial. But in a matter as important as the liberty of the suspect, no responsible prosecutor can avoid his or her duty to properly assess the evidence. After all, the prosecutor is a gatekeeper, charged with the duty of ensuring that only meritorious cases proceed to trial. Just as the judge must scrupulously protect the interests of the accused who stands trial, so should the prosecutor be vigilant in defence of the rights of the suspect who does not. Once the trial starts, the suspect enjoys certain fundamental rights, including the right to question the witness who accuses him or her, to know exactly what the prosecution case is, and to give and call evidence in his or her own defence.

Evidential test for prosecution

No citizen should ever be subjected to a criminal trial unless the evidence warrants that course. Prosecuting, after all, is the art of the possible. A suspect can only ever properly be prosecuted if there is sufficient evidence to justify that course. Prosecution policy in this area is clear and unambiguous. Those who prosecute in Hong Kong apply the guidance contained in *The Statement of Prosecution Policy and Practice* (Department of Justice 2002), which, in turn, reflects the English approach and that of the wider common law world.

The Department of Justice does not support the proposition that a mere prima facie case suffices to ground a prosecution. In deciding whether to start proceedings, the single most important consideration for the prosecutor is the likelihood of conviction. But a conviction can never be guaranteed, and the system of justice could not operate effectively if the prosecutor pursued only those cases where there was an absolute certainty of conviction. However, the enforcement of the law would be brought into disrepute if there were an inordinate number of failed prosecutions. This could also affect public confidence in the efficacy of the criminal process.

The duty of the prosecutor is to institute criminal proceedings against a suspect in accordance with prosecution policy guidelines. It is then for the court, if guilt is disputed, to decide if the charge has been proved beyond reasonable doubt. A prosecution may properly be started once it is decided that the evidence is capable of proving the guilt of the suspect. The decision to prosecute has usually to be taken by the prosecutor without the opportunity of seeing or hearing the witnesses, and is based invariably upon an assessment of the papers submitted by the investigator. The prosecutor must satisfy himself that there exists at least a reasonable prospect of conviction. Mere suspicion, no matter how great, falls well short of what is required.

A suspect should not be prosecuted on the basis of what lawyers sometimes call 'a bare case', by which is meant a case that proceeds on no more than the basis of a 51 per cent prospect of conviction. Just as the prosecutor will wish to see that those against whom the evidence is compelling face trial, so also will he or she wish to avoid unnecessary proceedings. A proper evaluation of the case will involve an assessment of the evidence as well as of the law. It is also necessary to take account of such matters as the availability, competence and credibility of witnesses, their likely impression on the court, and the prospects for the admissibility of evidence implicating the accused, such as alleged confessions. The prosecutor should also consider any defences that are plainly open to the accused, such as alibi evidence, by which is meant evidence which puts the accused somewhere else when the crime occurred, and which may affect directly the prospects of conviction.

Article 87 of the *Basic Law* recognizes the right of those accused of crime to be presumed innocent. It is only if the court is satisfied of guilt beyond reasonable doubt that the prosecutor will secure a conviction. But even if the prosecution fails, it by no means follows that the case ought not to have been brought. Prosecutions fail for all sorts of reasons. Witnesses may not come up to proof, or may be shaken in cross-examination, or may even fail to appear. The judge may sometimes exclude crucial items of evidence on legal grounds. Such factors are imponderables, and cannot be predicted with certainty prior to trial.

Public interest factors

If a proposed prosecution satisfies the evidential test, the prosecutor must then assess the impact of the public interest factors, if any. As a rule of thumb, the more serious the offence the more likely it is that the public interest will require a prosecution. Factors which might suggest to the prosecutor that proceedings are inexpedient include the triviality of the offence; the medical condition of the suspect, his antecedents, and his age, whether very young or very old; the viability of any alternative to prosecution, such as a discretionary warning from a superintendent of police; the likelihood of a nominal penalty upon conviction; the staleness of the offence; any assistance which has been provided by the suspect to the authorities; the attitude of the victim, most obviously if it is forgiving; the indicia of remorse, such as the payment of compensation by the suspect to the victim.

Alternatively, factors may exist which aggravate the seriousness of the offence and emphasize the public interest in the prosecution of the suspect. Into this category fall such considerations as an abuse of trust by someone in authority; premeditation; the use of a weapon or the threat of violence; the prevalence of the offence; the role played in the offence, particularly if the suspect was a ringleader; any element of corruption; the criminal record of the suspect; the prospects of repetition. If any of these factors are combined with others the case for prosecution may become overwhelming, but that of itself does not absolve the prosecutor of the duty to evaluate the significance of each factor in the overall scheme of things.

Prosecutor at court

At court, the prosecutor represents the Hong Kong Special Administrative Region. He or she is not the representative of the government or the law enforcement agency. He or she is, in his or her own way, as independent as the judge, and his or her interest throughout is the just disposal of the issues joined. The prosecutor has no client in the conventional sense, and his or her duty is to act impartially and objectively in the public interest. He or she operates not as an adversary, but as a minister of justice. Rightly has it been said that the prosecutor secures no victories and sustains no defeats.

When he or she prosecutes a suspect, the prosecutor is himself or herself on trial. The public perception of the administration of justice may be affected if he or she badly manages the case, displays discourtesy, or is deficient in advocacy. Fairness by the prosecutor does not, however, make him or her some sort of 'soft touch'. He or she must be vigorous in prosecuting his or her case, but restrained and courteous throughout. He or she may strike hard blows, provided they are not foul ones. Evidence should be efficiently marshalled and cogently adduced.

The duty of the prosecutor is to call evidence which is relevant to prove the case, and to present it with appropriate fairness. He or she should not advance submissions to the court in which he or she does not truly believe, and he or she must never conceal material which may benefit the accused. The function of the prosecutor is to ensure that every material point is made which supports the prosecution case or undermines the defence case. At the same time, he or she should not press for a conviction at all costs.

Properly seen, the interest of the prosecutor is to ensure that the right person is convicted and that the truth emerges. If it becomes apparent to the prosecutor during the course of the trial that a reasonable prospect of securing a conviction no longer exists, he or she should acquaint the court with his or her view and seek to terminate the proceedings. In such a scenario, the sooner the ordeal the accused is undergoing is ended the better it will be for him or her, as well as for the public purse.

Duty of disclosure

The right of the accused to a fair trial is enshrined in Article 87 of the *Basic Law*. No trial can be fair if the prosecutor does not observe his or her disclosure obligations. The general duty upon the prosecution is to provide the defence in advance of trial with the evidence upon which reliance is intended to be placed. This ensures that the accused is aware of the case he will be required to meet, and enables him or her to prepare his or her position accordingly. Also disclosable, and often more problematic, is material upon which the prosecution does not intend to rely, but which might undermine the prosecution case or advance the defence case. The duty to disclose applies not only to previous convictions of a prosecution witness, but also to discreditable conduct by the witness which might affect his credibility. This, for example, might include disciplinary proceedings against an investigator. This duty is continuing, and matters not previously disclosable may have to be revealed in consequence of developments at trial. If there is a dispute as to whether evidence is in fact disclosable, it is for the court to resolve the issue, not the prosecution.

Victims and witnesses

Both at trial and before the case begins, the prosecutor should safeguard the interests of victims of crime and witnesses. The co-operation of such people is essential if offenders are to be brought to justice. They must have faith in the system, and the prosecutor should uphold their rights. These rights are reflected in *The Statement on the Treatment of Victims and Witnesses* (Department of Justice 2004), which the Director of Public Prosecutions issued to prosecutors in 2004, as well as in *The Victims of Crime Charter* (Department of Justice 2007). The rights of victims and witnesses include:

- the right to witness protection;
- the right to information throughout proceedings;
- the right to liaison at each stage;
- the right to assistance at court;
- the right to seek compensation or restitution;
- the right to protection from unjust criticism;
- the right to have the court appraised of the consequences of crime;
- the right to seek witness expenses;
- the right to information on appeals or reviews; and
- the right to have property disposed of appropriately once proceedings conclude.

Prosecutor and sentence

Once an accused has been convicted, the prosecutor plays an important role in the sentencing process, not least in ensuring that the exercise proceeds on a correct factual basis. He or she has the right to alert the court to guideline and tariff cases, including those which prescribe relevant sentencing principles. If requested, the prosecutor should be in a position to advise the court of the prevalence of the offence, and of the broad range of sentences passed generally for a particular offence. The prosecutor should ensure that any sentence which is in contemplation is in fact within the jurisdiction of the court, and an accurate record of previous convictions should be supplied. The court should be advised if the accused has assisted the authorities, and also if he or she faces satellite proceedings in other courts. In some situations, the prosecutor will be entitled to seek an enhanced sentence under the provisions of the *Organized and Serious Crimes Ordinance* (Cap. 455), most notably if the offence involves an organized crime. If a dispute arises over matters asserted in mitigation of sentence by the defence, the court should be alerted, so that it may, if necessary, conduct an inquiry to resolve the issue. In a nutshell, the duty of the prosecutor at the point of sentence is to assist the court to achieve a correct disposal, and to avoid appealable error. At the same time, it is no part of his or her function to press by advocacy for a more severe sentence.

Appeal against conviction and sentence

Article 39 of the *Basic Law* stipulates that the *International Covenant on Civil and Political Rights* (ICCPR) as applied to Hong Kong shall remain in force, and shall be implemented through the laws of the Hong Kong Special Administrative Region. Article 14(5) of the ICCPR provides that everyone 'convicted of a crime shall have the right to his conviction and sentence being reviewed by a higher tribunal according to law.' When those convicted of offences exercise their rights of appeal against conviction or sentence, or both, much is required of the prosecutor in the determination of the case before the appellate tribunal (see also Chapter 10 of this volume).

If there is an appeal against conviction, the duty of the prosecutor is to assist the court to achieve a just disposal of the case. To succeed, an accused must be in a position to show that his or her conviction is unsafe or unsatisfactory, or that the judgment of the trial court involves a wrong decision on a question of law, or that there was a material irregularity at trial. If an accused relies on any such ground of appeal, the prosecutor must evaluate it, settle his or her response, and identify relevant case law to assist the court. If he or she sees a basis for appeal which has not hitherto been noticed, the prosecutor should alert the court. Although the prosecutor will generally seek to uphold a conviction, if he or she concludes that the appeal is meritorious he or she should acquaint the court with his or her view and explain the reason for the concession. If the court disagrees with the reasoning, the prosecutor is entitled to adhere to his or her view of the merits and is not required to conduct himself or herself in a way which conflicts with his or her own judgement.

If an accused appeals against his or her sentence, he or she will generally need to demonstrate that the penalty imposed was unlawful, wrong in principle, or manifestly excessive. If the prosecutor decides that on the facts and the authorities the sentence does in fact fall into one of those categories, it is not his or her function to seek to uphold it. But once he or she decides that the sentence is legitimate and falls within an acceptable range, he or she should settle his submissions accordingly, and fortify them, if necessary, by reference to case law and, on occasion, to statistics which illustrate such things as prevalence or the customary range of sentence for the offence in question. The prosecutor must also be aware of the jurisdiction of the court when it disposes of an appeal.

Review of sentence

In some situations, it is open to the Secretary for Justice to apply to the Court of Appeal for leave to challenge a particular sentence. While this power is only invoked in exceptional cases, it is deployed most commonly where the sentence is considered to be manifestly inadequate, wrong in principle or contrary to law. Every application is carefully vetted by the Director of Public Prosecutions, who must usually be satisfied not only that the sentencing court has committed a serious error, but also that it is in the public interest for the matter to be corrected. In practice, the situation in which a review is most usually pursued is where a sentence has been imposed which is unduly lenient, by which is meant that it falls outside the range of sentences which in all the circumstances could reasonably be regarded as appropriate. In 2000–7, there were 64 applications for review of sentence initiated.

If leave is granted to the Secretary for Justice to seek a review of sentence, the duty of the prosecutor at the hearing is to identify for the Court of Appeal the precise nature of the error alleged to have been made. If the application is based on an error of law or principle, the prosecutor should indicate the substance of the complaint, making reference as required to relevant authority. If the sentence is said to be unduly lenient, the prosecutor will refer to guideline or tariff cases, if any, and to cases which establish points of principle. He or she may also indicate the approach which the sentencer ought to have applied, perhaps by reference to material which illustrates the prevalence or heinousness of the offence. The prosecutor may draw attention to matters appearing on the court record, although it is not open to him to rely on new evidence as a basis for a higher sentence. Just as at trial, the prosecutor must be restrained and balanced at a review hearing, ever mindful of his or her role as a minister of justice.

Private prosecution

If the citizen is aggrieved by the decision of the prosecutor not to bring a prosecution, he may himself institute a private prosecution. In *Gouriet v Union of Post Office Workers* [1978] AC 435, Lord Wilberforce described the right of the citizen to start a prosecution as 'a valuable constitutional safeguard against inertia or partiality on the part of authority'. This device provides a remedy to the individual who wishes to see the law enforced. At common law, every citizen has exactly the same right to institute proceedings as the public prosecutor. The right originated in the Middle Ages, and it continues, subject to certain restrictions, to enjoy a respectable position in modern schemes of criminal justice. In 2000–7, there were 17 private prosecutions in the local courts, involving 30 summonses (Department of Justice 2007).

The right of private prosecution is not absolute. A private prosecutor has two hurdles to surmount. He or she must first persuade a magistrate to issue a summons. Then, if he or she wishes to retain control of the case, and not everyone does, for it can be an expensive process, he or she may have to persuade the Department of Justice not to take it over. The criteria will be different.

The magistrate has a discretion whether to issue a summons. Before so doing, the magistrate should ascertain (i) whether the allegation is of an offence known to law and, if so, whether the essential ingredients of the offence are prima facie present; (ii) whether the time limits have been complied with; (iii) whether the court has jurisdiction; and (iv) whether the informant has the necessary discretion to prosecute (*R v West London Metropolitan Stipendiary Magistrate, ex p Klahn* [1979] 1 WLR 933). The magistrate should also consider if the allegation is vexatious, and before issuing a summons he must be satisfied that this is a proper thing to do (*R v Bros* [1901] 85 LT 581).

Once a private prosecution has started, it is open to the Secretary for Justice to intervene. Such intervention may be with a view to continuing or terminating the private prosecution. In *Dowson v R* [1983] 62 CCC (2) 286, Howland CJO recognized the right of a private citizen to lay an information, and added that the 'right and duty of the Attorney General to supervise criminal prosecutions are both fundamental parts of our criminal justice system'. As indicated, the *Basic Law* vests the ultimate control of prosecutions in the Department of Justice.

The taking over of a prosecution is exceptional. But if the right of private prosecution is abused, intervention may be unavoidable. The procedure is open to the intrusion of improper personal or other motives. It may be used to bring groundless, oppressive, or frivolous prosecutions. The state of the evidence may be such that there will clearly be no case to answer if the case is pursued. There may be a duplication of proceedings. The prosecution may be contrary to the public interest, included in which is a consideration of the likelihood of conviction, and of the appropriateness of proceedings. In any such situation the power and the duty of the Secretary for Justice will be to take over the conduct of the case and to offer no evidence. While this is a sensitive area, section 14 of the *Magistrates Ordinance* (Cap. 227) recognizes that the Secretary 'may at any stage of the proceedings before the magistrate intervene and assume the conduct of the proceedings'.

Judicial review of prosecution decisions

Although great deference must, on constitutional grounds, always be accorded to decisions reached on prosecutions by the Department of Justice, the jurisprudence which has developed in recent times in major common law jurisdictions suggests that in some circumstances the courts are prepared to intervene and to hold the prosecutor to account if there is irregularity in the decision-making process. Although this is an evolving area of the law in Hong Kong, in *R v Director of Public Prosecutions, ex p Kebilene* [2002] 2 AC 326 (HL) Lord Steyn indicated that if a prosecution decision was reached by dishonesty or in bad faith, it would be amenable to judicial review. Quite clearly, if the prosecutor acts corruptly or out of some base motive an aggrieved party ought to have a means of redress.

In *Keung Siu Wah v Attorney-General* [1990] 2 HKLR 445, Fuad VP said it was *'a constitutional imperative'* that the courts would not interfere with the discretion of the Attorney-General to prosecute. This, however, did not mean that there was no remedy if the discretion to prosecute was improperly exercised, as the court 'retained an inherent jurisdiction to prevent an abuse of process'. This, presumably, referred to the power of the court to order the stay of proceedings which were improperly instituted. If, however, the decision not to prosecute was taken for irregular reasons, the remedy would seem to lie in the right of the citizen to institute a private prosecution.

In *Kwan Sun Chu, Pearl v Department of Justice* [2005] 3 HKC 441, the Court of First Instance noted developments elsewhere, but concluded that as the law stood in 2005 it was not open to an applicant to obtain leave to judicially review a decision of the Director of Public

Prosecutions not to prosecute. At the same time, the Court recognized that even if a judicial review were possible in cases where abuse of process was identified, it would be necessary for an applicant to point to dishonesty, bad faith or some other exceptional circumstance. In *RV v Director of Immigration* HCAL 12 of 2008, however, the Court of First Instance reviewed the position under the Basic Law, and concluded that, to a very limited extent, a prosecutorial decision is indeed amenable to judicial review. In any event, judicial review, if granted, would have the effect of requiring a reconsideration of the original decision, and the court could not require the prosecutor to change his or her view.

Guidelines on the role of prosecutors

In 1990, in Havana, Cuba, the Eighth United Nations Congress on the Prevention of Crime and the Treatment of Offenders adopted 'The Guidelines on the Role of Prosecutors' (see Appendix I of *The Statement of Prosecution Policy and Practice*, Department of Justice 2002). These affirm the important responsibilities of the prosecutor in the administration of justice. At paragraph 12, they state:

> Prosecutors shall, in accordance with the law, perform their duties fairly, consistently and expeditiously, and respect and protect human dignity and uphold human rights, thus contributing to ensuring due process and the smooth administration of the criminal justice system.

Human rights of the accused

In any criminal case, the human rights of the accused are engaged, and these include the right to liberty and the right to a fair trial. In the course of a trial, it is the prosecutor who must supply the perspective which may sometimes be lacking. The prosecutor, after all, has no vested interest of his or her own to pursue, and no client to serve. This means that he or she is well placed to ensure that the court is in a position to make decisions that take full account of the rights of the accused and serve the wider public interest. The prosecutor will, for example, need to disclose to the court that a witness is testifying pursuant to an immunity from prosecution, for this may mean that the witness has an interest of his or her own in testifying against the accused. If the prosecutor becomes aware of the existence of a witness who can help the defence case, this also should be revealed.

Conclusion

It is crucial for the prosecutor to be recognized as an integral part of the means by which our society maintains personal liberty. He or she must be viewed as the public prosecutor, not because he or she prosecutes the public, but because he or she prosecutes on behalf of the community. The prosecutor is uniquely placed to protect human rights, and in the course of a trial he or she must conduct himself or herself in a way which takes account of the rights of the accused as well as the rights of the public. Rights, that is, may be either personal or public in nature. Just as it is important that the individual should not be wrongly prosecuted, convicted, or punished, so must members of the public be free to walk the streets, to live in their homes without fear of violation, and to enjoy their rights as citizens to the full.

Review questions

1 How should the prosecutor decide whether or not to prosecute a suspect?
2 How important is it for the prosecutor to obtain a conviction of an accused?
3 How should the prosecutor ensure that victims of crime co-operate in the prosecution of crime?
4 How should the prosecutor respond when he or she considers there is not enough evidence to prosecute, but the law enforcement agency insists that there is?

References

Crown Office and Procurator Fiscal Service (2005) *COPFS Roles and Responsibilities*. Scotland: Crown Office and Procurator Fiscal Service. Available at: http://www.procuratorfiscal.gov.uk/About/roles/remit

Department of Justice (2002) *The Statement of Prosecution Policy and Practice*. Hong Kong: Department of Justice. Available at: http://www.doj.gov.hk/eng/public/pub20021031toc.htm

Department of Justice (2003) *The Victims of Crime Charter*. Hong Kong:

Department of Justice. Available at: http://www.doj.gov.hk/eng/public/pub200004.htm
Department of Justice (2004) *The Statement on the Treatment of Victims and Witnesses*. Hong Kong: Department of Justice. Available at: http://www.doj.gov.hk/eng/public/pub20040407.htm
Department of Justice (2006) *Department of Justice*. Hong Kong: Department of Justice. Available at: http://www.doj.gov.hk/eng/public/pdf/doj2006e.pdf

Legislation cited

The Basic Law of the Hong Kong Special Administrative Region
International Covenant on Civil and Political Rights
Magistrates Ordinance (Cap. 227)
Organized and Serious Crimes Ordinance (Cap. 455)

Cases cited

Dowson v R [1983] 62 CCC (2) 286
Gouriet v Union of Post Office Workers [1978] AC 435
Keung Siu Wah v Attorney-General [1990] 2 HKLR 445
Kwan Sun Chu, Pearl v Department of Justice [2005] 3 HKC 441
R v Director of Public Prosecutions, ex p Kebilene [2002] 2 AC 326(HL)
R v West London Metropolitan Stipendiary Magistrate, ex p Klahn [1979] 1 WLR 933
R v Bros [1901] 85 LT 581
RV v Director of Immigration HCAL 12 of 2008

Useful websites

Crown Office and Procurator Fiscal Service (UK)	http://www.procuratorfiscal.gov.uk/ and http://en.wikipedia.org/wiki/Crown_Office_and_Procurator_Fiscal_Service
Customs and Excise Department	http://www.customs.gov.hk/
Department of Justice	http://www.doj.gov.hk/
Hong Kong Police Force	http://www.police.gov.hk
Independent Commission Against Corruption	http://www.icac.org.hk/
The Basic Law of the Hong Kong Special Administrative Region	http://www.info.gov.hk/basic_law/flash.html

The Code for Crown Prosecutors (UK)	http://www.cps.gov.uk
The Statement of Prosecution Policy and Practice	http://www.doj.gov.hk/eng/public/pub20021031toc.htm

Chapter 7

Criminal trial courts

Tony Upham

Introduction

Despite the return of sovereignty over Hong Kong to the People's Republic of China on 1 July 1997, Hong Kong remains a common law jurisdiction, as set out in Article 8 of *The Basic Law of the Hong Kong Special Administrative Region* (the *Basic Law*). The reversion of sovereignty inevitably brought about changes in nomenclature and the establishment of the Hong Kong Court of Final Appeal (CFA) gave Hong Kong a self-contained legal system, but overall there has been little change in the way Hong Kong's criminal courts operate. There is understandably more use of Cantonese in the criminal courts these days and the Judiciary is more localized than before 1997, but the principle of 'one country, two systems' set out in the *Basic Law* leaves the previous system very much intact.

The courts in the Special Administrative Region of Hong Kong (HKSAR) with a criminal jurisdiction are the Magistrates' Court (MC), the District Court (DC), the Court of First Instance of the High Court (CFI), the Court of Appeal of the High Court (CA), and the CFA. The MC, the DC, and the CFI are first instance trial courts, though the CFI also hears appeals from magistrates. Both the CA and the CFA have exclusively appellate jurisdiction (see Chapter 9 of this volume). Those courts can only be reached after going through a trial court.

Each of Hong Kong's criminal courts has its structural Ordinance from which it takes its powers. Procedure in the criminal courts is governed by the *Criminal Procedure Ordinance* (Cap. 221) (CPO). Section 9(3) of that Ordinance provides that subject to the provisions of the Ordinance and to any other local enactment, the practice and procedure in criminal causes and matters in Hong Kong shall be the same as the practice and procedure from time to time and for the time being in force for similar cases in England.

Criminal offences in Hong Kong fall into three broad categories. The first category contains the most serious offences which are triable only upon indictment. They can only be tried before a judge and a jury in the CFI. The second category is offences that may be tried either upon indictment or summarily. These are sometimes referred to as offences triable either way, which means they can be tried in the CFI or in the DC or by a magistrate. They may be described as offences in the middle range of seriousness. The third category is offences triable only summarily. These are the least serious criminal offences and can only be tried by a magistrate.

Whether or not an offence is triable upon indictment depends upon the wording of the Ordinance creating the offence. The use of such wording as 'indictable' or 'upon conviction on indictment' means that the offence is indictable. Some indictable offences can, with the consent of the prosecution, be tried summarily. According to section 10 of the *Offences Against Property Ordinance* (Cap. 210), robbery, for example, is an indictable offence but it can be tried either in the CFI, in the DC, or by a magistrate. The Secretary for Justice, who is in charge of criminal prosecutions in Hong Kong, decides which court will deal with an indictable offence triable summarily depending upon the likely sentence upon conviction after trial. Where the provision creating the offence uses the wording 'triable summarily' or 'on summary conviction', the offence is triable only before a magistrate.

The Magistrates' Court

This court has exclusively criminal jurisdiction. All criminal cases start in the MC and most end there. Those that do not are either transferred to the DC or committed, either for trial or for sentence, to the CFI. Section 94A of the *Magistrates Ordinance* (Cap. 227) (MO) states that where an offence can be tried on indictment or summarily the prosecution must consent to it being dealt with by a magistrate. That consent is given by the prosecution proceeding with an offence which can be tried either upon indictment or summarily before a magistrate rather than asking for it to be transferred to the DC or committed to the CFI.

Magistrates are either Permanent Magistrates (PM) or Special Magistrates (SM). They are appointed by the Chief Executive of the HKSAR and take their powers from the MO. If that Ordinance does not give a magistrate the power to do what he or she has done, the act is *ultra vires* and cannot stand. There are seven Magistracies (or Magistrates' Courts) in Hong Kong. Each one of them is headed by a Principal Magistrate who sits in Court No. 1. Each Magistracy contains a number of courts. Cases will normally be brought to the Magistracy which is nearest to the police station dealing with the offence.

Permanent Magistrates are professionally qualified. They must be qualified to practise as a barrister, solicitor, or advocate in a court in Hong Kong or any other common law jurisdiction having unlimited jurisdiction either in civil or criminal matters and have had five years' practice as a barrister, solicitor, or advocate or have held other specified appointments: section 5AA of the MO. SMs may be professionally qualified or have substantial experience in the legal field. They may have been court clerks, court interpreters, or lay prosecutors: section 5AB of the MO. Both PMs and SMs are judicial officers. The difference is in the cases they deal with and their powers of punishment.

The normal maximum sentence a PM can impose is two years' imprisonment and a fine of $100,000: section 57 of the MO. Where, however, two or more indictable offences are dealt with by the same magistrate at the same time, imprisonment of up to three years may be imposed (see section 92A of the MO; for a practical example of this see *R v Pau Chi Keung* [1987] HKLR 1148). This general power in the MO gives way to specific provisions in a particular Ordinance which may provide for a lower maximum sentence than two years or enable a PM to impose more than three years' imprisonment. Section 4 of the *Dangerous Drugs Ordinance* (Cap. 134), for example, enables a magistrate to impose three years' imprisonment and a fine of $500,000 for trafficking in dangerous drugs. SMs have a general power to impose imprisonment not exceeding six months and fines not exceeding $50,000: section 91 of the MO. They deal with such offences as hawking (which means illegal selling of goods in public), traffic offences, construction site safety, and littering.

There is no jury in the MC. The magistrate is both judge and jury. Issues of law, such as the admissibility of evidence, must be dealt with as they arise. At the end of the evidence the magistrate considers the factual question of guilt or innocence. Magistrates must, however, keep the two roles separate and give themselves the same directions, for example about the burden and standard of proof and evaluation of evidence, as would have been given to a jury had there been one.

Barristers and solicitors have the right of audience before magistrates. Defendants can appear in person when the magistrate must ensure their rights are protected. Defendants who cannot afford to pay a lawyer may be represented at the public expense through the Duty Lawyer Service (DLS). Representation through the DLS is only available once the case is before the court. The DLS does not provide representation after arrest and before charge. Representation at the first court appearance is available without any means test. Representation at subsequent appearances is means tested and subject to a fixed handling charge of HK$400.

Procedure in the Magistrates' Court

Defendants appear first of all in Court No. 1 of the Magistracy for the area where the alleged offence was committed. This court is known variously as the Plea Court, the Principal Magistrate's Court or Court No. 1. Defendants are brought to the court in police custody if they have been charged but refused police bail. If they have been granted police bail they will attend court No. 1 to answer their bail. Similarly, if the case is being dealt with on summons the first appearance will be in court No. 1.

Assuming the case will be dealt with by a magistrate and all parties are ready to proceed, the magistrate in Court No. 1 will take a plea. If the prosecution wants a triable either way case dealt with by a magistrate, the magistrate must deal with the case (see, for example, *R v Pau Chi Kung* [1987] HKLR 1148). The charge, or the summons, is read to the defendant, the defendant is asked if it is understood and, if it is, whether the plea is guilty or not guilty. If the defendant pleads guilty the prosecutor hands a brief statement of the facts to the magistrate. The magistrate must be satisfied that the brief facts establish the offence charged. If it does, the facts are read aloud to the defendant who is asked whether they are understood and, if so, whether they are accepted or disputed. If they are accepted, the magistrate convicts. If they are disputed, a not guilty plea is entered or the case is stood down for discussion between the defendant and their lawyer.

Once the facts are admitted and the magistrate has convicted, the prosecution hands up a list of any previous convictions. Relevant convictions are put to the defendant. The magistrate then hears mitigation and either sentences or adjourns for reports. The defendant may be bailed pending the obtaining of reports and completion of sentence. If, however, the magistrate is considering a Drug Addiction Treatment Centre Order, a Detention Centre Order, a Rehabilitation Centre Order, or a Training Centre Order the remand will be in custody while the defendant's suitability for those orders is assessed.

If the defendant pleads not guilty in Court No. 1, the case will be listed for trial in one of the trial courts in that Magistracy. The trial date will be sufficiently far ahead for both the prosecution and the defence to be ready for trial.

The not guilty plea before a magistrate

On the trial date the practice is to read the charge or complaint again. This need not strictly be done as the defendant has pleaded not guilty in Court No. 1. If nothing else, this is a convenient opportunity for a change of plea. If it is still a not guilty plea the trial proceeds.

It is sensible at this stage for the magistrate to announce that all prosecution witnesses and any possible defence witnesses (other than the defendant) who are in court should leave the court. Though a witness who has been in court throughout the proceedings can still be heard, that must be taken into account when assessing their overall credibility.

The prosecution then presents its case. There may be a short opening speech but this is not usual in the Magistracy. The cases are usually relatively straightforward. Not infrequently the prosecution will adopt the Brief Facts as its opening statement. The prosecution then calls its witnesses into court one by one.

Each prosecution witness is examined in chief by the prosecutor. The objective is to draw out from the witness by a series of structured questions what was seen, heard, or done in their own words. What is known as leading questions, that is questions which contain the answer within the question or which assume the existence of facts not yet proved, should be avoided. The witness is then cross-examined by the defence. Cross-examination is the opportunity to confront the witness, to undermine credibility, to weaken their evidence, and to put the defence case to the witnesses. Leading questions are used in cross-examination, as indeed they must be if the defence case is to be put to the witness. Closed questions will be used to avoid the prosecution witness giving more evidence by way of explanations.

The witness can then be re-examined by the prosecutor. Re-examination is the opportunity to deal with ambiguities and inconsistencies and points arising for the first time from cross-examination. Re-examination is not an opportunity for the witness to repeat what was said in examination in chief.

The procedure is repeated until the prosecution has called all its evidence, after which the prosecution closes its case. The magistrate then rules whether there is a case for the defendant to answer: that is, whether the prosecution has produced sufficiently cogent evidence so that there could be a conviction if no more evidence was heard. The defence will take the initiative in raising the issue. A ruling that there is a case to answer means that the prosecution has discharged the evidential burden in that it has put sufficient evidence before the court so that there could be a conviction if no more evidence is heard.

If there is a case to answer, the defendant can either give evidence in his or her own defence or not give evidence, give evidence and call witnesses, give evidence but not call witnesses, or remain silent and call witnesses. The magistrate must explain these rights to an unrepresented defendant and some magistrates will do this with a represented defendant. An unrepresented defendant should also be told that whatever is done about evidence and/or witness there is the right to address the court at the end of the case but that evidence cannot be given by means of such an address.

A defendant who elects to give evidence goes into the witness box, is sworn or affirmed, and then examined in chief by defence counsel, cross-examined by the prosecution and, if necessary, re-examined by defence counsel. Any defence witnesses are then similarly examined in chief, cross-examined, and re-examined. After the defence has called all its witnesses there will be a closing address. In that address defence counsel will highlight perceived weaknesses in the prosecution case and perceived strengths in the defence case. The magistrate then considers the verdict. If the verdict is not guilty the defendant is free to leave. If the verdict is guilty the magistrate proceeds to sentence or adjourns for reports. The defendant may be remanded in custody or bailed pending sentence.

Challenging the magistrate's decision

The cheapest and quickest way of challenging a magistrate's decision is by a review under section 104 of the MO. A review is a reference back to the original magistrate asking that magistrate to think again. This is a simple way of correcting errors, for example an excess of jurisdiction, overlooking a relevant Ordinance or a relevant case, or making a wrong decision. There is no similar review procedure in the DC or the CFI.

Either the prosecution or the defence can seek a review. The prosecution can seek a review of a not guilty verdict and of sentence. The defence can seek a review of a guilty verdict and/or sentence. A section 104 review is not an appeal: only the original magistrate can be asked for a review. A review can only be sought once there has been a final determination by the magistrate of any matter which the magistrate has power to determine in a summary way. The verdict and/or the sentence can be the subject of a section 104 review as there has then been a determination in the sense of a final decision on the issues. Decisions to grant or refuse bail or to grant or refuse an adjournment are not final decisions and are not reviewable under section 104. Decisions about bail and about adjournments are stages in the proceedings: they do not determine guilt or innocence.

The application for a review must be made within 14 clear days after the determination of any matter which the magistrate has power to determine in a summary way. It is made in writing to the magistrate's clerk. An application for review cannot be made where the original decision is already the subject of challenge by way of appeal.

The application for a review cannot be rejected without the applicant or his counsel (or solicitor) being given an opportunity to make representations to the magistrate in open court. Provided the application for a review is made within the time allowed, the actual review can be heard outside that time.

While applications for a review are normally made by the prosecution or the defence, magistrates can also review their decisions. The magistrate's decision to review must be made within 14 clear days from the determination. A magistrate may discover, for example, that a relevant authority was overlooked when reaching the earlier decision or may become concerned that an incorrect decision was made.

If the magistrate decides to review, the case can be reopened. Fresh evidence and further argument could be heard on the review and the earlier decision can either be confirmed or set aside either completely or in part and a new decision made. Where appropriate, the magistrate could set everything aside and send the case to be reheard before another magistrate.

The application for a review interrupts the running of time for an appeal. This means that a magistrate's decision could be challenged by a review under section 104 and, if the magistrate confirms the original decision, there could still be an appeal either against conviction and/or sentence. Particularly where there has been a conviction followed by a short prison sentence it is appropriate to seek a review as that can be done more quickly than by appealing. Appeals from magistrates are not prejudiced by an application for a section 104 review.

Appealing the decision of a magistrate

A magistrate's decision can be challenged on appeal either by a case stated under section 105 of the MO or by the alternative procedure under section 113 of the same Ordinance. The appeal goes to a single judge of the CFI. The single judge may, however, reserve (which means refer) an appeal under section 113 or any part of it to the CA: section 118(1)(d) of the MO. This power could be used where an important issue of law arises (see *R v Pau Chi Kung* [1987] HKLR 1148).

Until 1 July 1997, appeals from a magistrate ended with the single judge. Even if the decision on the appeal was considered wrong, it was not possible to take it further. Since 1 July 1997, however, it is possible to appeal to the CFA against a decision made by a single judge on appeal from a magistrate.

Section 105 of the Magistrates Ordinance*: the case stated*

This procedure is complicated and can take time. It is designed for appeals on points of law, for example the interpretation of an ordinance (see, for example, *AG v John Lok & Partners & George Wimpey International Ltd.* HCMA000062/1985). The case stated enables a judge of the CFI to consider whether the magistrate's decision is correct or incorrect in law. It is not the appropriate procedure where the challenge to the magistrate's decision involves issues of fact or mixed fact and law. Nor is it the appropriate procedure to challenge a sentence imposed by a magistrate. As it is designed to deal with issues of law, the case stated is available to both the prosecution and the defence. The prosecution can therefore appeal a magistrate's decision to acquit provided the appeal is upon a point of law.

An appeal by case stated must be commenced within 14 days of the magistrate's decision. Only the final decision can be appealed. The appeal is commenced by the party aggrieved by the decision writing to the magistrate and asking the magistrate 'to state and sign a case setting forth the facts and the grounds on which the conviction, order or determination was granted and the grounds on which the proceeding is questioned, for the opinion of a judge': section 105 of the MO.

The magistrate then prepares a statement of findings setting out what facts were found and the reasons for the decision. Though the magistrate states the case, the questions to be answered by the judge are the questions the party aggrieved wants answered. That party therefore formulates the questions which the magistrate incorporates into the case stated. It might be, for example, a magistrate stopped the defence case before all the defence witnesses had been called and convicted the defendant. The defence would contend this was an error of law and the magistrate had no power to stop the defence case in this way. The magistrate would set out in the case stated why that action was taken. The question the defence would want the judge to answer might then be formulated as 'whether I was right in law to stop the defence case and convict the defendant while the defence still had witnesses to call?'

Once the paperwork is complete, the case is listed for argument before the judge. The judge hears argument on the question or questions asked and then rules whether the decision was correct in law. If the judge decides it was wrong, the decision will be set aside and the case will be sent back to the magistrate to continue with it. The magistrate would then have to hear the remaining defence witnesses and then decide upon guilt or innocence.

Section 113 of the Magistrates Ordinance*: the alternative procedure*

Section 113 allows for a challenge both to the factual and the legal merits of the magistrate's decision. This section applies where the judge is being asked to substitute a different view to that of the magistrate and is especially appropriate where the appeal is against sentence. Most appeals are by the alternative procedure.

As the section refers to a person aggrieved by a conviction, only the defence can appeal by this route. The appeal can be against conviction and/or sentence. A notice of appeal must be lodged with the clerk to the magistrate within 14 days of the magistrate's decision. It is not unusual for a magistrate to obtain reports before sentencing. There is no final determination until sentencing is complete. The time for appealing conviction and/or sentence therefore runs from the date of sentence. There cannot be an appeal against conviction before sentence. According to section 114A(1) of the MO, the time limit for appealing may be extended for good reason either by the magistrate or by a judge of the High Court. What is, or is not, good reason will depend upon each case.

Either the magistrate whose decision is the subject of a notice of appeal or a judge may grant bail pending the appeal. This is not however automatic, even where the sentence is short. Bail pending appeal cannot be granted until the notice of appeal has been lodged with the magistrate's clerk.

Referring to section 114(b) of the MO, once a notice of appeal has been given the magistrate must prepare a written statement of findings (with reasons for verdict) within 15 days after the day upon which the notice of appeal was given. A copy of that statement of findings is served upon the parties to the appeal. Once the magistrate has prepared the statement of findings, the clerk of the magistrate's court where the case was dealt with prepares a basic appeal bundle as required by Practice Direction 9.6 titled *Magistracy Appeals in the Court of First Instance* (Chief Justice 2000). The basic appeal bundle includes the notice of appeal, any agreed facts, and a transcript of the proceedings before the magistrate, but limited to the plea, oral closing submissions, verdict, and reasons for verdict or order.

Once the basic appeal bundle has been prepared, it is sent to the Registrar of the High Court together with the notice of appeal. The appeal is then included in the list of appeals and the parties will be notified of the hearing date. The procedure on the hearing is that the appellant goes first and the respondent replies. Additional evidence may be heard during the appeal, though this is not usual. The appeal is a review of the evidence before the magistrate and an examination of the magistrate's reasons for convicting and/or for imposing the sentence that was imposed.

On the appeal the judge can confirm, reverse, or vary the magistrate's decision, direct that the case shall be heard again by another magistrate, remit the matter with his opinion thereon to the magistrate, or make such other order as thought just. The judge can exercise any power which the magistrate might have exercised. An appeal against sentence reopens the whole question of sentence and the judge can impose any sentence the magistrate could have imposed. On an appeal against sentence, the sentence imposed by the magistrate may be increased: section 119(e) of the MO.

Review of sentence by the prosecution

Though the prosecution cannot appeal sentence, sections 81A, 81B, and 81C of the CPO enable the prosecution to seek a review of sentence by the CA. As this procedure applies to sentences imposed by magistrates, DC judges, and CFI judges, and involves an application to the CA, it will be addressed in the CA section in Chapter 9.

Transferring to the District Court

Where the prosecution wants an indictable offence which can be tried either way dealt with in the DC, the prosecutor asks the magistrate not to take a plea. When the prosecution is ready to proceed, the prosecutor asks the magistrate, in open court and in the presence of the defendant, to transfer the case to the DC and hands up a written transfer request (see section 88 of the MO). Though put as a request, the magistrate must order transfer as choice of venue for an offence triable either way is with the prosecution. The defendant cannot oppose the transfer. Once the request is made, the magistrate announces that the charge or charges are transferred to the DC and that all further proceedings will take place in that court. The defendant will either be bailed to appear at the DC for plea on a specified date or remanded in custody. The remand in custody cannot exceed 20 clear days: section 90(2) of the MO. When ordering transfer the magistrate must advise the defendant of the right to apply for legal aid and give the defendant an alibi warning: section 90(1)(d) of the MO.

Committing to the Court of First Instance

A DC judge has the power to imprison for a maximum period of seven years. Cases triable only upon indictment or those either way cases where the likely sentence upon conviction after trial will exceed seven years are dealt with in the CFI. In those situations the magistrate conducts committal proceedings. At one time, the prosecution witnesses attended court at the committal stage and gave their evidence orally and the magistrate then considered whether the prosecution case was sufficiently strong for the defendant to be put on trial before a judge and a jury. Nowadays most committals are on paper and the prosecution evidence is not tested before the magistrate (the paper or short committal). There can still be an old-style committal (now called a Preliminary Inquiry (PI)), but most defendants waive the right to a PI and are committed to the CFI without the magistrate considering the prosecution evidence.

Where a case will be dealt with in the CFI there will be a number of appearances before the magistrate without any plea being taken from the defendant while the prosecution prepares its case. When the prosecution is ready to proceed, the prosecutor asks the magistrate to appoint a Return Day for the continuation of committal proceedings:

section 80A(1) of the MO. This application is made in open court in the presence of the defendant. The magistrate must then appoint a Return Day for the continuation of committal proceedings not less than 10 days nor more than 42 days ahead: section 80A(3) of the MO. Asking for the appointment of a Return Day is the 'official' start of committal proceedings. Legal aid is then available to the defendant: section 80A(4)(a) of the MO.

As the CFI takes its jurisdiction from the committal proceedings, it is important the committal proceedings are properly conducted and recorded. Upon appointing the Return Day the magistrate must tell the defendant of the right to apply for legal aid; that not less than seven days before the return date they will receive copies of the complaint/information, witness statements, documentary exhibits; that on the Return Day they will have the right to require a PI and call witnesses on their own behalf; if there is more than one charge and a PI is required on any one of those, there will be a PI on all charges and only at the end of the PI will it be possible to plead guilty; and that if PI is not required, they will be committed for trial unless there is a guilty plea, in which case there will be a committal for sentence.

The prosecution discloses the whole of its case at trial at this stage. The statement of each prosecution witness must be signed by the witness and contain a declaration that it is true to best of knowledge and belief and that he/she is aware that making a false statement is an offence under section 33 of the *Crimes Ordinance* (Cap. 200). If the statement is made by a person under 21 years of age, the age must be given. Each statement must contain a caption that the statement either has been read to the witness in their own language or has been read by the witness: section 80B(2) of the MO. These requirements are important as the written statement is the evidence upon which the prosecution is asking for a committal to the CFI and the statement takes the place of oral evidence at this stage.

On the Return Day, provided all the requirements of section 80B(1) have been complied with, the prosecutor hands the magistrate the originals of the documents served upon the defendant. The magistrate tells the defendant (now referred to as the accused) that the prosecution is seeking a committal to the CFI and there will be that committal unless there is an election for a PI. The accused is again reminded of the opportunity for a PI and told that the committal will only proceed on the Return Day if a PI is not required.

If the accused elects to have a PI the proceedings are adjourned to a later date for the PI. The accused is informed that unless notice is given to the magistrate and the prosecution not less than seven days before the date of the PI which of the prosecution witnesses will be needed at the PI, that witness will not be available at the PI. The onus is upon the accused to tell the magistrate and the prosecution what witnesses are required to attend the PI. The magistrate can either bail the accused or remand in custody to the date of the PI.

If the accused does not elect a PI, the magistrate must tell the accused that there is no obligation to say anything in respect of the charge(s) but that the accused may plead guilty, in which case there will be a committal to the CFI for sentence, and if there is no guilty plea there will be a committal for trial. The accused must also be told that after the committal there is the right to apply to a judge for a discharge on the grounds there is no prima facie case to answer. Having done that, the magistrate then finds out whether the accused wants to plead guilty and if there is no guilty plea commits the accused for trial in the CFI.

Pleading guilty at the committal proceedings

Where the case will be dealt with in the CFI, the Return Day is the first opportunity for a guilty plea. A guilty plea generally attracts a discount of one-third from the sentence that would have been imposed upon conviction after trial. The magistrate is required to find out whether the accused wants to plead guilty at the committal stage, whether the committal is with a PI or without a PI.

If there is a guilty plea the prosecutor must outline to the accused the facts upon which the charge is based: section 81B of the MO. The magistrate must then explain the offence and its legal ingredients to the accused and record any statement made by the accused in pleading guilty and also that the offence and its ingredients was explained. Provided the magistrate is satisfied the plea is voluntary, the accused is committed for sentence to the CFI either on bail or, more likely, in custody. A guilty plea at committal stage can only be withdrawn with the consent of a judge of the CFI: section 81B(3) of the MO.

The Preliminary Inquiry

If on the Return Day the accused asks for a PI, there will be an adjournment to a later date. The committal will continue on that date as a PI at which evidence is called and witnesses can be cross-examined. The PI is not a trial but part of the process by which the magistrate examines the prosecution case to see if it is apparently strong enough for there to be a trial (see *HKSAR v Tsoi Kei-lung & Anor* HCMA 000340/200). As the PI is not a trial, considerations about openness of the trial process do not apply. It may indeed be prejudicial to the eventual trial to give publicity at this stage. Accordingly, some special considerations apply.

The room where the PI takes place is not an open court: section 80 of the MO. There are substantial restrictions on reports in news media: section 87A of the MO. News media reports can only contain such matters as the identity of the court and the magistrate's name, names, addresses, occupations, and age of the parties and witnesses, the offence charged, names of counsel and solicitors, decision of the magistrate, charge (or details of charge) on which the accused was committed, and whether legal aid has been granted. These reporting restrictions apply to the whole of the committal proceedings. The restrictions must, however, be lifted by the magistrate if the accused wants them lifted. If one of several accused wants the reporting restrictions lifted, the others cannot oppose that and the restriction must be lifted: section 87A(2) of the MO. An accused might want the restrictions lifted to try to find witnesses. It is not usual for the restrictions to be lifted as publicity is not generally in the best interests of the accused.

Procedure at the Preliminary Inquiry

If the accused is unrepresented, the magistrate must explain the procedure, the provisions about reporting restrictions, and generally ensure the accused understands the procedure. The prosecutor then opens as if it was a trial. The prosecution witnesses give evidence, are cross-examined and re-examined, in the usual way. Evidence is given on oath or under affirmation, recorded, read back to, agreed with, and signed by the witness and by the magistrate. This record then becomes the deposition of the witness. The witness may be shown their witness statement which has been served upon the accused and asked to adopt that statement as evidence in chief and then be cross-examined by the defence.

There may be a submission of no case at the end of the prosecution case. This is a claim that the prosecution case is too weak for the accused to be put on trial before a judge and a jury. The test is whether on the prosecution evidence, and provided that evidence is believed at trial, the accused could be convicted. Submissions of no case will rarely be made. The PI is not a trial and the accused is not at risk of being convicted. If the submission succeeds, the accused is simply released from bail or released from custody. If there is no submission or it is rejected, the magistrate must then read the charge to the accused, explain it in ordinary language, inform the accused of the right to give evidence and call witnesses, find out whether the accused wishes to plead guilty, and, if not, administer a caution. Before the accused replies, the magistrate must state that there is nothing to hope from any promise of favour and nothing to fear from any threats which may have been held out to induce the accused to make any admission or confession of guilt, but whatever is now said may be given in evidence at the trial notwithstanding such promises or threats. Whatever reply is made to the caution must be recorded. The accused must be invited to sign that reply. Even if the accused does not reply, the magistrate must record that and invite the accused to sign the recording.

Absent any submission of no case or after a ruling there is a case to answer, the magistrate then asks whether the accused wishes to give evidence or call witnesses. If the accused gives evidence and/or calls witnesses, the procedure is the same as at a trial, again with the evidence being recorded and signed by the witness. It is not usual for an accused to give evidence at a PI. There is obvious potential danger in so doing.

The magistrate then decides whether or not to commit for trial. If the magistrate decides not to commit, the accused is discharged (released and allowed to leave). A decision not to commit is not an acquittal. It does not prevent a further arrest and the start of new committal proceedings on exactly the same charge.

Procedure after committal (Section 85A of the Magistrates Ordinance*)*

Once the magistrate has decided to commit the accused to the CFI the committal can be on bail or in custody: if the committal is in custody the magistrate must advise the accused of the right to apply to a judge for bail. Whether the accused is bailed or remanded in custody the magistrate must inform the accused of the right to apply for legal aid: section 85A(1)(c) of the MO (the accused is given a form about that), give the alibi warning (and if necessary explain what an alibi is and what must be done if there is to be an alibi defence): section 85A(1)(d) of the MO. If the committal is without a PI (that is, the committal is on the Return Day), the magistrate must advise the accused of the right to apply to a judge for a discharge on the grounds that the prosecution papers do not show a prima facie case for trial: section 85A(1)(e) of the MO.

The committal is to the CFI for trial. As case listing in that court is not under the control of the magistrate, the accused is simply committed to the CFI, either on bail or in custody, for trial on a date to be notified.

Application for discharge

Under section 80C(4) of the MO and section 16 of the CPO, an accused committed for trial without a PI can apply once to a judge of the CFI for a discharge on the grounds the evidence disclosed by the documents before the magistrate on the committal is insufficient to establish a prima facie case on the offence charged. This procedure is not an appeal against the committal but an attempt to put an end to the proceedings after the committal and before trial. A discharge under this procedure is an acquittal. The prosecution could not then begin again. The prosecution can, however, appeal an order for discharge to the CA (see, for example, *Attorney-General v Phung van Toan & Others* CACC000082/1991 and *HKSAR v Yan Panyue* HCC137/2004 (successful application to a judge of the CFI for a discharge after a committal) and *HKSAR v Yan Panyue* CACC 128/2005 (successful appeal by the prosecution to the CA against the CFI judge's discharge order).

Juvenile Court

The Juvenile Court takes its jurisdiction from the *Juvenile Offenders Ordinance* (Cap. 226) (JOO). A Juvenile Court is presided over by a permanent magistrate appointed by the Chief Justice. The magistrate sitting in the Juvenile Court has all the powers of a permanent magistrate under the MO and additional powers under the JOO. There is complete separation between the Juvenile Court and the adult court. Like the permanent magistrate, the Juvenile Court magistrate sits alone and is responsible for findings of both fact and law.

Juvenile courts hear and determine criminal charges against a child or young person for any offence other than homicide: section 3C of the JOO. The age of criminal responsibility in Hong Kong is 10 years of age. A child is a person who is under the age of 14 years, while a young person is a person of 14 years of age and upwards and under the age of 16 years. The Juvenile Court therefore has criminal jurisdiction, except in homicide, over persons aged from 10 to 16 years of age. It has concurrent jurisdiction with the CFI of the High Court for indictable offences.

As the Juvenile Court has no jurisdiction over persons who have attained 16 years of age where a person aged between 10 years and 16 years is charged jointly with a person who has attained 16 years of age, that charge cannot be heard in the Juvenile Court. Where a child or young person is charged with aiding and abetting, causing, procuring, allowing, or permitting an offence with which a person who has attained 16 years of age is charged, that charge need not be tried in the Juvenile Court. Similarly, where a child or young person is charged with an offence arising out of circumstances which are the same or connected with those giving rise to an offence with which a person who is 16 is charged, that offence need not be heard in a Juvenile Court: section 3C of the JOO. The ratio is that it is in the public interest for offences which are in common sense so connected that they form part of the overall picture of criminality to be dealt with together.

The principle of separating juvenile offenders from adult offenders is reflected in the way juveniles come before the court. Ideally there will be a separate court used only for juveniles. However, that may not be practical and an adult court may be used as a juvenile court. In that event there must be at least a one-hour gap between the use of the court for adults and for juveniles. There must similarly be a one-hour gap after its use as a juvenile court before being used as an adult court: section 3D(2) of the JOO.

The Juvenile Court sits in private in the sense that access to the court is restricted. Only officers of the court, the parties to the case and witnesses, bona fide representatives of newspapers, and persons specifically authorized by the court may be present in the court: section 3D(3) of the JOO. These restrictions on access are part of the policy of reform and rehabilitation. They do not contravene the general principle of the openness of the criminal courts. The restrictions are proportionate and justified.

As well as restrictions on access to the Juvenile Court, there are restrictions upon what can be reported in the news media: section 20A of the JOO. The news media cannot report or broadcast anything that might reveal the identity of a child or young person. This is not restricted to name and address but extends to anything calculated to lead to identification. A particular characteristic might lead to identification. If so, there must be no reference to that in the reports. The court can lift this restriction if it considers it right and appropriate to do so. This will depend upon the particular circumstances. Where a young person has been responsible for a series of particularly anti-social and dangerous offences, a court might lift the reporting restrictions to reassure the public. These restrictions on reporting also apply to appeals from the Juvenile Court: section 20A(1)(a) of the JOO. Appeals lie from the Juvenile Court in the same way that appeals lie from the adult court.

Procedure in the Juvenile Court

In terms of calling witnesses, burden of proof, and submissions, the procedure is the same as in the adult court. Where the juvenile is unrepresented, the magistrate must assist the juvenile. In such situations questions may be put either by the juvenile or by its parents and the magistrate will be much more interventionist. Overall the procedure is more relaxed than in the adult court: juveniles are often referred to by their family name, and everyone sits down during the proceedings except when pleas are taken or verdicts given. The terminology is different from that used in the adult court. Reference is made to findings of guilt rather than conviction and defendants are asked whether they admit or deny the charge rather than whether they plead guilty or not guilty. This is all part of the rehabilitative approach of the court.

Police bail for juveniles

The approach to bail for juveniles is again consistent with rehabilitation. Section 4 of the JOO requires a juvenile to be bailed by the police where the juvenile cannot immediately be brought before the Juvenile Court. An exception applies where the charge is homicide or other grave offence, where the juvenile needs to be detained for their own interest (personal protection, personal welfare) or where bail would defeat the ends of justice. There is therefore a very strong presumption in favour of bail. Persons not released on bail will be detained in a place of detention until they can be brought before the court (see section 5 of JOO; also consult *Places of Detention (Juvenile Offenders) Appointment (Consolidation) Order* (Cap. 226A)).

Court bail for juveniles

The presumption in favour of bail in the CPO applies across the board. Where a juvenile is not bailed the remand is to a place of detention (a Boys' Home or a Girls' Home) for a person under 14 and to a place of detention or a Training Centre for a person aged 14 to

16. Where the juvenile is too unruly or too depraved to be detained in those places, the detention is in Correctional Services premises.

Where juveniles are remanded in custody, great care must be taken to keep them separate from adult prisoners. This includes taking them from court and bringing them back to court and waiting before or after a court attendance. They must not be allowed to associate with any adult other than a relative or an adult with whom they are jointly charged. Female defendants must be under the care of a female during transportation and waiting (see section 6 of the *Places of Detention (Juvenile Offenders) Appointment (Consolidation) Order*).

Parents or guardians

Parents or guardians of juveniles must attend the Juvenile Court at each stage of the proceedings (see section 9 of the *Places of Detention (Juvenile Offenders) Appointment (Consolidation) Order*). Parents or guardians who do not attend when required can be compelled to attend in the same way that a reluctant witness can be compelled to attend by the issue of a witness summons: section 21 of the MO).

As well as requiring the attendance of parents and guardians at all stages of the proceedings, the Juvenile Court can order parents or guardians to pay any fine, damages, or costs awarded against the juvenile. This cannot be done, however, if the court finds that the parent or guardian has not conduced to the commission on the offence by neglecting to exercise due care of the child or young persons: section 10 of the JOO.

Remitting to the Juvenile Court

Where a juvenile is tried and convicted before an adult court, that court must send the juvenile to the Juvenile Court for sentence unless satisfied it would be undesirable to do so: section 3F of the JOO. The intention is that juveniles convicted in adult courts will be sent to the Juvenile Court for sentence as that will generally be in their best interests (see, for example, *Cheng Shu-wai Magistracy Appeal* No. 982 of 1985; *Ip Wai-Hung v The Queen* CACC000151/1982). The adult court can however sentence a juvenile (see, for example, *HKSAR v Yeung Sze Lun Magistracy Appeal* No. 717 of 1997). There is no prohibition upon depriving young offenders of their liberty, but detention centres or training centres will be more appropriate than imprisonment because of the emphasis placed on reform and rehabilitation (see, for example, *HKSAR v Lee Kwong Lap* [2002] HKCFI 1371, HCMA 001117/2002).

The District Court

The DC takes its powers from the *District Court Ordinance* (Cap. 336) (DCO). It has both criminal and civil jurisdiction but only the criminal jurisdiction is addressed in this section. Like the MC, the DC is a first instance criminal court. There is no jury and, like magistrates, DC judges decide issues of fact and of law. Again like magistrates, the powers of punishment are limited. A DC judge can impose a maximum of seven years' imprisonment in respect of one offence. Where two or more offences are dealt with at the same time and consecutive terms of imprisonment are imposed, the aggregate of those terms must not exceed seven years: section 82(2) of the DCO. Where the particular ordinance provides for a lesser sentence than seven years' imprisonment, that takes precedence over the sentencing powers in the DCO. There is the power to fine as an alternative to imprisonment even where the particular Ordinance does not provide for a fine as a penalty: section 82(3)(a) of the DCO.

District Court judges are professionally qualified. They are appointed from persons qualified to practise as a barrister, solicitor, or advocate in a court in Hong Kong or any other common law jurisdiction having unlimited jurisdiction either in civil or criminal matters. As well as the professional qualification there must be not less than five years' practice either as a barrister, solicitor, or advocate or the holding of certain other public appointments: sections 5(1)(a) and (b) of the DCO.

Criminal cases get to the DC by transfer from the Magistracy. Cases which have been committed to the CFI may also be referred back to the DC but this is not usual. Section 88 of the MO, provides that where any person is charged with an indictable offence not included within Part 111 of the Second Schedule to the MO, the magistrate shall upon the application of the prosecution transfer the charge to the DC. The charges which cannot go to the DC are the most serious charges such as murder, manslaughter, and rape. The procedure before the magistrate is that the prosecution tells the magistrate it wants the case dealt with in the DC, asks the magistrate to transfer the charge or charges to the DC, and hands up the transfer papers. Only the prosecution can ask for a transfer to the DC. Once the application to transfer is made, the magistrate must order the transfer. The transfer order is not appealable or reviewable as the magistrate is not making a determination of a matter dealt with summarily. If the defendant is also charged with an offence triable only summarily, that offence may also be transferred: section 88(1)(a) of the MO. There are obvious advantages in all matters arising out of the same incident being dealt with together.

Effect of the transfer order

The order for transfer removes the case from the jurisdiction of the magistrate and all further steps in the case will take place in the DC. Upon making the transfer order the magistrate must appoint a day for the defendant to appear at the DC for plea. The transfer papers will contain the date of that appearance. On transferring to the DC the magistrate may grant bail or remand the defendant in custody. Where the defendant is remanded in custody the remand can be for a maximum of 20 clear days: section 90(2) of the MO. The transfer order handed up to the magistrate will usually specify the date of the appearance in the DC as the 21st day after the day on which the transfer order is made. Where the defendant is on bail a later date may be specified.

After transfer

Once the charge is transferred to the DC the procedure is governed by Part V of the DCO. Within 14 days after the transfer order the prosecution must deliver to the registrar of the DC a charge sheet including all the charges against the defendant: section 75(2) of the DCO. A copy of the charge will be served upon the defendant. The form of the charge sheet is set out in the first Schedule to the DCO.

The District Court procedure

The procedure follows the procedure in the CFI, save that there is no jury in the DC: section 79 of the DCO. The procedure in the CFI follows the procedure of the Crown Court in England and Wales. The procedure in the DC is much the same as in the Magistrates' Court but is more formal. If the case proceeds to trial there will be a much more detailed opening statement by the prosecutor. If the defendant pleads guilty on the plea day the judge will proceed to sentence. If the plea is not guilty the case is listed for trial at a later date. The plea day gives the judge an opportunity to consider bail pending the trial.

Detailed guidance on the procedure in DC criminal cases is contained in Practice Direction 9.4 titled *Criminal Proceedings in the District Court* (Chief Justice 1998a). The pre-trial review referred to in the Direction is an example of case management. The judge will want to know whether any necessary alibi notice has been given, whether there will be expert witnesses and if so whether the expert's evidence or the substance of their evidence have been exchanged, and will deal with anything that is necessary to ensure the case is ready for trial on the date set. The objective is to ensure, as far as this can possibly be done in a criminal trial, that the trial will run smoothly and that court time is used properly and efficiently (see *R v Law Loi On* [1996] 1 HKC 738 for an examination of pre-trial procedures in the DC and the DC Criminal Listing and Pre-trial Procedures Directions).

Giving reasons

Unlike magistrates, DC judges must give oral reasons for their decision and to record those reasons in writing within 21 days of the decision: section 80 of the DCO. These reasons reflect the justification for the conviction and form the starting point for an appeal. The verdict and the reasons must be read aloud in open court.

Appeals

Appeals from the DC, either against conviction and/or sentence, go to the CA. The provisions about appeals from the CFI to the CA in sections 80 to 83Y of the CPO apply to appeals from the DC with such verbal alterations and modifications as are necessary to make them conveniently applicable to the DC: section 83 of the DCO. A convicted person can appeal as of right to the CA against conviction on any ground which involves a question of law alone. Where, however, the appeal involves a question of fact alone or a question of mixed fact and law, leave to appeal is needed from the CA unless the trial judge grants a certificate that the case is fit for appeal on a ground which involves a question of fact or a question of mixed law and fact.

Section 84 of the DCO enables the prosecution to appeal an acquittal in the DC but only on a point of law. This is an appeal by way of case stated and the procedure is the same as where the prosecution appeals a magistrate's decision by the case stated procedure: section 84(a) of the DCO. The application to the judge to state a case is made in writing and the application must be made within seven clear days after the reasons for verdict have been recorded or after the order of acquittal. This period can be extended by a judge of the High Court. As with a case stated by a magistrate, the procedure brings the decision to a higher level to review the legal correctness of that decision. On an appeal by case stated the CA can dismiss the appeal, reverse the verdict and order the resumption of the trial, record a conviction and proceed to sentence, or give any directions it considers necessary (see, for example, *Secretary for Justice v Lam Tat Ming & Anor (No. 2)* [1999] 2 HKLRD 735 (CA) and *Secretary for Justice v Lam Tat Ming & Anor* [2000] 2 HKLRD 431 (CFA)). Where the CA quashes an acquittal it is suggested that the most appropriate course of action would be to remit the case to the DC for the judge to continue with the trial (see *Secretary for Justice v Wong Sau Fong* [1998] 2 HKLRD 254).

The Court of First Instance

The CFI or, to give it its full title, the CFI of the High Court of the HKSAR, has both civil and criminal jurisdiction. Only the criminal jurisdiction will be discussed in this chapter. In its criminal jurisdiction it is a first instance court. It also hears appeals from magistrates. These have already been discussed.

Cases get to the CFI either through committal proceedings before a magistrate, by an order for transfer under the *Complex Commercial Crimes Ordinance* (Cap. 394) (CCCO), or by the issue of a Voluntary Bill of Indictment. Committal proceedings have already been addressed. A transfer order to the CFI can be made where a person is accused before a magistrate of an indictable offence and the Secretary for Justice considers that the evidence would be sufficient for the accused to be committed for trial and it reveals a case of fraud or dishonesty in a commercial context of such seriousness and complexity that it is appropriate to transfer it to the CFI: section 3 of the CCCO. A Voluntary Bill of Indictment enables an offender to be put on trial in the CFI without going through committal proceedings before a magistrate: section 24A(1)(b) of the CCCO.

The CFI deals with the most serious criminal charges: those which can only be tried upon indictment and those offences triable either way where the prosecution anticipates a sentence of more than seven years' imprisonment upon conviction after trial. Trials in the CFI are before a judge and a jury. The judge is responsible for overall control of the trial and decides upon matters of law, for example the admissibility of evidence. The jury is the sole decider of fact, for example which witness to believe, what the evidence amounts to, and whether the accused is guilty or not guilty.

Court of First Instance judges are professionally qualified. They must be qualified to practise as a barrister or advocate in a court in

Hong Kong or any other common law jurisdiction having unlimited jurisdiction either in civil or criminal matters and have practised as such for at least 10 years. Solicitors may be appointed if they are qualified as solicitors and have had at least 10 years' practice. Section 9 of the *High Court Ordinance* (Cap. 4) sets out the alternative ways in which the 10 years' practice requirement can be satisfied, for example service as a DC judge.

Procedure in the Court of First Instance

The court's procedure is governed by the CPO. That procedure follows the procedure in the Crown Court in England and Wales with appropriate local variations. The CFI is Hong Kong's most senior criminal trial court and has unlimited jurisdiction. That means it can impose any sentence up to the maximum provided by the particular ordinance which governs the offence.

Within seven days of an accused being committed for trial or transferred under the CCCO, the prosecution must file an indictment with the registrar of the CFI. The indictment is the formal allegation of crime which is read to the accused at the start of the trial. That indictment may contain any charge revealed by the committal papers, not simply the charge on which the accused was committed. An accused may have been committed for trial on a charge of manslaughter. The indictment might however allege murder if the committal papers apparently show the ingredients of murder rather than the ingredients of manslaughter.

As with the DC the concern is that trials should run smoothly and that court time will be used efficiently. Use is made of pre-trial directions hearings to attempt to achieve those objectives. By the stage of committal the prosecution will have made full disclosure of the case it intends to present at trial to the defence. The trial judge will require counsel for the prosecution and the defence to attend a meeting in chambers. At that meeting the trial judge will expect to be informed of such matters as the plea to be entered, whether there will be objections to the admissibility of evidence and any significant matter which might affect the proper and convenient trial of the case (see Practice Direction 9.3 titled *Criminal Proceedings in the Court of First Instance* (Chief Justice 1998b)). Although the prosecution must make full disclosure of its case ahead of trial, the defence need not disclose its case before trial. Where however there will be an alibi defence, particulars of the alibi must be given to the prosecution before the trial: section 65D of the CPO. Similarly, where the defence will call expert evidence there must be advance disclosure to the prosecution: section 65DA of the CPO. The trial judge is concerned to ensure that these requirements have been complied with for an efficient trial.

On the trial day the accused will be arraigned (which simply means brought in front of the court to plead to the charges). The indictment is read to the accused. If there is a guilty plea the prosecutor reads out a summary of the facts, hands up any previous convictions and reads out an antecedent statement prepared by the officer in charge of the case.

Trials in the CFI are before a judge and a jury. The *Jury Ordinance* (Cap. 3) (JO) sets out the qualifications for jury service and the role and responsibility of the jury. A jury in Hong Kong has seven members, though exceptionally it can have nine members: section 3 of the JO. A nine-member jury will be used where it is anticipated the trial will be long, so that the trial will continue if any member of the jury withdraws. Whether the starting number is seven or nine, the jury remains properly constituted as long as there are five jurors.

According to section 4 of the JO, persons aged between 21 years of age and 65 years of age are eligible to sit on a jury. In addition to age and residence requirements, jurors must be of sound mind, and not be blind, deaf, or have other disability preventing them from serving as a juror. Jurors must be of good character and have sufficient knowledge of the language in which the proceedings are to be conducted to understand the proceedings. The trial is, in effect, a re-enactment of the incident giving rise to the allegation of crime and jurors must be able to understand and assess the evidence if they are to render a true verdict on the merits.

Certain persons such as the Executive Council and Legislative Council members, public officers, legal officers, and barristers and solicitors in practice, who meet the criteria for jury service, are exempt from jury service, as set out in section 5 of the JO. As the jury must take the law from the judge, it would not be appropriate to have a practising lawyer on the jury as the jury could be exposed to conflicting views of the law when considering their verdict. Similarly, as criminal charges are brought by the HKSAR it would not be appropriate for persons seen as part of the government, for example police officers, to sit on the jury. Eligibility for jury service is much narrower in Hong Kong than in England and Wales. Recent changes in England and Wales to eligibility for jury service by the *Criminal Justice Act 2003* have widened the category of persons who can sit on a jury. A police officer, for example, could sit on a jury in the Crown Court in England and Wales (for a discussion of issues of potential bias in such situations see, for example, *R v Abdroikov & Others* [2005] EWCA Crim 1986).

Persons apparently eligible for jury service are included in the List of Jurors (the List). Before a person's name is included in the List, the registrar of the High Court will give them notice that their name is to be added to the List. This enables a person who claims to be within the provisions of section 5 of the JO and exempt from serving as a juror to claim that exemption. A provisional List is compiled by 1 October every two years and the List is confirmed by the registrar of the High Court by the end of the following February. The List is published in the *Government Gazette*.

A person whose name is included in the List may have their name removed from the List for good cause. What will be good cause depends on the particular circumstances. An application for removal from the List is made by summons to the court. However, as jury service is an important public duty, an application for removal either completely or for a specified period of time will rarely succeed (see *In Re Lau Ko Yuen, Tom* [1998] HKCFI 73, HCMP 5664/98).

Persons whose names are on the List may or may not be called for jury service. Names are drawn at random from the List by the registrar: section 13 of the JO). A person selected for jury service will receive a summons requesting their presence in the High Court on a certain date: section 17 of the JO). A juror who has attended in response to a jury summons will not normally be summoned again within two years. Persons called to court form the Panel of Jurors (the Panel). Those who will form the jury at trial are selected from that Panel. To ensure that there are sufficient persons to form the actual jury, a large Panel will be formed. A person summoned for jury service may be excused from attending for good reason. A written application must be made to the registrar of the High Court. What is or is not a good reason depends upon the facts of each case. It must, however, be something substantial, and mere inconvenience or reluctance to serve on a jury is not enough. If the registrar refuses to excuse attendance, an application can be made to the trial judge for exemption from sitting as a juror in the particular trial: section 28 of the JO.

Forming the jury

After the accused has pleaded not guilty, the judge will ask for the Panel to be brought into the court. The name of each juror is printed on a card and the cards are put into a ballot box. The clerk of the court then draws out names from the ballot box. Before the ballot begins, the accused will be told that the names of the jurors to try the case are to be called and if there is an objection to any of them the objection must be made before they are sworn. Those selected then walk across the court to the jury box unless they successfully claim exemption from serving or are successfully challenged.

Challenges to jurors

A challenge to a person being on the jury is an objection to that person being on the jury to try the case. Challenges are made immediately after the name is drawn in the ballot and before the juror is sworn. The accused can challenge (object to) not more than five jurors without cause (reason) and to any number of jurors for cause. A challenge without cause might be made where the manner or appearance of a person whose name has been drawn in the ballot causes unease in the mind of the accused or, more likely, of the defence counsel. Defence counsel simply says 'Challenge' and that is the end of the matter. A challenge for cause is where the juror is thought not to be qualified or there are concerns about bias or prejudice or connection with the case. In essence the defence is claiming that the person objected to should not in the overall interests of justice be a decision maker in the case. The judge then rules upon the challenge. If the challenge succeeds, that person will not be part of the jury. If the challenge fails, the person is part of the jury.

The prosecution may similarly object to a juror for cause. The prosecution can also ask for a juror or jurors to 'stand by'. No reason need be given. The prosecution is simply saying it does not want that person on the jury.

A juror may be removed by the judge during the trial where this is required in the interests of justice. What will trigger removal depends on the particular case. If removal is due to misconduct by a juror, for example showing obvious bias or hostility towards the prosecution or the accused, the judge will consider whether such damage has been done to the jury overall that the trial should start again before a different jury.

After the jury has been selected, the jurors take their seats in the jury box and take the jurors' oath or affirmation. The judge will then address them and tell them the timetable and how long the case is expected to last. Jurors will be warned not to talk about the case with anyone other than fellow jurors. There may then be a short recess so that the jurors can make telephone calls to arrange personal or business matters. The jury is then told what it is that the accused has pleaded not guilty to. The jury will also be told to select one of their number to act as the foreperson to lead their discussions and to deliver the verdict.

The trial

Before the trial starts in front of the jury, the judge will have ruled on matters of admissibility of evidence, for example whether a confession was voluntary, and have dealt with any matters of case management. These issues are not issues of fact and the jury is not concerned with them. At the start of the trial, judges normally tell the jury what its role is. The role of the jury during the trial is to listen to the evidence. Members of the jury are not allowed to put questions to the witnesses or to interrupt the proceedings with comments or suggestions.

The trial procedure is the same as in the DC and in the MC with appropriate variations to take account of the presence of the jury. The prosecution goes first. There will be an opening address by the prosecutor. In that opening the prosecutor will introduce themselves and defence counsel to the jury, explain the jury's role and outline the prosecution case. The objective is to set the scene for what is to come. The outline must be confined to admissible evidence and must not be inflammatory, emotional, or unfair to the accused. Prosecutors are officers of the court. Their role is not to obtain a conviction at all costs and by any means but to put the case fully and fairly before the jury so that an informed and reasoned decision can be made. If the opening becomes inflammatory, unfair to the accused, or discloses inadmissible evidence, the judge will intervene. If necessary the jury will be discharged and the trial will start again before a new jury.

The prosecution then calls its witnesses one by one. Those witnesses are examined in chief by the prosecution, cross-examined by the defence, and, if necessary, re-examined by the prosecutor. At the end of the prosecution case there can be a submission of no case to answer. As this is a legal argument that the case is too weak to be allowed to continue, the jury is not present at this stage. Having heard submissions, the judge rules whether there is a case for the accused to answer, that is whether assuming the prosecution witnesses are believed the accused could be convicted if no more evidence was heard. If the judge rules that there is a case to answer, the jury returns to court and the trial proceeds. If the judge rules that there is no case to answer, the jury returns to court and the judge will direct the jury to return a not guilty verdict. A jury verdict is necessary as once a jury has started to try the case, the jury must give a verdict either of guilty or not guilty. Where the judge rules there is no case to answer, the not guilty verdict is a directed verdict but it is, nonetheless, the verdict of the jury. The jury cannot refuse to return a not guilty verdict: they are directed to do so as a matter of law.

If there is a case to answer, the accused has the same rights about evidence and witnesses as in DC or MC trials. At the end of the defence case there will be closing speeches for the prosecution and for the defence. The closing speeches are an opportunity to draw things together and to concentrate the mind of the jury on the relevant matters for their consideration. The defence has the last word. In the closing speech, defence counsel will highlight perceived weaknesses of the prosecution case and perceived strengths of the defence case.

After the closing address for the defence, the judge sums up to the jury. The summing up is intended to guide the jury. The judge will review the evidence and direct the jury on what the law is if certain facts are proved. Care must be taken to ensure that the jury fully understands the defence case. In summing up the judge can make comments and express opinions. Indeed, this is often an essential part of the guidance the judge gives to the jury. However, the jury must be told it can reject or adopt those comments and opinions as it wishes and it is solely responsible for deciding upon issues of fact. Where appropriate, the judge should discuss with the prosecution and the defence the wording of the directions to be given to the jury (see, for example, *HKSAR v Sham Ying Kit* [2001] 1 HKLRD 52). This discussion will take place in the absence of the jury. It is in everyone's interest that the jury should be properly directed on all relevant matters and both prosecuting counsel and defence counsel have a responsibility to help the judge do this.

The verdict

Once the summing up is complete, the jury goes to its private room, the jury room, to consider its verdict. The jury is taken to that room by an officer of the court (jury bailiff) who takes an oath or an affirmation not to communicate with the jury about the case until they have reached their verdict or allow anyone else to do so. The bailiff is the channel for communication between the judge and jury or, more accurately, from the jury to the judge. The jury may, for example, want more help on a particular point from the judge. The bailiff will relay this to the judge so that the jury can be called back into court for further directions on that point. There must not be any secret communication between the judge and jury so prosecuting counsel and defence counsel will be advised of the jury's request. Unless the request can be answered with a simple 'yes' or 'no', the jury is brought back to the court for further directions. Particularly at this stage, the judge will try to agree the wording of these further directions with both prosecuting counsel and defence counsel.

Once the jury has started to consider its verdict it is kept together to avoid extraneous influence or contamination. Because of that, judges will avoid sending the jury out to consider its verdict late in the day. If the defence case concludes in the afternoon, the judge will start to sum up but then adjourn until the following day when the summing up will be concluded. The jury then has most of the day to consider its verdict. If it cannot reach a verdict during the day it will be accommodated overnight in a hotel or in rooms in the High Court building.

Ideally the verdict should be unanimous either to convict or to acquit. The judge will tell the jury to try to reach a unanimous verdict. However, the jury will also be told that if after a reasonable period it cannot reach a unanimous verdict there can be a majority verdict. Where the jury has seven members a majority verdict is only acceptable where the majority is not less than five to two either to acquit or to convict. Where only five members of the jury remain, the verdict must be unanimous. Where the jury has nine members, the majority either to acquit or to convict must be not less than seven. If eight jurors remain a majority of not less than six is acceptable and if six or seven jurors remain a majority of not less than five is acceptable (see section 24 of the JO; and for cases on majority verdicts see, for example, *HKSAR v Kwok Chi Wai* CACC 300/2003 and *HKSAR v Shek Wai Chiu* CACC 445/2004).

If the jury cannot reach either a unanimous verdict, or a majority verdict, a mistrial must be directed. The prosecution then has the option of offering no further evidence, when the jury will be directed to acquit, or starting again before another jury. There is sometimes said to be a tradition that if two juries cannot reach a verdict either unanimously or by a permitted majority the prosecution should offer no further evidence, but each case must depend upon its own facts (see *HKSAR v Hau King Yeung* [2006] HKEC 2070).

The jury deliberates in secret. No records are kept and jurors must not disclose what was discussed. When the jury has reached its verdict, it informs the bailiff of that, but not what the verdict is.

The bailiff informs the judge's clerk and the court reassembles. The jury is asked in open court if it has reached a verdict. If it has, the indictment is read out and the jury is asked, 'How do you find the accused – guilty or not guilty of [the offence]?' If there is more than one count on the indictment each count is put separately and the jury gives its verdict on each count. The verdict is given by the foreperson who speaks on behalf of the jury.

After the foreperson has given each verdict, the foreperson is asked whether the verdict is unanimous or by a majority. If the verdict is by a majority, the foreperson is asked whether the verdict accords with the requirements of section 24 of the JO. A majority verdict that does not comply with section 24 must not be accepted. When directing the jury on a majority verdict, the trial judge must ensure the jury fully understands the requirements for a majority verdict and similarly when taking the verdict care must be taken to ensure that the majority verdict accords with section 24 (see *HKSAR v Chau Hon-Kwong* [2004] HKCA 279).

The jury does not give reasons for its verdict. It cannot be questioned about its reasons. Such questions would undermine the integrity of the jury system. Similarly, members of the jury cannot be asked, for example if a case goes to appeal, why they reached the decision they did reach. Even where it is suspected something improper occurred in the jury room to lead to the verdict that was reached, members of the jury cannot be questioned about that. If the jury convicts then the judge proceeds to sentence either at once or after obtaining any necessary background reports. The jury plays no part in sentencing.

Conclusion

This chapter has outlined the role and responsibilities of Hong Kong's criminal trial courts. The reader should now have an appreciation of how cases are allocated to the trial courts, the relationship between the trial courts, and the powers of those courts. The procedure in the trial courts is adversarial: the HKSAR against the defendant. The prosecution must prove guilt with certainty and the procedure by which each trial court operates is designed and intended to ensure a fair trial. It is for the prosecution to prove guilt. That means the prosecution must bring into the trial sufficient cogent evidence so that the decision maker, whether magistrate, judge, or jury, is certain of the guilt of the defendant both in fact and in law.

An offender appears first of all in the MC. Most cases will finish in that court. The more serious cases pass from the MC either to the CFI or to the DC. The most serious criminal charges can only be tried in the CFI. It is only in the CFI that the trial is before a judge and a jury. There is no right for a defendant to elect a jury trial in Hong Kong. Some charges must be dealt with in the CFI. Charges which are triable either way will be dealt with in the CFI or in the MC or the DC. The prosecution decides upon the venue of trial where the charge can be heard either way. To that extent the prosecution is in charge but, even so, the procedures laid down in the ordinances which govern each trial court and in the CPO must be adhered to if the trial is to be fair and just. Chapter 10 will examine how the decisions of the trial courts can be challenged.

Review questions

1 What is meant by the 'venue' of a trial? Who decides on the venue of trial in Hong Kong and by what criteria?
2 Stephen has been charged with murder. What courts would be concerned with his case and why?
3 What might be the situation if at Stephen's trial three jurors want to convict him of murder and four jurors want to acquit him of murder?
4 D is convicted after trial by a magistrate and sentenced to 9 months' imprisonment. Can D challenge the conviction and if so, how?
5 Six days ago John, a magistrate, convicted a defendant of assault occasioning actual bodily harm and imposed a fine by way of punishment. John now feels that the sentence he imposed was too lenient. Is there anything John can do about that?
6 Six weeks ago John, a magistrate, convicted Sam of theft. The theft involved pickpocketing on the Mass Transit Railway. Sam had two previous convictions for pickpocketing and John imposed 15 months' imprisonment. John now feels that he was wrong to convict Sam. Is there anything that Sam can do?
7 D aged 15 and E aged 18 have been arrested and charged with theft from a shop. Both intend to plead not guilty. D asks whether he will be tried in the Juvenile Court. What would you tell him and why would you do that?
8 J aged 15 is jointly charged with X aged 21 of robbery. The charge has been transferred to the District Court. J, who has no previous convictions, has pleaded guilty in the District Court? What, if any, issues arise about the sentencing of J?
9 Frank's son J, aged 14, has been arrested and charged with theft from a shop. J has to attend the Juvenile Court next week. Frank is worried

that when J's school friends find out about this they will make fun of J. Frank wants to know whether he can do anything to stop the newspapers reporting J's case. Frank also says that he does not want to go to court with J but he has been told by the police officer in charge of the case that as J's parent he must attend the court. What would you say to Frank?

References

Chief Justice (1998a) *Practice Direction – 9.4: Criminal Proceedings in the District Court*. Hong Kong: The Judiciary. Available at: http://legalref.judiciary.gov.hk/lrs/common/pd/pdcontent.jsp?pdn=PD9.4.htm&lang=EN

Chief Justice (1998b) *Practice Direction – 9.3: Criminal Proceedings in the Court of First Instance*. Hong Kong: The Judiciary. Available at: http://legalref.judiciary.gov.hk/lrs/common/pd/pdcontent.jsp?pdn=PD9.3.htm&lang=EN

Chief Justice (2000) *Practice Direction – 9.6: Magistracy Appeals in the Court of First Instance*. Hong Kong: The Judiciary. Available at: http://legalref.judiciary.gov.hk/lrs/common/pd/pdcontent.jsp?pdn=PD9.6.htm&lang=EN

Legislation cited

The Basic Law of the Hong Kong Special Administrative Region
Complex Commercial Crimes Ordinance (Cap. 394)
Criminal Justice Act 2003 (England and Wales)
Crimes Ordinance (Cap. 200)
Criminal Procedure Ordinance (Cap. 221)
Dangerous Drugs Ordinance (Cap. 134)
District Court Ordinance (Cap. 336)
High Court Ordinance (Cap. 4)
Jury Ordinance (Cap. 3)
Juvenile Offenders Ordinance (Cap. 226)
Magistrates Ordinance (Cap. 227)
Offences Against Property Ordinance (Cap. 210)
Places of Detention (Juvenile Offenders) Appointment (Consolidation) Order (Cap. 226A)

Cases cited

AG v John Lok & Partners & George Wimpey International Ltd. HCMA000062/1985
Attorney-General v Phung van Toan & Others CACC000082/1991
Cheng Shu-wai Magistracy Appeal No. 982 of 1985

HKSAR v Chau Hon-Kwong [2004] HKCA 279
HKSAR v Hau King Yeung [2006] HKEC 2070
HKSAR v Kwok Chi Wai CACC 300/2003
HKSAR v Lee Kwong Lap [2002] HKCFI 1371, HCMA 001117/2002
HKSAR v Sham Ying Kit [2001] 1 HKLRD 52
HKSAR v Shek Wai Chiu CACC 445/2004
HKSAR v Tsoi Kei-lung & Anor HCMA 000340/200
HKSAR v Yan Panyue HCC137/2004
HKSAR v Yan Panyue CACC 128/2005
HKSAR v Yeung Sze Lun Magistracy Appeal No. 717 of 1997
In Re Lau Ko Yuen, Tom [1998] HKCFI 73, HCMP 5664/98
Ip Wai-Hung v The Queen CACC000151/1982
R v Abdroikov & Others [2005] EWCA Crim 1986
R v Law Loi On [1996] 1 HKC 738
R v Pau Chi Kung [1987] HKLR 1148
Secretary for Justice v Lam Tat Ming & Anor (No. 2) [1999] 2 HKLRD 735 (CA)
Secretary for Justice v Lam Tat Ming & Anor [2000] 2 HKLRD 431 (CFA)
Secretary for Justice v Wong Sau Fong [1998] 2 HKLRD 254

Useful websites

Bilingual Laws Information System (BLIS) (Hong Kong)	http://www.legislation.gov.hk/eng/index.htm
Department of Justice	http://www.doj.gov.hk
Duty Lawyer Service	http://www.dutylawyer.org.hk/
Legal Aid Department	http://www.lad.gov.hk/english/home/home.htm
The Judiciary	http://www.judiciary.gov.hk

Chapter 8

Sentencing

Simon N.M. Young

Introduction

Sentencing is one of the most important aspects of the criminal process. The sentencing judge must take into consideration a multitude of factors including the interests of the offender, the victim, and society in arriving at a balanced and appropriate sentence. Errors made in the sentencing process can result in the excessive detention of an individual, the premature release of a dangerous offender, aggrieved victims who feel justice has not been done, and other issues. Sentencing can also be highly political, with governments using sentencing reform as a way to curry favour with voters attracted to 'get tough on crime' policies. In Hong Kong, however, with its developing state of democracy, the politicization of sentencing has not been seen, and indeed one might criticize the legislature for giving insufficient attention to the topic generally.

This chapter outlines the main sentencing options currently available in Hong Kong before discussing the various purposes and principles of sentencing which the judge must consider and apply in arriving at a just and appropriate sentence.

Punishment and sentencing

Every child knows (or should know) that doing something 'bad' or 'wrong' might be met by some form of 'punishment' from one's parents. In this everyday sense, punishment is a response from an authority figure to misbehaviour. In law, the word 'punishment' is reserved for the category of misconduct that constitutes a criminal offence. Punishment is the response of a court to a person's criminal conduct. By contrast, if a person is ordered to pay damages in a civil lawsuit or disciplined by a professional body, these measures are not typically described as punishment. Thus the word punishment carries with it a special meaning and signifies censure from a court for breaching criminal laws (von Hirsch 1993). Easton and Piper (2005) note that punishment 'rests on a moral foundation' and 'stems from an authoritative source, usually the state' (p. 4).

Sentencing is the legal process by which a person is punished by a court. The law of sentencing is concerned with how and how much a person should be punished for the criminal offence(s) he has committed. In every case, the court balances the purposes of sentencing and applies established sentencing principles in accordance with the law to reach a just and appropriate sentence given the circumstances of the offence and the offender.

Before moving on, a word should be said about the classical debate over the theories and justification of punishment. Punishment theories generally fall within two schools of thought. The *utilitarian* school justifies punishment as a means to achieving the greatest good for the greatest number. While punishment is a source of unhappiness for the offender, it is nevertheless able to bring about a greater good in its direct and indirect consequences, for example deterring the offender and others from causing further harm in society. The competing school of thought is concerned more with the particular offender and his criminal offence. Punishment is justified as *just desert* for the crime committed by the offender. In other words, a person who commits a criminal offence deserves to be punished and how much he or she deserves is measured by the extent of the offender's wrongdoing and blameworthiness. The essential difference between the two schools is that the former treats the offender and his punishment as a means to a greater end while the latter respects the autonomy of the offender and treats his punishment as an end in and of itself. As will be seen, Hong Kong's system of sentencing may appear incoherent at times as it reflects elements of both schools of thought.

Sentencing options

Sentencing options lie along a spectrum of severity and can serve different purposes. The range of options changes with time and place.

As you read about the different sentencing options, reflect upon why certain options exist and the purposes they are meant to achieve. Describing them as options is not meant to suggest that the court can freely choose any option to apply in a given case. Both the law and sentencing principles will constrain the range of options on the basis of the circumstances of each case.

Death and corporal punishment

The death penalty in Hong Kong was abolished in 1993, and the last execution by hanging took place in 1966 (Cross and Cheung 1994: 32). Death was the punishment for the offences of murder, treason, and piracy with violence (Liu 1992). In the period before the formal abolition of the death penalty, death sentences imposed were commuted to sentences of life imprisonment. Corporal punishment, although it once existed in Hong Kong primarily in the form of caning, was abolished in 1990 (Cross and Cheung 1994: 20). While both these sentencing options are now part of Hong Kong's criminal justice history, it should not be forgotten that they remain popular sentencing measures in many other Asian jurisdictions.

Imprisonment[1]

Jail is the typical sentencing option in the mind of most people. Jail sentences can range from a term as short as 'to the rising of the court' (see *White v Brown* [2003] 175 FLR 325) to one as long as life imprisonment, the most severe sentence available in Hong Kong. Statutory offences will normally specify a maximum term of imprisonment, and very few offences in Hong Kong carry a minimum term. When a judge orders different terms of imprisonment for several offences, he must specify whether the terms are to run at the same time (i.e. concurrent terms) or one after another (i.e. consecutive terms). It is a constitutional principle that a person who is imprisoned must 'be treated with humanity and with respect for the inherent dignity of the human person': Article 6(1) of the *Hong Kong Bill of Rights*.

Murder is the only offence which must be punished by life imprisonment, and a small category of serious offences, such as manslaughter, rape, and robbery, can attract discretionary life sentences. When the judge sentences someone to a discretionary life sentence, the judge must also specify a minimum term in years which the person will have to serve before he can be released. There is no guarantee that the person will in fact be released after he or she has served the minimum term. Decisions concerning the release of such persons are made by the Long-term Prison Sentences Review Board (LTPSRB) and the Chief Executive (CE) in accordance with the *Long-term Prison Sentences Review Ordinance* (Cap. 524). A person who receives a mandatory life sentence for murder is not given a minimum term by the judge. Instead, his or her sentence is reviewed by the LTPSRB after five years of the sentence and every two years thereafter until he or she is released under the terms of the Ordinance.

Fine

The sentencing court has a discretionary power to impose a fine in lieu of or in addition to other forms of punishment. A fine serves a punitive purpose but should only be given if the offender is in a position to pay the fine. To enforce the fine, a default period of imprisonment up to 12 months may have to be served by the offender if he fails to pay the fine. Fines can range from HK$1 to HK$100,000 according to Schedule 8 in the *Criminal Procedure Ordinance* (Cap. 221); however, other ordinances may provide for much higher upper limits. For example, the indictable offence of making child pornography carries with it a maximum fine of HK$2,000,000. For some offences, the fine is at large, and there is no ceiling, although regard will be had to the capacity of the offender to pay in the calculation of the amount.

Suspended sentence

A person who receives a suspended sentence gets a chance to keep his freedom and to demonstrate his or her potential to rehabilitate. This option is only reserved for less serious wrongdoing, i.e. when the court orders a jail term of 2 years or less. Schedule 3 of the *Criminal Procedure Ordinance* lists a number of excluded offences including manslaughter for which no suspension is possible even if the actual sentence is a term of jail within the 2 year period. Before suspending a sentence, a court should first decide that a term of imprisonment is required, and then satisfy itself that exceptional circumstances exist to justify its suspension (Cross and Cheung 2003: 466).

For a period of at least one year and up to 3 years, the offender must not recommit another offence in Hong Kong punishable with imprisonment. Otherwise he or she will have to serve the original sentence which had been suspended along with any other sentence he or she might receive for the subsequent offence. When imposing a suspended sentence the court may also impose reasonable conditions to which the offender must adhere during the period of suspension. Breach of a condition is tantamount to recommitting a further offence and can result in having to serve the original sentence. As conditions can attach to suspended sentences, the imposition of a simultaneous probation order for other offences is not allowed: section 109B(2) of the *Criminal Procedure Ordinance*. This prohibition does not, however, extend to the making on a later occasion of a probation order for some other offence (see *R v Tarry* [1970] 2 QB 560 (CA)).

Probation

A probation order requires the offender to be under the supervision of a probation officer and to adhere to certain conditions during the period of the order which must be at least one year in duration but no more than 3 years: section 3 of the *Probation of Offenders Ordinance* (Cap. 298). The conditions aim at securing the good conduct of the offender or to prevent reoffending by the offender. They can provide that the offender reside at a particular residence or approved youth institution but cannot require the offender to pay compensation (as compensation orders are provided for separately). The probation officer plays an important supervisory role in respect of the discharge, amendment, and review of probation orders.

Like the suspended sentence, the probation order has rehabilitative aims and is a measure that gives the offender a second chance, albeit with some restrictions on his liberty. It is not available for offences whose sentence is fixed by law (for example, murder), and when the judge orders probation he or she is not allowed to sentence the offender any further, see *R v Isherwood* [1974] 59 Cr App R 162 (CA). Thus, probation is only an option for less serious offending and will not be available for serious offences, even if the offender has an impeccable background. It is a common method of dealing with juvenile offenders.

A probationer who breaches a condition of his or her probation order is required to return to court where he or she may be cautioned, fined up to HK$500, or in serious cases resentenced for the original offence as if he or she had just been convicted of it. If the probationer commits another offence during the period of the probation order, he or she will also be liable to be resentenced for the original offence in addition to any sentence he or she receives for the new offence (see Chapter 10 of this volume).

Community service

Many people still remember the controversial community service order which actor Nicholas Tse Ting-fung received in 2002 for perverting the course of justice by trying to conceal his responsibility for a vehicle accident. A community service order requires the offender to perform unpaid work in the community up to a maximum of 240 hours: *Community Service Orders Ordinance* (Cap. 378). Such orders can only be given to an offender of or over 14 years of age who consents to the order and only after conviction for an offence punishable with imprisonment. The order will not be made if the judge finds that the offender is not a suitable person to perform work under such an order.

As with probation and suspended sentences, the community service order serves the primary purpose of rehabilitation with a meaningful degree of liberty restriction to convey a punitive message. This sentencing option was first introduced in 1984 following a study and report on the topic by the Law Reform Commission of Hong Kong (1983, see Chapter 10 of this volume).

Discharge

Where an offender is convicted of an offence, he may receive a conditional or absolute discharge by a magistrate (section 36 of the *Magistrates Ordinance* (Cap. 227)) or a conditional discharge by the Court of First Instance or District Court (section 107 of the *Criminal Procedure Ordinance*). An absolute discharge is reserved for wrongdoing of a very low order while conditional discharges serve a similar purpose to probation orders. Absolute discharges are typically not appropriate for shoplifting cases given the offender's moral blameworthiness: *Secretary for Justice v Tse Sheung Kai & Others* [2001] 3 HKLRD 487 (CA).

When a person is discharged he or she cannot also be given a custodial sentence, fine, or community service order. Before ordering a discharge, the court must find that it is 'inexpedient to inflict any punishment or any other than a nominal punishment' on the offender having regard to 'the character, antecedents, age, health, or mental condition of the person charged, or to the trivial nature of the offence, or to the extenuating circumstances under which the offence was committed': section 36 of the *Magistrates Ordinance*; section 107 of the *Criminal Procedure Ordinance*.

Binding over

The power to bind over an individual is a non-custodial measure that helps to keep the peace in a potentially violent context and/or to ensure good behaviour from that individual. 'The making of binding-over orders is sometimes explained as constituting "preventive"justice': *HKSAR v Lau Wai Wo* [2003] 6 HKCFAR 624 at para. 39.

Under section 109I of the *Criminal Procedure Ordinance*, the judge or magistrate has the power to bind over a person who or whose case was before the court irrespective of whether he has been convicted of an offence. But where the court proposes to bind over an acquitted person, the court must give him or her fair notice of this proposal and an opportunity to make representations. The power obligates the person to enter into his or her own recognisance or to find sureties or both, and for the duration of the recognisance (usually one year but not more than 3 years) to keep the peace and/or be of good behaviour. Failure to enter into the recognisance can result in contempt proceedings against the person who has been bound over. In fixing the amount of the recognisance, the judge or magistrate should try to satisfy himself that the amount is such that the person could reasonably be expected to be able to pay: *Lau Wai Wo* at para. 55. If the recognisance is breached then the amount of the recognisance may be forfeited.

Restitution and compensation

In recent times, victims of crime have been given a greater role in the trial of persons accused of crime. It has been recognized that victims should not have to bring their own legal proceedings (and suffer all the costs of doing so) to obtain either the return of property from the offender or compensation for harm caused by the offender. The restitution order and compensation order are two different orders available to the sentencing judge in order to effect corrective justice to the victim: sections 73 and 84 of the *Criminal Procedure Ordinance*. Both orders are made in addition to the sentence which the offender receives.

Forfeiture and confiscation

Forfeiture and confiscation orders aim at depriving the offender of property related to crime. Such crime-related property is of three kinds: (1) property which is in itself illegal to possess (i.e. contraband); (2) property used in the commission of the offence (i.e. an instrument of crime); and (3) property derived directly or indirectly from crime (i.e. proceeds of crime). In respect of contraband and instruments of crime, there are a number of disparate provisions which allow the court to forfeit property ranging from dangerous drugs and counterfeit goods to detained property used in the commission of an offence.

In respect of proceeds of crime, there exists a complex legal regime in the *Drug Trafficking (Recovery of Proceeds) Ordinance* (Cap. 405) and *Organized and Serious Crimes Ordinance* (Cap. 455) that allows the sentencing court to order the offender to pay a confiscation order in an amount equivalent to the degree to which the offender has benefited from drug trafficking and/or serious crime. If the offender fails to pay the confiscation order, he or she may be liable to serve an additional term of imprisonment up to 10 years.

Other orders

Disqualification orders prohibit the offender from engaging in certain activities as a preventative measure to possible reoffending. Such orders include disqualifying the offender from driving or in cases of white-collar crime from being a company director for fixed periods of time. A criminal bankruptcy order, which can only be made by the District Court or Court of First Instance, can force the offender's bankruptcy and assist in ensuring that the proceeds of crime are returned to victims. A judge or magistrate can also order a hospital order for an accused where there is medical evidence that the person is a mentally disordered person and the nature and degree of the mental disorder from which the person is suffering warrants his detention in a mental hospital for medical treatment: section 54(3) of the *Mental Health Ordinance* (Cap. 136).

Sources of purposes and principles

Surprisingly, while most of the above sentencing options are clearly spelled out in legislation, the statutes are silent when it comes to the purposes and principles of sentencing. In other words, the Hong Kong ordinances contain no express guidance on when a certain sentencing option should be given and on how much a person should be sentenced. This of course does not mean that there are no rules which govern a judge's exercise of his sentencing powers in a particular case. Rather, the purposes and principles of sentencing are found in the common law and have been developed over the years by judges in England and Hong Kong.

In 1991 Hong Kong passed the *Hong Kong Bill of Rights Ordinance* (Cap. 383) (BORO) as the means to implement the United Kingdom's international treaty obligations in respect of Hong Kong under the International Covenant on Civil and Political Rights. After 1997, China allowed the BORO to continue alongside the many human rights protections under Hong Kong's constitution, the *Basic Law of the Hong Kong Special Administrative Region* (the *Basic Law*). As will be seen, both the BORO and the *Basic Law* contain very important constitutional principles relevant to sentencing.

The purposes of sentencing

There are many varied sentencing purposes which express themselves more or less strongly in any given case. It would be incoherent if all the sentencing purposes were to have full expression in every case. Instead, the relative emphasis given to the different purposes varies depending on the nature of the criminal offence of which the offender is convicted, its prevalence in a particular community, public attitudes to that offence, the harm caused to the particular victim, and the moral culpability and background of the offender (see the discussion in *R v Sargeant* [1974] 60 Cr App R 74).

While sentencing purposes can explain what the sentence is trying to achieve, they are poor indicators of how much punishment should be given in a particular case. For this, it is necessary to apply established sentencing principles which provide greater guidance on the quantum of punishment. Even greater precision comes from the development of caselaw by appellate courts establishing certain guidelines and precedents as to sentences for certain types of cases.

Public protection

It is uncontroversial that one of the main purposes of sentencing is to protect the public. Imprisoning the offender is not the only means to protect the public but can be an effective one. Any measure including a binding-over order which can prevent the offender from reoffending would also achieve the purpose. In cases where the offender is a habitual one and his criminal record shows an escalation of seriousness in his offending, the purpose of public protection will find strong emphasis in the sentence.

Deterrence: general and specific

Deterrence sees punishment for a particular offence as a means to lower the incidence of that offence. In this respect, deterrence has much in common with public protection since lowering the incidence of crime has the effect of protecting the public. General deterrence uses the offender as an example to deter others from committing the same or a similar offence. Specific deterrence punishes the offender to deter him from recommitting offences.

At a theoretical level, deterrence 'works' because of the basic notion that humans are rational beings who will choose to avoid conduct that can result in a deprivation of liberty or other personal discomfort. In respect of imprisonment, however, this theory breaks down for two categories of offenders: rational decision makers, often motivated by profit, who are prepared to take the risk of non-apprehension, and those with mental disorders or substance abuse problems who do not think rationally before committing an offence. For these offenders, other sentencing purposes and options may need to find more prominent expression in the sentence.

When sentencing judges have regard to the prevalence of the offender's offence in the community, they are giving effect to the purpose of general deterrence. In Hong Kong, section 27 of the *Organized and Serious Crimes Ordinance* allows the court to take into consideration admissible evidence concerning the prevalence of the offence committed by the offender to order a more severe sentence than it would have ordered had it not considered this evidence. For example, in *HKSAR v Ma Suet Chun & Others* [2001] 4 HKC 337, the Court of Appeal approved an enhancement of sentence in a case concerning street deception. The prosecution had called three police officers to testify to the increasing number of street deception complaints made in the New Territories and West Kowloon region. The Court held that in future cases of this kind the enhancement could be as great as 50 per cent. While there has yet to be a constitutional challenge to section 27, courts will need to be wary that giving general deterrence such great emphasis could well put the sentence in conflict with other established sentencing purposes and principles.

Retribution

If public protection and deterrence were the only sentencing purposes then long custodial sentences would be the norm. Retribution reins in excessive punishments by ensuring that the offender is only punished for what he deserves. There is a misconception that retribution is the same as vengeance. This passage from a Canadian judgement explains the difference (see *R v M(CA)* [1996] 1 SCR 500, para. 80, per Lamer CJC):

> Vengeance … represents an uncalibrated act of harm upon another, frequently motivated by emotion and anger, as a reprisal for harm inflicted upon oneself by that person. Retribution in a criminal context, by contrast, represents an objective, reasoned and measured determination of an appropriate punishment which properly reflects the moral culpability of the offender, having regard to the intentional risk-taking of the offender, the consequential harm caused by the offender, and the normative character of the offender's conduct. Furthermore, unlike vengeance, retribution incorporates a principle of restraint; retribution requires the imposition of a just and appropriate punishment, and nothing more.

Retribution is closely related to the principle of proportionality, which is a fundamental principle that informs all sentences.

Denunciation

There are times when the circumstances of the offence are so aggravating in terms of the harm done to the victim and society that it calls for denunciation by the court. To achieve this purpose, the court denounces the offender and his crime in the public forum of the courtroom and orders a severe sentence to reflect the denunciation. Thus there is a strong communicative element when giving effect to the purpose of denunciation. The court sends a message voicing the sentiments of the victim and community that the offender's conduct is wrong and must be sharply condemned.

Denunciation was voiced in the case concerning the infamous Yip Kai Foon, who, after escaping from jail, led a criminal gang armed with assault rifles and explosives in a street battle with the police. He was sentenced to 30 years' imprisonment on top of the 11 years and 3 months he had left to serve when he escaped custody.

As a result of the shootout with the police, Yip became paralysed from the waist down. The Appeal Committee of the Court of Final Appeal (by majority) refused to hear Yip's appeal and held that even if appropriate weight was given to Yip's paralysed condition, his offences were so extremely grave that they deserved the sentence given (albeit reduced slightly by the Court of Appeal): *HKSAR v Yip Kai Foon* [2000] 3 HKCFAR 31. The Appeal Committee described the actions of Yip and his gang as coming 'very close to declaring war on society' and approved of the Court of Appeal's statement in this case that '[s]entences must be imposed which, to use the words of Lord Denning, express the emphatic denunciation by the community of such crimes': cited in the Committee's determination at p. 37.

Rehabilitation

Rehabilitation aims to address the underlying causes of the offender's criminal behaviour and thereby serves to prevent a reoccurrence of the offending. Rehabilitative aims are often served by non-custodial orders such as the suspended sentence, community service order, probation, discharge, and binding-over order. If the offender has a drug or alcohol addiction problem which caused him to commit the crime, rehabilitation would require the offender to be treated for this substance abuse problem.

Long terms of imprisonment are often perceived as being inconsistent with achieving rehabilitative aims. Article 6(3) of the *Hong Kong Bill of Rights* requires that custodial institutions 'comprise treatment of prisoners the essential aim of which shall be their reformation and social rehabilitation'. This, however, relates not to the appropriateness of the sentences passed, but to the treatment of offenders who are detained: *R v Chu Man Chiu*, Cr App 198/1991 (CA). In Hong Kong, specialized custodial settings have been established to pursue specific rehabilitative aims. For example, young offenders can be sentenced to serve a term in a reformatory school or training centre. Those with drug problems can be sentenced to a term in a drug addiction treatment centre.

Reparation for victims

While the victim is not a formal party to criminal proceedings, modern criminal justice systems have accorded the victim a greater role, particularly in the sentencing stage. The restitution and compensation orders are two mechanisms by which the sentencing court can achieve a degree of civil justice between the victim and the wrongdoer. The availability of such orders at sentencing saves the victim time and money from having to bring his own lawsuit.

There are, however, limits to the ability of the sentencing court to make full reparation to the victim(s). Sentencing proceedings are intended to be held immediately after conviction and once commenced, expeditiously completed; they are not supposed to be long drawn-out hearings in which complex factual and legal issues are decided. Ultimately, it is at the discretion of the sentencing judge to decide whether and how much reparation should be made for victims. Where the issues are likely to distort and delay the sentencing process (for example, many victims, each raising contested factual and liability issues), the judge may decide not to order restitution or compensation and to leave such issues for a civil court to resolve.

Restoration

A separate but related sentencing purpose to reparation is restoration, sometimes known as restorative justice. Where all parties are willing, restorative justice aims to reintegrate the offender back into the community by having him accept responsibility for his wrongdoing and make amends to the victim for the harm caused. The process by which this is achieved typically involves the offender and victim agreeing to meet in mediation conducted by a neutral mediator. While achieving acknowledged responsibility and reintegration is an end in itself, restorative justice can also protect the public by lowering the risk of reoffending by the offender. While much literature now exists on restorative justice, it has yet to be generally accepted in Hong Kong sentencing law, nor has the legislature enacted provisions aimed at furthering restorative justice.

The principles of sentencing

It is imperative that the courts apply the correct principles of sentencing in every case, as an error of principle is a recognized ground of appeal. Where an appeal court has found an error of principle in the reasons for sentence, the appeal court will sentence the offender afresh applying the correct principles. Some of the major sentencing principles are discussed below.

Proportionality

The principle of proportionality requires that the sentence and punishment be calibrated according to the seriousness of the offence and the circumstances of the offender. Seriousness of the offence will depend on the nature of the offence, the gravity of the harm caused to individual victims and society generally, and the degree of moral culpability of the offender. The maximum sentence for the offence is often a reliable indicator of the relative seriousness of different offences. The circumstances of the offender, including his criminal history and the consequential hardship which the sentence will have on him, are all relevant to the application of the proportionality principle. However, in general, a person with a long criminal record should have already received proportionate punishment for all of his past crimes and should not be punished again for them. That said, a recidivist must expect to receive a longer sentence than a first offender: *HKSAR v Chan Pui Chi* [1998] 2 HKLRD 830 (CA).

Proportionality is a fundamental principle since all sentences are liable to be altered on appeal if they are manifestly excessive or inadequate. A good illustration of the application of this principle is found in *HKSAR v Wong Chun Cheong* [2001] 4 HKCFAR 12. Wong, who was aged 16 at the time of the offence, pleaded guilty to participating in a lion dance in a public place without a permit. The magistrate sentenced Wong to be detained in a training centre where the period of detention would range from a minimum of 6 months up to a maximum of 3 years. However, the maximum sentence for the offence for which Wong was convicted was only a $2,000 fine and imprisonment for 6 months. In allowing the appeal and substituting a fine of $100 (Wong had already served 4 months in the training centre), the court found that detention in a training centre for the period allowed by the legislation would be a 'wholly disproportionate period given the triviality of the offence' (p. 25). This was true even if Wong was a suitable candidate for rehabilitation in a training centre. The case stands for the proposition that a man should not lose his liberty in the name of rehabilitation if it would be disproportionate to do so.

Proportionality in the sentence is also a constitutional principle. Article 28 of the *Basic Law* protects individuals from 'arbitrary or unlawful … detention or imprisonment', and Article 3 of the *Hong Kong Bill of Rights* provides that '[n]o one shall be subjected to torture or to cruel, inhuman or degrading treatment or punishment'. In *HKSAR v Lau Cheong & Another* [2002] 5 HKCFAR 415, the Court of Final Appeal held that a sentence would give rise to arbitrary imprisonment if the sentence was 'manifestly disproportionate' (at para. 110). In relation to Article 3 of the *Bill of Rights*, the Court held that the threshold test for determining whether a sentence constituted cruel, inhuman, or degrading punishment was either the same or higher than the threshold for arbitrary imprisonment. *Lau Cheong* was concerned with a challenge to the mandatory life imprisonment sentence for murder. In rejecting all the constitutional arguments, the Court noted the 'inherent and unique gravity of the offence' and the 'legislative judgment' to have the mandatory sentence together with a statutory regime for review of all life sentences by an independent board: at paras. 123–5.

Totality

The principle of totality ensures proportionality when the offender is sentenced for multiple offences. It is said that the principle 'requires the court which passes a series of sentences, each perfectly proper in its own right, to consider whether the aggregate which is achieved is just and appropriate' (Cross and Cheung 2003: 487). The principle was applied in *HKSAR v Chung Yiu Ming* [2003] 3 HKLRD K14 (CA), where the offender was sentenced to 5 years' imprisonment for drug trafficking to be served consecutively to a sentence of 3½ years' imprisonment he was already serving also for drug trafficking. The Court of Appeal held that the total 8½-year term was excessive and had the judge properly applied the totality principle the total custodial sentence should have been 7 years. The principle was applicable because the offence for which he was being sentenced related to the previous charges which concerned drug trafficking in the same premises and were closely related in time. The Court looked to see what the appropriate sentence would have been had all the charges been dealt with at the same time.

Parity of sentencing

Another important principle of sentencing requires parity of sentencing between offenders. In theory, this principle requires that two offenders with similar backgrounds committing the same offence receive the same sentence. In practice, this position is rarely seen since the circumstances in any two given cases invariably differ in some respect. Nevertheless, the principle, like the principle of *stare decisis*, still holds to ensure that like cases are decided alike and any material differences in two similar cases are reflected in the difference between the two sentences.

The sentencing of co-accused in the same case will usually put this principle to test. Two co-accused whose degree of involvement in the crime is the same and whose backgrounds are similar should in principle receive the same sentence. But if different sentences were accorded to the co-accused they must be justified according to the gravity of their role in the offence and/or their backgrounds, particularly in terms of their criminal record.

Aggravating and mitigating factors

It is a basic principle that the presence of aggravating factors will tend to make the sentence more severe, while mitigating factors will lighten the sentence. From time to time, appellate courts in Hong Kong will provide guidelines on sentencing for a given offence having certain factual characteristics. For example, in *Secretary for Justice v Ho Mei Wa* [2004] 3 HKLRD 270 (CA), the Court set a new starting point sentence of 3 months' imprisonment in cases where an employer knowingly or recklessly employed an employee who was not lawfully employable. This sentence applied where there was casual employment and no aggravating factors. The case was important because previous appellate authority had set the starting point at 15 months' imprisonment but magistrates had for many years not followed this guideline.

Aggravating factors are those which highlight the seriousness of the offence and the criminal record of the offender. Circumstances such as the planning and premeditation of the offender, a breach of trust owed to the victim, and the degree of violence involved are some aggravating factors pertaining to the offence. Mitigating factors are generally factors concerning the background of the offender, the remorse of the offender, and consequential hardship of the sentence on the offender. In 2001–2, there was a lively debate on whether the fact the offender was a foreigner could constitute a mitigating factor given the hardship of serving the sentence in an alien jail in Hong Kong. Despite one appellate judgement showing sympathy for this position, the prevailing position was that for serious offences, particularly drug trafficking, the element of foreignness will carry little if any weight: see *HKSAR v Rohrer* [2001] 3 HKC 371 (CA) and *HKSAR v Hong Chang-chi* [2002] 1 HKC 295 (CA) which are discussed by Young (2001).

No retrospective punishment

It is a constitutional principle that an offender shall not be sentenced retrospectively to a heavier penalty than the one that was applicable when the offence was committed: Article 12(1) of the *Hong Kong Bill of Rights*. For example, if at the time the offence was committed, the maximum sentence for the offence was 10 years' imprisonment and by the time the offender was sentenced the maximum had been increased by the legislature to 14 years, it would offend the principle if the judge imposed a jail sentence of 12 years under the new law. The principle does not apply in respect of a lighter penalty applied retrospectively: Article 12(1) of the *Hong Kong Bill of Rights*. If, in the same example, the law was changed by lowering the maximum sentence to 5 years' imprisonment, at the time of sentencing the offender would be entitled to benefit from this change in the law as it could result in a lighter penalty. This principle of benefiting from a change in the law that results in a lighter penalty applies even if the change is by way of a reformulated offence with a lower maximum sentence: *R v Chan-Chi Hung* [2005] 2 HKCLR 50 (PC). In *Seabrook v HKSAR* [1999] 2 HKCFAR 184, the court held that the principle also applied to judge-made changes in the law so that an accused could benefit from a change which lowered the guideline sentences for a particular offence.

Separation of powers between the executive and judiciary

In *Yau Kwong Man & Another v Secretary for Security* [2002] 3 HKC 457 (CFI), Mr Justice Hartmann found that the old scheme whereby the Chief Executive would fix the minimum term of imprisonment for a young person convicted of murder was unconstitutional as it infringed the principle of separation of powers. The scheme infringed the *Basic Law* as it conferred what amounted to a judicial power on the Executive and according to the judge this was not permitted under our constitution. However, it is clear that under the *Basic Law*, the administration of a sentence and the granting of a pardon or commutation of penalties are matters within the authority of the Executive (see Articles 48(12) and 62(2) of the *Basic Law*).

Rehabilitation of juvenile offenders

In Hong Kong the current minimum age of criminal responsibility is 10 years: section 3 of the *Juvenile Offenders Ordinance* (Cap. 226). In the *Juvenile Offenders Ordinance*, a child is defined as a person under the age of 14 years and a young person is defined as a person 14 years of age or upwards and under the age of 16 years. There is a general principle that in the sentencing of children and young persons, rehabilitation above all other purposes of sentencing should be emphasized, see *HKSAR v Law Ka Kit & Others* [2003] 2 HKC 178 (CA). There are at least two reasons for this.

First, young offenders who commit the same crime as an adult will generally do so with a lower degree of moral culpability since their mental faculties have not been fully formed. Secondly, and perhaps more importantly, even if the young offender acts with full moral culpability the principle reflects the policy that one's misdeeds in childhood should not haunt one's future as an adult and thus there should be a clean break as one makes the transition from being a young person to an adult. For these reasons a sentence that emphasises rehabilitation will generally be a more lenient sentence, attentive to the needs and problems of the individual young person. The juvenile offender is to be 'accorded treatment appropriate to their age and legal status': Article 6(3) of the *Hong Kong Bill of Rights*. But if the principle could result in an excessive deprivation of liberty, the principle of proportionality will step in to limit the rehabilitative measures, as was seen in *Wong Chun Cheong*'s case.

In giving effect to this principle, legislation prohibits imprisoning children in default of payment of fines, damages, or costs: section 11(1) of *the Juvenile Offenders Ordinance*. No young person is to be sentenced to imprisonment if he can be suitably dealt with in any other way: section 11(2) of the Ordinance. For persons 16 years or over and under 21 years of age, the court must not sentence the person to imprisonment unless it is of the opinion that no other method of dealing with the person is appropriate: section 109A(1) of the *Criminal Procedure Ordinance*. Thus, imprisonment is a last resort. This rule, however, does not apply to a list of serious offences including murder, manslaughter, rape, serious drug offences, and so on: see Schedule 3 of the *Criminal Procedure Ordinance*. A person who was under the age of 18 years when he committed murder may be sentenced to imprisonment for life or a lesser period at the discretion of the court: section 2 of the *Offences Against the Person Ordinance* (Cap. 212).

A related principle is the one found in the *Hong Kong Bill of Rights* and elsewhere that juvenile accused and offenders shall be segregated from adults: Article 6(3) of the *Hong Kong Bill of Rights*; sections 6 and 11(3) of the *Juvenile Offenders Ordinance*.

Conclusion

It must always be remembered that the purposes and principles of sentencing operate in the real world of criminal proceedings. Thus efficiency and judicial economy are also important considerations that can affect the sentence and punishment of an offender. These considerations are the basis for the rule which reduces an offender's sentence up to as much as one-third from the starting point if he pleads guilty without going to trial. Similarly, another rule exists to disallow the offender from counting the time which he spends in jail pending the determination of his application for leave to appeal as part of his sentence if the application was totally without merit: *HKSAR v Hau Kin & Others* [2005] 8 HKCFAR 63. But however important these considerations may be, the constitutional safeguards in Hong Kong ensure that the offender's dignity and liberty interest will be of paramount importance in the law of sentencing.

Note

1 Please refer to Chapter 11 of this volume for a fuller discussion of the custodial sentences for offenders in Hong Kong.

Review questions

1 Why is it said that the purposes of sentencing are often in conflict?
2 What are the constitutional principles of sentencing that exist in Hong Kong?
3 What sentencing purpose was emphasized in Yip Kai Foon's case?
4 Why should juvenile offenders be sentenced differently from adult offenders?
5 Is remorse an aggravating or mitigating factor on sentence? Why?

References

Cross, I.G. and Cheung, P.W.S. (1994) *Sentencing in Hong Kong*. Hong Kong: Butterworths Asia.
Cross, I.G. and Cheung, P.W.S. (2003) *Sentencing in Hong Kong* (4th edn). Hong Kong: LexisNexis Butterworths.
Easton, S. and Piper, C. (2005) *Sentencing and Punishment: The Quest for Justice*. Oxford: Oxford University Press.

Law Reform Commission of Hong Kong (1983) *Report – Community Service Orders (Topic 7)*. Hong Kong: Law Reform Commission of Hong Kong.
Liu, A. (1992) 'The right to life', in R. Wacks (ed.) *Human Rights in Hong Kong* (pp. 264–300). Hong Kong: Oxford University Press.
von Hirsch, A. (1993) *Censure and Sanctions*. Oxford: Clarendon Press.
Young, S.N.M. (2001) 'Justifying sentencing discounts for foreigners', *Hong Kong Law Journal*, 31 (3): 369–79.

Legislation cited

The Basic Law of the Hong Kong Special Administrative Region
Community Service Orders Ordinance (Cap. 378)
Criminal Procedure Ordinance (Cap. 221)
Drug Trafficking (Recovery of Proceeds) Ordinance (Cap. 405)
Hong Kong Bill of Rights
Hong Kong Bill of Rights Ordinance (Cap. 383)
International Covenant on Civil and Political Rights
Juvenile Offenders Ordinance (Cap. 226)
Long-term Prison Sentences Review Ordinance (Cap. 524)
Magistrates Ordinance (Cap. 227)
Mental Health Ordinance (Cap. 136)
Offences Against the Person Ordinance (Cap. 212)
Organized and Serious Crimes Ordinance (Cap. 455)
Probation of Offenders Ordinance (Cap. 298)

Cases cited

HKSAR v Chan Pui Chi [1998] 2 HKLRD 830 (CA)
HKSAR v Chung Yiu Ming [2003] 3 HKLRD K14 (CA)
HKSAR v Hau Kin & Others [2005] 8 HKCFAR 63
HKSAR v Hong Chang-chi [2002] 1 HKC 295 (CA)
HKSAR v Lau Cheong & Another [2002] 5 HKCFAR 415
HKSAR v Lau Wai Wo [2003] 6 HKCFAR 624
HKSAR v Law Ka Kit & Others [2003] 2 HKC 178 (CA)
HKSAR v Ma Suet Chun & Others [2001] 4 HKC 337
HKSAR v Rohrer [2001] 3 HKC 371 (CA)
HKSAR v Wong Chun Cheong [2001] 4 HKCFAR 12
HKSAR v Yip Kai Foon [2000] 3 HKCFAR 31
R v Chan-Chi Hung [2005] 2 HKCLR 50 (PC)
R v Chu Man Chiu, Cr App 198/1991 (CA)
R v Isherwood [1974] 59 Cr App R 162 (CA)
R v M(CA) [1996] 1 SCR 500
R v Sargeant [1974] 60 Cr App R 74 (Eng CA)

R v Tarry [1970] 2 QB 560 (CA)
Seabrook v HKSAR [1999] 2 HKCFAR 184
Secretary for Justice v Ho Mei Wa [2004] 3 HKLRD 270 (CA)
Secretary for Justice v Tse Sheung Kai & Others [2001] 3 HKLRD 487 (CA)
White v Brown [2003] 175 FLR 325
Yau Kwong Man & Another v Secretary for Security [2002] 3 HKC 457 (CFI)

Useful websites

The Basic Law of the Hong Kong Special Administrative Region	http://www.info.gov.hk/basic_law/flash.html
Department of Justice	http://www.doj.gov.hk/
Restorative Justice Online	http://www.restorativejustice.org/
Sentencing Law and Policy, Law Professors Blog Network	http://sentencing.typepad.com/sentencing_law_and_policy/

Chapter 9

Criminal appeal courts

Tony Upham

Introduction

This chapter examines Hong Kong's criminal appeal courts and how final decisions of trial courts can be challenged. As a generalization defendants can appeal conviction and/or sentence, but the prosecution cannot appeal an acquittal. Where, however, a defendant is acquitted in the District Court (DC) or in the Magistrates' Court (MC), the prosecution can challenge the legal correctness of that acquittal by case stated. The decision of the lower court is brought up to, and examined by, a higher court. If the acquittal is on an error of law as opposed to factual merits, the acquittal may be overturned. An acquittal by a jury cannot however be challenged: jury verdicts are sacrosanct.

Sentencing is for the court and not for the prosecution (see Chapter 8 of this volume). However, where the prosecution considers the sentence imposed by a trial court was wrong in principle or was manifestly excessive or manifestly inadequate, it may apply to the Court of Appeal (CA) to review that sentence. This can result in an increased sentence.

The Court of Final Appeal (CFA), as the name implies, is the highest court of appeal in Hong Kong. It is a new court and is much more than simply another level of appeal. A unique feature of the court is the presence of judges from other common law jurisdictions. There is therefore substantial input from other common law jurisdictions, which enriches and vitalizes Hong Kong's legal system.

The Court of Appeal

The CA takes its powers from the *High Court Ordinance* (Cap. 4) (HCO). In its criminal jurisdiction the CA, or to use its full title, the CA of the High Court (HC), hears appeals from the DC and from the Court of First Instance (CFI). It can also hear an appeal from the decision of a magistrate if that appeal is remitted to the CA from the CFI. There is also jurisdiction to review sentences imposed by a trial court: section 81A of the *Criminal Procedure Ordinance* (Cap. 221) (CPO). The court consists of the Chief Judge of the HC and such Justices of Appeal as the Chief Executive may appoint: section 5 of the HCO. A CFI judge may sit as an additional judge of the CA. The Court is divided into three Divisions, each presided over by a Vice-President.

Eligibility to sit in the CA is dependent on professional qualification to practise as a barrister or advocate in a court in Hong Kong or any other common law jurisdiction having unlimited jurisdiction either in civil or criminal matters. There must also be at least 10 years' practice as a barrister, solicitor, or advocate in such a court. A number of public appointments will also satisfy the 10 years' practice requirement, as set out in section 9 of the HCO.

Appeals against conviction and/or sentence

Appeals to the CA may be against conviction and/or against sentence. As already discussed in Chapter 7 of this volume, the prosecution can challenge an acquittal in the DC by the case stated procedure. Unlike the magistrate, a DC judge does not have a power of review. Challenges to decisions of DC judges must therefore be by appeal to the CA. Appeals to the CA, whether from the DC or the CFI, are governed by sections 80 to 83Y inclusive of the CPO and by the *Criminal Appeal Rules* (Cap. 221A). The Schedule to the *Criminal Appeal Rules* contains the Notices to be used in appeals to the CA. Practice Direction 4.2 titled *Criminal Appeals to the Court of Appeal* must also be complied with (Chief Justice 1998).

Whether the appeal is from the DC or from the CFI, leave to appeal must be obtained from the CA unless the appeal is on a question of law only. What is a question of law is not always an easy decision. If the appeal involves reference to or examination of any of the facts alleged at trial, the appeal is not solely on a question of law but on a question of mixed law and fact. A question of law would relate to such issues as jurisdiction and interpretation of an ordinance. Most appeals will involve questions of mixed law and fact and leave of the CA will be needed. Where, however, the trial judge grants a certificate that the case is fit for appeal on a ground which involves a question of fact, or a question of mixed law and fact, an appeal lies without leave of the CA: section 82 of the CPO.

An appeal against conviction can only be allowed where the CA thinks that the conviction should be set aside either because it is unsafe or unsatisfactory, there was a wrong decision on a question of law, or there was a material irregularity in the course of the trial. Unless one of those reasons is established, the appeal must be dismissed: section 83(1) of the CPO. Even where the court is of the opinion that the point raised in the appeal might be decided in favour of the appellant, the appeal may still be dismissed if it is considered that no miscarriage of justice has actually occurred. This is what is known as 'applying the proviso' and is designed to prevent a perfectly good conviction being quashed where a mistake has been made which cannot and did not affect the overall correctness of the conviction. The court has to consider whether, had the error not been made, the jury would have convicted in any event.

In deciding whether a conviction is unsafe and unsatisfactory, the CA examines what happened at the trial. This does not mean the CA tries the case again, but looking back on the trial it considers whether there is 'A not insubstantial doubt but a substantial remaining doubt' about the correctness of the conviction (see *R v Copper* [1969] 1 QB 267). The court must bear in mind it has not seen the witnesses at trial but nonetheless where the transcript of the evidence shows serious and unresolved inconsistencies between the witnesses there may well be a substantial doubt about the correctness of the conviction and the appeal will be allowed (see *R v Kwong Kin Hung* [1995] HKCA 25).

Where the appeal is based on a wrong decision on any question of law, the CA considers whether there was the wrongful admission or exclusion of evidence and/or whether the jury was misdirected. In an appeal based on a material irregularity in the course of the trial the CA will consider, for example, whether there were constant interruptions by the trial judge and the effect of those interruptions on the appellant's case, whether there was improper behaviour by a juror, whether the trial judge failed to respond correctly to that behaviour, whether the jury were incorrectly informed of the appellant's previous convictions, and the effect of such errors.

The prosecution cannot appeal an acquittal by a jury even if the acquittal was against the weight of the evidence or was caused by some impropriety. There is therefore nothing akin to the appeal by case stated procedure in the Magistrates' Court or the DC for the CFI. Even if the acquittal by the jury is seen as perverse or tainted, there is at present no provision in Hong Kong to set aside that acquittal and order a new trial. The verdict of the jury is sacrosanct. Where there has been impropriety leading to an acquittal, criminal charges such as perverting the course of public justice or perjury may be brought against those responsible but the acquittal stands.

Appeal against conviction after a guilty plea

Though most appeals against conviction will follow conviction after trial, it is possible to appeal conviction even though a guilty plea was entered. It might be, for example, that the only issue for decision in the DC or in the CFI was whether the facts amount to an offence in law. Argument would be heard in the trial court on that and there would then be a ruling by the judge. If the ruling was that the facts did amount to an offence in law, the accused would then enter a guilty plea. That would preserve the entitlement to a one-third discount from the sentence that would have been imposed upon conviction after trial and at the same time leave the door open for an appeal to the CA that the ruling of the trial judge was wrong in law. The same principle applies in the MC and allows for an appeal to the CFI (see Chapter 7 of this volume).

There can also be an appeal against conviction where the guilty plea in the trial court was not voluntary. To be a valid guilty plea, the plea must be the expression of the defendant's free will. Both understanding and appreciation of the alleged criminality is required before there can be an expression of free will. If there was a lack of understanding or if the guilty plea was brought about by improper pressure or subterfuge by a third party, the guilty plea is not given voluntarily. There are obvious difficulties about appealing conviction where it is alleged the guilty plea was not voluntary but it can be done.

Bail pending appeal

The procedures to be followed on an appeal against conviction mean that there will be quite some time between conviction and the appeal being heard. Inevitably therefore the question of bail pending appeal arises. Under section 83R of the CPO, the CA can admit an appellant to bail pending appeal. In deciding whether to do so, section 83Z of the Ordinance requires the court to consider all relevant circumstances and, in particular, the likelihood of the sentence being completed before the disposal of the appeal or of the appeal being allowed. The longer the sentence the less likely it will be that the sentence will have been completed before the appeal is heard. In that event the appellant must show there is a reasonable prospect of the appeal succeeding, for example that there was a substantial misdirection of the jury which could result in the conviction being quashed. The issue is whether there are 'exceptional circumstances, which would drive the Court to the conclusion that justice can only be done by the granting of bail?' (see *R v Watton* 68 Cr. App. R. 293, 297, CA).

Making the appeal

A convicted person who wishes to appeal conviction or sentence may apply to the CA for leave to appeal within 28 days from the date of the conviction or sentence. If the application is not made within that time, leave may be granted out of time. What will or will not be a good reason for granting leave out of time will depend on the particular case.

It is the responsibility of trial counsel to see the accused after conviction and give preliminary advice about an appeal against conviction and/or sentence. This is a professional duty. If counsel considers there are reasonable grounds for appeal, counsel will formulate what are termed 'initial grounds' of appeal. A reasonable ground of appeal is one that has a real chance of succeeding. At this stage counsel will not have the benefit of any transcript of evidence or of the judge's summing up to the jury and will be relying upon their own notes and the notes made by the instructing solicitor during the trial.

Once counsel has formulated the initial grounds of appeal, a notice of application for leave to appeal is lodged with the registrar of the HC. The Clerk of Appeals will then obtain the 'appeal bundle' from the judge's clerk. In the CFI the appeal bundle will contain the indictment, a transcript of the summing up, the shorthand note of the verdict, the criminal record, if any, and where the appeal is against sentence the transcript of sentence and copies of any pre-sentence reports. The appeal bundle is sent to the person seeking leave (the applicant) or the applicant's solicitors. If legal aid has been applied for a copy of the appeal bundle is sent to the Director of Legal Aid. A copy is also sent to the Secretary for Justice and to a Justice of Appeal for directions. If any additional papers are considered necessary, for example a transcript of the evidence or parts of the evidence, an application for those items can be made to the registrar. The application will be referred to the Directions Judge. Once any necessary additional papers are received, counsel can settle the Perfected Grounds of Appeal. The Perfected Grounds of Appeal should bring together all the grounds of appeal in one document and refer to any authorities relied upon. This document becomes the grounds of appeal to be argued at the hearing of the application for leave.

The application for leave to appeal is heard by a single judge. If leave to appeal is granted, a date will be fixed for the hearing of the appeal. Appeals against both conviction and sentence are heard by a three-judge court. Appeals against sentence are heard by a two-judge court. If the single judge refuses leave to appeal, the applicant can renew the application to the CA when the application will be considered by three judges.

The appellant will be present on the hearing of the appeal. On that hearing, the CA can allow or dismiss the appeal. Where on an appeal against conviction the appellant has been convicted of an offence and the jury could on the indictment have found him or her guilty of some other offence, and it appears that the jury must have been satisfied of facts which proved guilt of the other offence, the court may substitute a verdict of guilty on that other offence and impose a sentence that the lower court could have imposed: section 83A of the CPO.

On the hearing of an appeal against sentence, the CA can quash any sentence or order which is the subject of the appeal and replace it with such sentence as it considers appropriate, whether that sentence is more or less severe than the sentence under appeal. It is important to appreciate that an appeal against sentence reopens the whole issue of sentencing. A warning to that effect now appears on prescribed forms for appeals against sentence in the Schedule to the Criminal Appeal Rules: section 83I of the CPO.

On both appeals against conviction and appeals against sentence the judges will be much more involved than a judge at a trial. They will be aware of the issues and arguments from the Perfected Grounds of Appeal and accordingly their approach will be more inquisitorial. An appeal often becomes a series of exchanges between one or more of the judges and the appellant's counsel. Decisions on appeal against conviction are by a majority. If all three judges are agreed, usually one judge will give the judgement of the court. If there is a disagreement there will be a dissenting judgement.

New evidence on appeal

Though appeals against conviction are an examination of the correctness of events at the trial, the CA can receive new evidence on the hearing of the appeal in accordance with section 83V of the CPO if it thinks it is necessary or expedient in the interests of justice to do so. The court must be satisfied that the evidence is credible, would have been admissible at the trial, and that there is a reasonable explanation why that evidence was not called at the trial. This is a substantial hurdle and is designed to avoid evidence being held back from the trial for tactical reasons and then brought into the appeal. There is also concern to avoid evidence that may have been manufactured either in anticipation of an appeal or to support an appeal. The court will therefore scrutinize the proposed new evidence, the circumstances leading to the request to introduce it in the appeal, and the reasons why it was not available at the original trial. If the evidence does not present as credible it will not be allowed into the appeal (see *R v Ch'ng Poh* [1996] HKCA 17).

Orders for retrial

The quashing of a conviction by the CA does not necessarily put an end to the case. Referring to section 83E of the CPO, where the CA considers that the interests of justice so require, it may order the appellant to be retried. The appellant can only be retried on the offence in respect of which the appeal was allowed, or an offence on which there could have been a conviction at the original trial on that indictment or an offence which was shown on the original indictment as an alternative and in respect of which the jury was discharged from giving a verdict by reason of the conviction appealed against. This power is used where the CA considers that overall there is strong evidence of guilt but errors at the trial make the conviction unsafe and the errors are such that the proviso cannot be applied. No question of double jeopardy arises here as the original conviction is set aside. However, the prosecution on the retrial does have the advantage of the CA having pointed out the reasons why the first conviction was set aside. Where the conviction is quashed, the prosecution can also consider an appeal to the CFA.

Review of sentence by the prosecution

Traditionally the prosecution is not concerned with sentence but where the sentence, either in the Magistrates' Court, the DC, or in the CFI, was not authorized by law, was manifestly inadequate, or wrong in principle, the prosecution may seek to intervene in the public interest by applying to the CA to review the sentence under sections 81A, 81B, and 81C of the CPO.

Where the prosecution is seeking to challenge the sentence of a magistrate there could first be a request to the magistrate to hold a review under section 104 of the *Magistrates Ordinance* (Cap. 227) (MO). If the magistrate refused to review the sentence, the prosecution could then apply to the CA to hold a review of sentence. As there are no such review provisions in the DC or in the CFI, an application under the CPO is the only route available to the prosecution.

The application to the CA must be in writing, accompanied by a record of the case, and be filed with the registrar within 21 days of the sentence in respect of which the review is sought. On the hearing of a review of sentence the CA may, if it finds that it was not authorized by law, was wrong in principle, or manifestly inadequate, quash that sentence and substitute such other sentence (whether more or less severe) as it considers ought to have been passed.

The CA reviews the sentence imposed in the light of the information before the lower court at the time the sentence was imposed. No new material can be put before the CA as this would make the procedure an appeal against sentence rather than a review of the correctness of the sentence imposed.

Three cases, *AG v Dil Bahadur Guring* [1994] 2 HKC 476; *AG v Li Ah-sang* Application for Review No. 10 of 1995 [1995] 2 HKCLR 239, and *Secretary for Justice v Tse Sheung Kai & Others* CAAR000003/21, (CAAR 2/2001, CAAR 3/2001, CAAR 4/2001, CAAR 5/2001, CAAR 6/2001), adequately show how the review of sentence provision operates. *Tse*'s case is particularly informative as it shows how an application for a review under section 104 of the MO can precede an application for a review of sentence to the CA. *Tse*'s case also illustrates the control the Secretary of Justice has over whether or not to bring a prosecution in the particular case.

Referrals and references

The common law system does not provide for the courts to answer hypothetical questions. The criminal courts decide whether conduct giving rise to the particular prosecution is, or not, an offence by looking at the events that have occurred. However, where an issue of law arises on the trial of any indictment, the trial judge may refer that question of law to the CA for its consideration under section

81 of the CPO. This power should be used sparingly. As stated in Judge's Reservation (No. 1) of 1994 HKCA 171:

> in our view resort should only be made to section 81 in the most exceptional cases. It is the duty of a judge to ensure that the trial over which he presides proceeds to conclusion with a minimum of disruption. To that end it is his duty to resolve issues of law, be they simple or difficult, as they arise in the course of a trial. It hardly needs stating that reference of any but the most exceptional points of law to the Court of Appeal would inevitably seriously disrupt the orderly disposal of other appeals that have already been listed for hearing and, where the trial is before a jury, result in inconvenience to jurors. We do not think that it was the intention of the legislature that other than in wholly exceptional cases the continuity of trials should be interrupted by references under section 81. (Per Macdougal, V.P.)

The CA can then give an opinion on that issue of law if it is appropriate to do so. There will be few occasions when references will be made under section 81. Nevertheless the power is there.

While the CA has no power to answer hypothetical questions, section 81D of the CPO enables the Secretary for Justice to ask for an opinion on a question of law which arose in a case where a person tried on indictment has been acquitted. This procedure enables the court to give an authoritative answer on the question referred to it so that the question is resolved for the future without affecting the decision in the case giving rise to the question of law.

The Court of Final Appeal

Prior to 1 July 1997, the highest court of appeal for Hong Kong was the Judicial Committee of the Privy Council. The Hong Kong CFA replaced the Privy Council on 1 July 1997. It takes its powers from the *Hong Kong Court of Final Appeal Ordinance* (Cap. 484) (HKCFAO). As with the CA, the CFA only has appellate jurisdiction.

The court is presided over by the Chief Justice and consists of the Chief Justice and not less than three Permanent Judges. A unique feature of the court is the provision for Non-Permanent Judges: sections 5(2) and 5(3) of the HKCFAO. Five judges sit to hear an appeal. When hearing appeals the court normally consists of the Chief Justice, three Permanent Judges and either one Non-Permanent Hong

Kong Judge or one judge from another common law jurisdiction: section 16 of the HKCFAO.

To be eligible for appointment as Chief Justice a person must be a Permanent Judge of the court, the Chief Judge of the HC, a Justice of Appeal or a judge of the CFI, or a barrister with at least 10 years' practice in Hong Kong. A person who has been Chief Judge of the HC, a Justice of Appeal or a judge of the CFI, or a barrister with at least 10 years' practice in Hong Kong is eligible for appointment as a permanent judge. Retired Chief Judges, retired Chief Justices, retired Permanent Judges, Justices of Appeal or retired Justices of Appeal, and barristers with at least 10 years' practice in Hong Kong may be appointed as a Non-Permanent Judge.

Persons eligible to be appointed as a judge from another common law jurisdiction are judges or retired judges of a court of unlimited jurisdiction in either civil or criminal matters in another common law jurisdiction who are ordinarily resident outside of Hong Kong and who have never been a member of the Judiciary of Hong Kong: section 12 of the HKCFAO.

In the exercise of its criminal jurisdiction the CFA hears appeals from the CA and from any final decision of the CFI from which no appeal lies to the CA. This means decisions of a judge on an appeal from a magistrate. On the hearing of such an appeal, the court may confirm, reverse, or vary the decision of the court below, or remit the matter to that court with its opinion. In disposing of an appeal, the court may exercise all the powers of the court from which the appeal came: section 17 of the HKCFAO. Either the prosecution or the defence may appeal.

The CFA is not simply a second level of appeal. In the exercise of its criminal jurisdiction it deals with points of law of great and general importance and issues of 'substantial and grave injustice' arising from the decision in the court below.

Appealing to the Court of Final Appeal

The procedure for appeals is governed both by the court's ordinance and by the *Hong Kong Court of Final Appeal Rules* (Cap. 484A). Leave is needed for an appeal to the CFA. That leave must be from the CFA. Leave shall not be granted unless the CA or the CFI (on an appeal from a magistrate) certifies that a point of law of great and general importance is involved in the decision or it is shown that substantial and grave injustice has been done. If the CA or the CFI declines to make that certification, an application for such a certificate may be made to the CFA. In that event, the CFA could make the certification and grant leave to appeal: section 32 of the HKCFAO.

According to section 33 of the HKCFAO, an application for leave to appeal must be made within 28 days from the date of the decision in respect of which leave is sought though this time limit may be extended by the court. Section 46 states that applications for extension will be dealt with by a single permanent judge. Applications for leave to appeal must set out the facts and relevant matters relied upon in support of the application for leave. The application is heard by the Appeal Committee, which consists of the Chief Justice and two Permanent Judges, or three Permanent Judges nominated by the Chief Justice. The decision of the Appeal Committee is final. If leave to appeal is given, the notice of appeal is filed. There are detailed provisions in the Appeal Rules as to the procedure to be followed between the grant of leave and the hearing of the appeal.

Five judges will sit to hear the appeal. These will be the Chief Justice (or a Permanent Judge sitting as Acting Chief Justice), three Permanent Judges and either one Non-Permanent Hong Kong Judge or one judge from another common law jurisdiction: section 16 of the HKCFAO. The judgement or order of the majority is the judgement or order of the court. If the court is unanimous one judgement may be given with which the other judges agree. The court may confirm, reverse, or vary the decision of the court from which the appeal lies or may remit the matter with its opinion thereon to that court, or may make such other order, including any order as to costs, as it thinks fit. In disposing of an appeal the court may exercise any of the powers of the court from which the appeal came.

Bail pending appeal

Bail pending appeal to the court is addressed by section 34 of the HKCFAO. The section provides that the court, the CA, or the CFI may grant bail to a person appealing or applying for leave to appeal. Conditions may be imposed upon that bail. Bail cannot be considered until the appeal process has been commenced. There must be either a notice of appeal or an application for leave to appeal. As an application for leave to appeal must be lodged with the CFA, an application for bail may be made to the court. That can be dealt with by a single Permanent Judge: section 46C of the HKCFAO. The single judge, as with an application for bail pending appeal against conviction from a magistrate, a DC, or a judge of the CFI, must consider whether there is a reasonable prospect of obtaining leave to appeal.

The role of the court

Relatively few appeals will reach the CFA. The references to 'a point of law of great and general importance' and to 'substantial and grave injustice' being involved in the decision under appeal in criminal cases in section 32(2) of the HKCFAO emphasize that the court is not simply a second level of appeal. A high threshold must be met before a criminal appeal gets to the court. As stated by Bokhary PJ in *So Yiu Fung v HKSAR* [1999] 2 HKCFAR 539; [2000] 1 HKLRD 179 at para. 7 of the judgement:

> This Court's primary role in the administration of criminal justice is to resolve real controversy on points of law of great and public importance. For this Court does not function as a court of criminal appeal in an ordinary way. However the 'substantial and grave injustice limb' of s. 32(2) exists as a residual safeguard to cater for those rare and exceptional cases in which there is a real danger of something so seriously wrong that justice demands an enquiry by way of a final criminal appeal despite the absence of any real controversy on any point of law of great and general importance.

Conclusion

This chapter has outlined the role and responsibilities of Hong Kong's criminal appeal courts. The reader should now have an appreciation of how those courts operate and how decisions by trial courts can be challenged. Unfortunately things do go wrong in the trial courts for a variety of reasons and appeal courts provide an essential safeguard both for defendants and for the system as a whole. Logically after conviction, the onus is upon the appellant to show a good reason why the conviction should be quashed. An appeal against conviction may therefore be described as an uphill task for the defendant, though if there is an obvious error during the trial which strikes at the fundamental correctness of the conviction, the prosecution should not oppose the appeal. Prosecutors are officers of the court and must serve the overall public interest of ensuring that only those who are guilty are convicted.

As would be expected, there are more opportunities for a defendant to challenge the decision of the trial court than there are for the prosecution to challenge the decision. The prosecution can only challenge an acquittal where it is founded upon an error of law by the trial judge. It follows therefore that only decisions by a DC judge or a magistrate can be challenged in this way. In a jury trial in the CFI the decision to acquit is the decision of the jury. The jury is solely responsible for facts. Even where an acquittal is considered unmeritorious, perverse, or contaminated, the acquittal stands. Inroads have been made into this principle, for example in England and Wales, but in Hong Kong the acquittal stands, though criminal charges may be brought against those responsible for, or contributory to, a contaminated acquittal.

An appeal against conviction is not a rehearing of the witnesses who gave evidence at the trial but an examination of the correctness of the conviction both in fact and in law in the context of the evidence given at trial. Most often the appeal is based on an allegation of an error by the trial judge. On appeals from the CFI, attention will generally be concentrated on the way in which the trial judge summed up to the jury.

In an attempt to avoid the time and expense of unmeritorious appeals, appeals to the CA from the CFI and the DC require leave unless the appeal is solely on a point of law. Requiring leave to appeal is an attempt to ensure that only those appeals with a real prospect of success actually get to an appeal hearing. The intention is that meritorious appeals are not kept waiting because the CA is overwhelmed with unmeritorious appeals.

The same screening applies for the CFA. That is again necessary if the CFA is to fulfil its role of resolving real controversy on points of law of great and public importance and being a residual safeguard where something has gone so seriously wrong in the lower court or courts that justice demands the court's intervention. A court which is overburdened with unmeritorious appeals will not be able to attend to the matters it should attend to and this would have adverse consequences for the criminal justice system as a whole.

Review questions

1 D was tried in the District Court. The prosecution case substantially depended upon confession statements made by D. The confession statements were ruled inadmissible. Taking the view that the remaining evidence would not be sufficient to obtain a conviction, the prosecutor offered no further evidence and D was acquitted. The prosecution considers the District Court judge's ruling on the admissibility of the

confession statements was erroneous and that D was wrongly acquitted. Is there any action the prosecution can take? If so, what is it and what procedure is involved?

2 D pleaded guilty before a magistrate to one charge of theft from a shop. She was fined $4,000. D now tells you that she had been taking medication which made her forgetful and she had not intended to steal from the shop. She also says that the police officer in charge of the case told her that if she pleaded guilty 'nothing will happen to you'. D wants to know whether she can appeal her conviction.
3 You are a District Court judge. Six weeks ago you convicted an unrepresented defendant of theft and sentenced him to 2 years' imprisonment. Yesterday you happened to read a law report which makes you doubt the correctness of your conviction. What could/should you do?
4 D was acquitted of murder after a trial before a judge and a jury in the Court of First Instance. The prosecution considers the jury was wrong to acquit. Is there anything the prosecution can do?
5 D was convicted of murder after a trial before a judge and a 7-member jury in the Court of First Instance. The conviction was by a majority verdict of 6 to 1. D intends to appeal conviction and wants to obtain a statement from the minority juror about his reasons for preferring an acquittal. How would you advise D?
6 What is the role and purpose of the Court of Final Appeal?
7 Why does the Court of Final Appeal have judges from outside Hong Kong on the court?

References

Chief Justice (1998) *Practice Direction 4.2 – Criminal Appeals to the Court of Appeal*. Hong Kong: The Judiciary. Available at: http://legalref.judiciary.gov.hk/lrs/common/pd/pdcontent.jsp?pdn=PD4.2.htm&lang=EN

Legislation cited

Criminal Appeal Rules (Cap. 221A)
Criminal Procedure Ordinance (Cap. 221)
High Court Ordinance (Cap. 4)
Hong Kong Court of Final Appeal Ordinance (Cap. 484)
Hong Kong Court of Final Appeal Rules (Cap. 484A)
Magistrates Ordinance (Cap. 227)

Cases cited

AG v Dil Bahadur Guring [1994] 2 HKC 476
AG v Li Ah-sang Application for Review No. 10 of 1995 [1995] 2 HKCLR 239
R v Ch'ng Poh [1996] HKCA 17
R v Copper [1969] 1 QB 267
R v Kwong Kin Hung [1995] HKCA 25
R v Watton 68 Cr. App. R. 293, 297, CA
Secretary for Justice v Tse Sheung Kai & Others CAAR000003/21, (CAAR 2/2001, CAAR 3/2001, CAAR 4/2001, CAAR 5/2001, CAAR 6/2001)
So Yiu Fung v HKSAR [1999] 2 HKCFAR 539; [2000] 1 HKLRD

Useful websites

Bar Association of Hong Kong	http://www.hkba.org
Bilingual Laws Information System (BLIS) (Hong Kong)	http://www.legislation.gov.hk/eng/index.htm
Department of Justice	http://www.doj.gov.hk
Law Society of Hong Kong	www.hklawsoc.org.hk
The Judiciary	http://www.judiciary.gov.hk

Chapter 10

Community sentences

Wing Hong Chui

Introduction

This chapter examines various issues surrounding the use of community sentences for juvenile and adult offenders. Issues such as the rationale for community sentences and the effectiveness of these sentences for offenders will be discussed. Broadly speaking, there are two main types of community sentence in Hong Kong, namely the probation order and community service order.[1] In contrast to other non-custodial sentences such as fines, disqualification, and compensation, these two specific community sentences involve both an element of active participation by the offender and close supervision or monitoring by a designated authority figure from the State. The intended goal of the community sentence is to 'help offenders reintegrate into the community as law-abiding citizens' through counselling, proper supervision, and social skills training (Director of Social Welfare 2007).

What is central to community sentences is the emphasis of social work approaches to rehabilitate offenders and encourage their pro-social behaviours. Registered social workers are employed to supervise all offenders on community sentences that are run by the Social Welfare Department (Chui 1999, 2002). While proponents of the criminal justice social work intervention for offenders firmly believe that 'a highly motivated individual can change into a productive and law-abiding citizen if he or she is given the right counselling (non-judgmental, empathetic, confrontative, reality-oriented, strengths-based, and cognitive-behavioural), as well as academic, vocational, and social education opportunities' (Brownell and Roberts 2002: 2; see also Barry 2000; Taylor 2001; Reynolds, Dziegielewski and Sharp 2004), others believe that the state should be tough on the convicted and that they should be deterred and incapacitated from further offending by imposing heavy penalties on them. For instance, in England and Wales, in order to give community sentences a new face, the probation order and community service order are now named the community rehabilitation order and community punishment order respectively (Nellis 2000). One major reason for renaming is largely driven by politics. The policy makers and politicians intended to convey to the public that these sentences are no longer 'soft' options and measures were taken to ensure community sentences were enforced (Raynor and Vanstone 2002; Worrall and Hoy 2005). Noted by Chui and Nellis (2003) is that probation training in England and Wales is no longer part of generic social work training and has become more criminologically focused since the early 2000s (see also Nellis 2003; Whitehead and Thompson 2004; Gregory 2007). In this respect, the paper will also speculate why the social work model of community sentences in Hong Kong has been able to preserve their social work identity, and discusses what should be done to improve the quality and effectiveness of these sentences.

This chapter consists of four main sections. The first section discusses the various justifications for community sentences such as diversion or deinstitutionalization, reintegration (or rehabilitation), and reparation. The second section describes the operation of community sentences, and relevant sections of the Ordinances will be cited to examine their operations. The third section examines the ingredients of effective intervention with offenders. In line with the 'What Works' movement, the chapter points to the importance of developing a more systematic and evidence-based criminal justice social work intervention for offenders.

The justifications for community sentences

Community sentences are formal control or penal measures to deal with certain selected offenders who are mostly first and second offenders. These offenders are not considered to pose any undue risk to the public for whom the increasing use of community sentences is appropriate. Community-based disposals are able to divert low-risk offenders from being incarcerated, help with their personal and social problems, and, most importantly, prevent them from causing further harm to the society. However, it appears that the community sentences do not have as high a profile within criminal justice as the police, law, and prisons in the media and research agenda (Chui 2002). Pollock (2004: 349) comments:

> Community corrections has a more positive and helpful image than does institutional corrections. However, even in this subsystem of the criminal justice system, the ideals of justice and care become diluted by bureaucratic mismanagement and personal agendas. Professionals in the community corrections do not have the same power as police or correctional officers to use physical force, but they do have a great deal of non-physical power over the clients they control.

While this chapter does not examine why community sentences have a low profile within the criminal justice system, it attempts to outline what community sentences can offer.

Diversion from custody

One justification for community sentences is diversion from custody, which is based on policy and practical consideration. It is unlikely to put all criminals in prison because of the huge costs involved, and some crimes are simply not serious enough to justify imprisonment. There are different kinds of diversion programmes available primarily for juvenile offenders in Hong Kong, and some examples are 'diversion from arrest' and 'diversion from prosecution' (Lo, Wong and Maxwell 2006). As argued by Klapmuts (1976), another type of diversion from the criminal justice system for adult offenders is 'associated with the movement away from the incarceration of offenders in penal institutions and their ostracism upon release, receiving impetus from the same pressures that account for the immense popularity of alternatives to incarceration and community-based treatment' (1976: 222). A specific example of the diversionary programme is the use of community sentences as an alternative to some shorter custodial sentences (Ashworth 2007). According to section 2(2) of the *Community Service Orders Ordinance* (Cap. 378), this order is suitable for those guilty of an offence to be treated as punishable with imprisonment.

With reference to section 109A of the *Criminal Procedure Ordinance* (Cap. 221), imprisonment is considered the last resort for young offenders between 18 and 21 years of age in both the Magistrates' Court and District Court:

> No court shall sentence a person of or over 16 and under 21 years of age to imprisonment unless the court is of opinion that no other method of dealing with such person is appropriate; and for the purpose of determining whether any other method of dealing with any such person is appropriate the court should obtain and consider information about the circumstances, and shall take into account any information before the court which is relevant to the character of such person and his physical and mental condition.

However, the above section shall not apply to a person who has been convicted of any of ten exempted offences in the Schedule 3 to the Ordinance, for example, manslaughter, rape or attempted rape, affray, any offence against section 4, 5, or 6 of the *Dangerous Drugs Ordinance* (Cap. 134), and any offence under section 4 or 10 of the *Weapons Ordinance* (Cap. 217).

Reintegration

One important role of penal sentences is to assist offenders in reintegrating into the community. Reintegration has a strong theoretical root in the rehabilitative theories of punishment (Gaines and Miller 2007). The rehabilitation model is based on the premise that an individual's offending is related to a wide range of personal and social factors such as personality problems, poor schooling, lack of parental supervision, and community disorganization, and the removal of these factors will bring about his or her positive changes. The model also places great emphasis on the treatment, welfare and therapy of the individual offender. The ultimate goal of community sentences is to strengthen the ties between an offender and the community, and to integrate the offender into community life by helping him or her to assume normal social roles. Supporters would see the probation and community service programmes being conducive to providing help with offenders to become law-abiding citizens. While the effect of incarceration on prisoners is primarily negative, the community correctional approaches are more reintegrative and have less stigmatization than imprisonment to encourage pro-social behaviour (Pollock 2004).

Reparation

Reparation or restoration is another justification for the use of community sentences as opposed to custodial sentences. Community service orders can provide general reparation to the community, whereas probation sentences and custody cannot. The community is a symbolic victim in need of reparation (McDonald 1986). On the one hand, the activities carried out during a community service order should deliberately be unpleasant in the expectation that this will deter the offender (that is, specific deterrence) and other potential offenders (that is, general deterrence). On the other, the convicted offender should make amends to society for his or her wrongdoing by performing unpaid manual labour or working with disabled or elderly people. While acknowledging this as a punishment, they are treated as volunteers to improve the environment or to help people in their communities. In England and Wales, various community groups, victim support groups, and voluntary organizations for victims are consulted on what reparation should be done, and what placements and projects are available for offenders to contribute to improve the community (Home Office 2003).

Types of community sentences

In this chapter the operation of two community sentences is considered. As shown in Table 10.1, probation is the most common form of community sentence in Hong Kong.

Probation orders

The emergence of probation orders

Probation was introduced in Hong Kong on a formal statutory basis right from its beginning and was basically an overseas import during colonial times. The historical roots of the system can be traced to the penal practice in the United Kingdom in the early twentieth century. Its inception was due to the belief in giving the offender a chance to reform through welfare advice, education, and counselling. The offender is allowed to return to the community to resume normal work and could then be an asset to the society as a whole from an economic point of view. Also, the offender is helped to obey the law under the supervision of a probation officer, thus saving the government any expense involved in holding the offender in an institution (Mak 1973; Lee 1973).

The first step towards putting the probation system into effect was the *Juvenile Offenders Ordinance* in 1933, under which juvenile offenders may be placed on probation at the direction of the court.

Table 10.1 Services for offenders by the Social Welfare Department from 2002–3 to 2005–6

	Number of supervision cases served			
	2002–3	2003–4	2004–5	2005–6
Probation Supervision	3,215	3,312	3,279	2,907
Community Service Order	993	970	910	883
Probation Home and Hostel*	134	107	94	109
Reformatory School**	41	29	24	32
Community Support Service Scheme ***	+	+	420 (Youth members) 197 (Parents members)	624 (Youth members) 298 (Parents members)
Post-release Supervision of Prisoners Scheme	546	490	490	526

* The Social Welfare Department operates probation homes for juvenile offenders aged between 10 and under 16 who are required by the court to receive residential training as part of the probation sentence.

** Reformatory school is a custodial sentencing option for young offenders under the *Reformatory Schools Ordinance* (Cap. 225).

*** The Community Support Service Scheme is available for those offenders aged below 25 under probation order, community service order or reformatory school order, and their parents.

\+ Data not available.

Source: Social Welfare Department (various issues, 2003–6)

The probation officers were attached to the Police Force until 1938, when the service was taken over by the Prisons Department. A further change took place in 1948, when the Probation Service was grouped under the Social Welfare Office established as a branch of the Secretariat for Chinese Affairs in post-war Hong Kong. The Probation Service was also upgraded to professional status upon the appointment in 1950 of the late Donald Peterson, a trained social worker from Australia, who headed the development of the Probation Section of the Social Welfare Office. By law, he was gazetted as Principal Probation Officer, the first one ever appointed in the history of Hong Kong (Chan 1996). All this indicated a recognition by the government of the importance of the Probation Service as a field of social work practice for offenders in the community since the early 1950s. The final *Probation of Offenders Bill* was passed in 1956, which extended the probation system to adult offenders (Huang 1970; Mak 1973; Lee 1973; Chan 1996).

Details of probation orders

The *Probation of Offenders Ordinance* (POO) (Cap. 298), as revised and amended, details the responsibilities and core tasks of probation officers, and how an offender should be supervised in legal terms. By definition, 'probation officer' is a person appointed under Section 9 of POO and 'probationer' denotes a person who is under supervision by virtue of a probation order. The order applies to all ages of 10 or above. It must clearly specify the period of probation, which should not be less than one year and no longer than three years. Probation orders are issued after the court has considered carefully the circumstances leading to the offence, the nature of the offence, the character of the offender, and the recommendation of the probation officer in the social inquiry report. A basic probation order requires the offender to keep in touch with the probation officer in person regularly and inform the officer of any change of address. If at any time during the probation period it appears that a probationer has failed to comply with any of the requirements of the order or has committed another offence, he or she is liable to be brought back to the court for resentencing in the light of both new and old offences.

To address special circumstances in a case, added conditions can be imposed on the standard probation. They are required to: (i) work and reside as directed (such as living at an approved institution for a period of time); (ii) abstain from dangerous drugs; (iii) submit a urine sample for drug testing; (iv) attend drug treatment programmes; (v) receive psychological treatment; (vi) obtain psychiatric treatment; (vii) comply with the curfew order (that is, remaining at home from 11:00 p.m. to 6:00 a.m.); (viii) attend the court usually at halfway through the sentence in order to demonstrate improvement in behaviour (that is, the progress report court attendance); and (ix) attend group and rehabilitative programmes (such as the Community Support Service Scheme). Probation officers in Hong Kong usually recommend additional conditions with reference to the needs and problems of offenders identified in the social enquiry report. In effect, the liberty of the offenders would be restricted by attaching added conditions on the sentence. However, the recommendations are subject to the approval of the court.

As a statutory requirement, a probation officer will endeavour to 'advise, assist, and befriend' a probationer under Section 19 of the POO. It is the duty of the supervising officer to reform an offender by virtue of his or her specialized social work knowledge and practical experience in the treatment of offenders and by arranging special services felt necessary for the successful offender rehabilitation within the community such as employment, schooling, and accommodation (Yip 1973; Corrections Section 1994). In other words, the medical or rehabilitative model of probation is still existent, with an emphasis on careful case planning and intervention in order to help probationers to improve their individual and social adjustment during the period of supervision.

The medical or treatment model emphasized the need 'to diagnose, treat and cure criminals', thereby reintegrating offenders into the community (Davies, Croall and Tyrer 2005). This led to a growing involvement of professional social work that overtly supported the use of casework counselling for offenders on probation supervision. The dominant approach in supervising probationers in the 1960s and early 1970s in the United Kingdom was to 'advise, assist and befriend' them with the aim of enhancing their ability to avoid committing further offences (Willis 1986). Given the penological optimism allied to the ethos of rehabilitation, McWilliams (1987) noticed the expansion of the probation caseload and the increasing number of probation staff between the 1960s and 1970s in the United Kingdom. In line with this development, Chan also reports that 'Starting in the 60s, the total number of probationers had been on the rise, and was almost double in the early 70s as documented in the 1973 White Paper *The Way Ahead* [in Hong Kong]' (1996: 102). In addition, during this period three approved institutions for juvenile and young offenders were established in Hong Kong with the aim of providing residential treatment programmes on top of the probation orders. The use of social work approaches to rehabilitate offenders was formally and explicitly spelt out in the *White Paper 1973* (Lee 1973).

Pre-sentence investigation

There are two major functions of probation, namely pre-sentence investigation and supervision of offenders. One of the official aims of probation is to give recommendations to the court on the suitability of offenders to be put on probation order or community service order in the form of a social enquiry report or pre-sentence report. In this respect, the probation officer is the servant of the court and the magistrate or judge will take the recommendation from the report into account when sentencing an offender. It should be noted that the pre-sentence investigation is needed upon the request from the magistrate or judge following the offender's conviction. These reports are often requested when dealing with juvenile offenders to assess basic background information and their suitability to be put on the community sentence.

The nature of the social enquiry report is to give a detailed account of the offence and the offender, but not to determine guilt or otherwise. By assessing the circumstances of the crime and the personal, family, and social background of the offender, the report proposes a recommendation with justification to the court in regard to the sentence (Clear and Dammer 2003). Several sources of information are relied upon by the probation officer to prepare the report. An in-depth interview with the individual offender and often with his or her family members or guardians is conducted. Those whose bail application was denied will be interviewed in the remand centre or in custody. Additionally, official records and reports on the arrest records, previous conviction, and sentence are consulted. Regardless of the brevity of the report, it must be succinct and contain facts and evidence to justify the perspectives about defendants in terms of their risk of reoffending or the likelihood of successful completion of the sentence. This information helps the court make its decision.

Supervision and enforcement

The main customers of probation are the offender and the community. Supervision begins as soon as an offender is sentenced to probation. Section 17 of the Rules of the POO requires the probation officer to explain the requirements and conditions of the probation order as clearly as possible. The expectation of the probation supervision should also be discussed between supervising officers and probationers. Clear and Dammer (2003) hold the view that 'the probation supervision process emerges from informal understandings and interdependence' (2003: 275). However, it should be emphasized that the way probation officers work with offenders is based on a professional relationship, which ensures the law is enforced in order to protect the interests of society.

An empirical study with 115 adult probationers aged between 18 and 35 found that the probation service in Hong Kong still places a great emphasis on an individualized casework treatment approach to the probationers (Chui 2003a, 2006). The one-to-one counselling sessions usually took place in the probation offices, and the three most commonly discussed topics during the sessions were issues related to 'personal problems', 'problems with family', and 'employment' of the offenders. A considerable number of probationers who misused drugs mentioned that they were asked to submit urine samples for drug testing. Those who were unemployed while on probation were asked to look for jobs in the newspapers during the sessions. This confirms that probation officers tend to discuss the topics and design tasks to be done according to the characteristics and problems of offenders. This probation practice in Hong Kong has been guided by a casework-type philosophical ideology which was dominant in the 1960s in the United States (Sluder, Sapp and Langston 1994) and United Kingdom (Bottoms and McWilliams 1979).

Apart from having regular face-to-face sessions, other means of contact with probationers that were rendered include family interviews during home visits and telephone interviews. Family interviews were usually arranged with the aim of assessing the family dynamics and interactions well before the probation officers had to prepare the social enquiry reports. It is not uncommon for family members to be involved in the treatment process with the offenders, especially for those who are still young. As might be expected, those who were given an added condition of a curfew order were more likely to receive telephone calls from the probation officers than those who were not in order to monitor whether they were at home after eleven o'clock in the evening as required.

A strong probation service develops close working relationships with a wide range of governmental and non-governmental organizations which can get offenders into education, training, and employment. The probationers may be encouraged to contact relevant governmental organizations or social welfare agencies for help. For example, they may be encouraged to participate in social and recreational activities organized by community centres. They may also be asked to contact the Labour Department and social service agencies for help with their employment. Drug offenders can be referred to non-residential (such as methadone treatment) and residential drug rehabilitation centres in the course of supervision to deal with their drug misuse. They may also be referred to clinical psychologists and psychiatrists to receive some form of psychotherapeutic counselling.

Outcome of probation orders

Table 10.2 shows the annual success rates of probation supervision for those cases completed in the financial years 2001–2 to 2004–5. Taking the face value of these statistics, close to or more than 80 per

Table 10.2 Annual success rates of probation orders in the financial years 2001–2 to 2005–6

Year	Total number of case completions	Total number of satisfactory case completions	Success rate* (%)
2001–2	3,457	2,667	77.1
2002–3	3,142	2,549	81.1
2003–4	2,716	2,247	82.7
2004–5	2,768	2,308	83.4

*The annual success rate is calculated by dividing the total number of satisfactory case completions by the total number of case completions each year.
Source: Derived data from the departmental *Annual Report*s (Director of Social Welfare 2002–5)

cent of probation cases completed their orders satisfactorily. However, care should be taken when interpreting these official figures for two main reasons. First, the compilation of these statistics largely relies on probation officers' detection of and willingness to report further offences. Such rates illustrate probation work as it is seen from the point of view of the probation officer (Maltz 1984). In addition, Harris (1992) contends that: 'No more would there be that awkward thought that, say, probation officers' "successes" might reflect no more than the good fortune of the probationer in not having been caught reoffending' (1992: 25). Second, it is worth giving our attention to the counting rules of these statistics. Even where a probationer's order has been extended for failure to comply with the conditions of probation or for committing some further offence, he or she is still not considered as an unsatisfactory completion. This counting rule therefore may underestimate the actual reoffending rates. Thus, the statistics are only a rough estimation of the effectiveness of the probation.

Community service orders

The emergence of community service orders

In 1983, community service was first introduced as an additional means of dealing with offenders as a result of a recommendation made by the Law Reform Commission of Hong Kong. A sub-committee was formed to examine this issue in a detailed manner and concluded that community service orders should be available to offenders aged 14 and over for the offences for which the offender is liable to punishment by imprisonment (Law Reform Commission of Hong Kong 1983; for detailed accounts of the development of the Community Service Orders Scheme, see Lo and Harris 2000). In 1984 the *Community Service Orders Ordinance* (CSOO) (Cap. 378) was enacted. The Community Service Orders Scheme was launched in 1987 as a pilot in three magistracies, and subsequently has been extended to all courts since 1998 (Harris and Lo 2002; Lo and Harris 2004). Since its inception, the Community Service Orders Scheme has been under the administration of the Probation Service of the Social Welfare Department.

Aims of community service orders

By enjoining an offender to carry out a task within the community for a specified number of hours, community service orders aim at being rehabilitative and reparative. More specifically, these orders are expected to fulfil three penological objectives:

(a) Rehabilitation – Through structured work/service placement and the guidance of probation officers (POs(CSO)), offenders are helped to observe regulations, take up their own responsibility for self-progress, broaden perspective, develop an enriched sense of self-worth, cultivate a more constructive pattern of living, and steer away from committing further crime;

(b) Constructive disposal – Offenders are allowed to remain in the community while serving the sentence; and

(c) Reparation – Offenders make a contribution to the community (Director of Social Welfare 2007).

In addition to these three objectives, the order is punitive by depriving the offender of their leisure time to undertake volunteer service experience. Unlike volunteering, which is influenced by an individual's altruistic motivation, offenders are coerced to perform this task while agreeing to be put on the scheme.

Details of community service orders

Section 4(1) of the CSOO enables the court to impose the order on those convicted of an offence punishable with imprisonment. It should be for any number of hours up to a maximum of 240 within a period of 12 months. Section 4(3) of the CSOO makes it clear that the court shall not make the order against an offender unless the offender consents to the making of such an order; and the court is satisfied after considering a social enquiry report as to the offender's suitability to be made the subject of such an order. Similar to the probation officer's report discussed above, the social enquiry report or the Suitability Report for community service orders provides information to the court to consider which sentence is the most appropriate for sentencing the convicted. The amount of community service work is largely determined by the seriousness of the offence committed. The study conducted by Lo and Harris (2000) indicated that the majority of community service orders required the offender to undertake between 101 and 120 hours of unpaid work in the period 1994–5 to 1997–8.

Section 6 of the CSOO explicitly outlines the obligations of offenders under community service orders: to perform community work as directed by the supervising probation officer in a satisfactory manner, to comply with any conditions and requirements specified in the order with the reasonable direction to enable that supervising probation officer to provide rehabilitative counselling and guidance, and to notify any change of residence. The probation officer is advised to take into account the offender's religious beliefs and practice, employment status, and personal circumstances when organizing work or placement. Among others, the two most important tasks of the supervising probation officer are to explain the objective of the community service order with the offender, and assign work placement according to the offender's and the community interest. By doing so, it is hoped that the offender not only enjoys the work itself but also finds the experience meaningful, constructive, and worthwhile. The mode of community service or work placement includes task-oriented work such as painting, carpentry, and gardening and service-type work such as organizing game stalls, escorting the disabled during outings, and visiting homes for the elderly. Each work normally lasts for about 4 to 8 consecutive hours, and for many it is their first experience of community work. Liaising with prospective voluntary agencies or governmental departments to identify possible suitable placements is indeed one of the core tasks of the probation officer.

Lo and Harris (2000) rightly point out that while the community service practice in Hong Kong is primarily modelled on the British experience, the Hong Kong model places more emphasis on the role of counselling by supervising probation officers. Probation supervision in the form of periodic counselling is an integral component of the order. The supervising officers pay site visits to monitor the performance of the offender and to engage the offender to address offending behaviour. The format in terms of content, frequency, and length of the supervisory meeting varies according to the individual, family, and social circumstances of the offender. During the course of the order, the supervising officer has regular appointments with the offender to evaluate the experience of community service with the aim of engaging the offender actively to redress the damage done to the community. The officer can also refer the offender and his or her family to participate in the Community Support Service Scheme, which consists of counselling services, mutual aid group activities, and recreational programmes (Director of Social Welfare 2007).

Outcomes of community service orders

Previous literature shows that there is considerable support for community service from offenders themselves and other stakeholders such as non-governmental organizations and governmental departments that provide placement opportunities and on-the-post supervision (Law Reform Commission of Hong Kong 1983; Lo and Harris 2000). They genuinely believe that the offender has to make reparation to the public through unpaid work and learn to be responsible for the harm caused to others. As indicated in Table 10.3, the annual success rate is high, which means that more than 90 per cent of the orders were terminated satisfactorily.

When dealing with a breach of a community service order, commission of a further offence while the order is in force, or revocation of the order, the court may impose a fine not exceeding

Table 10.3 Annual success rates of community service orders in the financial years 2001–2 to 2004–5

Year	Total number of case completions	Total number of satisfactory case completions	Success rate* (%)
2001–2	2,282	2,100	92.0
2002–3	1,880	1,779	94.6
2003–4	1,685	1,617	96.0
2004–5	1,857	1,782	96.0

*The annual success rate is calculated by dividing the total number of satisfactory case completions by the total number of case completions each year.

Source: Derived data from the departmental Annual Reports (Director of Social Welfare 2002–5)

$1,000, increase the number of hours specified in the order, or resentence the offender for the original offence for which the order was made. The last option may make the offender leave the service, which is counted as the case being closed unsatisfactorily.

Elements of successful community sentences intervention for offenders

In contrast to the use of imprisonment, a community approach to dealing with criminals is founded on the ground that a significant proportion of the causes of offending originates in their environment or community. This leads to a common-sense conclusion that it is more effective to devise intervention programmes which work within the given reality of their social environment, especially among juvenile offenders. Custody punishes but alienates, whereas community punishes but reintegrates (Vass 1990). It is not difficult to understand how people end up feeling isolated, resentful, and angry if the punishment experience is alienating and meaningless. This may explain why penal custody seems not to be the best way of reintegrating people into the community against which they offend, and where they ultimately must learn to live. For instance, probation supervision with a strong emphasis of social work and counselling attempts to integrate offenders into the community in a positive fashion, overcoming the problems which might exist in relation to school, employment, or family. Community service orders not only provide worthwhile experiences for offenders (McIvor 1992) but also create opportunities for them to contribute to the community, thus gaining status and approval for their actions. The visibility of community sentences creates advantages for the offender as well as opportunities for the community to benefit from a service and to strengthen its ties with individuals who might otherwise be excluded and resentful. Another benefit is that it encourages offenders, rather than becoming recipients of a service, to dispense a service in the form of work that tends to be greatly appreciated by its beneficiaries. A community is capable of forgetting and forgiving offenders' past criminal behaviour and this assists in the healing and reintegration process.

Also, being perceived as a kind of humane punishment, community sentences help offenders to remain part of their families, and to retain their schooling and employment. Through their supervised activities, offenders can contribute to their own well-being as well as that of the community. In many respects, probation orders and community service orders can be effective ways to strengthen offenders' links to the community and not weaken them. The Probation Service itself makes use of ordinary active citizens as volunteers to befriend offenders and to provide them with informal help and support. Effective links with employment training schemes can enhance an offender's capacity to become a law-abiding citizen. This strengthens offenders' links with the community and gives them a sense of their own worth, thereby improving the likelihood of their success in becoming law-abiding citizens.

Experience to date supports a number of generalizations about the apparent ingredients of effective community sentences. These generalizations are mainly derived from the meta-analytic reviews of interventions with offenders primarily in North America (Bernfeld, Farrington and Leschied 2001; McGuire 2002). The generalizations are also part of the 'What Works' initiative that was initiated jointly by the Home Office Probation Unit, HM Inspectorate of Probation, Association of Chief Officers of Probation, and Central Probation Council (but with interest from the Prison Service and other Home Office agencies) in England and Wales (Chui 2003b, Chui and Nellis 2003; Whitehead and Thompson 2004). In one of the earlier reports, the elements of effective interventions with offenders are: risk assessment and management, targeting and addressing the specific factors linked with offenders' offending, relevance to offenders' learning style, using promising intervention approaches with offenders, promoting community reintegration, and maintaining quality and integrity of programme delivery (Underdown 1998). More specifically, some of the principles are:

- Risk assessment and classification – matching between offender risk level based on criminal history and other variables and level of supervision or degree of service intervention by using existing actuarial assessment tools (Robinson 2003; Andrews, Bonta and Wormith 2006);
- Criminogenic needs – identifying the needs most related to offending by using the risk-need assessment tool and focusing intervention on these issues during the course of supervision (Ward and Stewart 2003; Hollin and Palmer 2006);
- Responsivity – matching learning styles between supervising officers and offenders (Ward, Melser and Yates 2007);

- Treatment modality – applying a variety of models or approaches such as skills-based training, pro-social modelling, and cognitive-behavioural theory to design and implement intervention programmes (see Fleet and Annison 2003; Cherry 2005; Trotter 2006);
- Programme integrity – ensuring that the stated aims of programmes are linked to the theories and methods being used, and that well-trained and supported staff deliver the programmes with adequate resources (Andrews and Dowden 2005); and
- Partnerships – encouraging multi-agency collaboration to provide the offender help with employment, health, welfare, and accommodation, and address the problems of specific groups of individuals involved in criminal activity in local districts (Rumgay 2003).

It is important to note that the above principles of effective practice with offenders are primarily the research evidence from the British and North American experience. Whether all these are transferable to the Hong Kong Chinese context is questionable due to the different social, cultural, and legal background. However, one lesson learnt from their experience is their commitment to evaluation research; they see research as a part of accountable criminal justice management to identify good practice as well as room for improvement in the quality of the Probation Service (Mair 2000; Chui 2002; Israel and Chui 2006).

Conclusion

The Social Welfare Department, which is responsible for administering the two community sentences, maintains a strong and cohesive professional identity as a social work agency. The cornerstone of the practice is to 'advise, assist and befriend' offenders under supervision. It may be true that frontline practitioners still have strong faith in the social work model of probation practice. The official data also confirms that a number of probation and community service orders were closed satisfactorily (see Tables 10.2 and 10.3). However, by using a different outcome measurement, slightly more than one-third of the adult probationers in Chui's (2004) study admitted to committing at least one further offence within one year of the order being awarded. This recidivism rate based on the offender's self-report is higher than the rate of unsatisfactory completion derived from the official records.

This further confirms the deficiency of using official data to measure the effectiveness of the sentence.

Vexing questions still remain unanswered, and some examples are: Among a broad range of social work intervention, what works or otherwise with Chinese offenders? On what grounds should a residential requirement in a probation home be attached to the probation sentence? How do the probation officers deal with revocation of the community sentence? Instead of using the completion rate as a measurement of recidivism, are there other outcome indicators? What is the short-term and long-term impact of the community sentence on offenders and the community? Does probation work better than community service in reducing offending behaviour? Should risk and needs instruments be introduced in Hong Kong? How do the magistrates and judge rate the quality of the social enquiry report? Is the public confident with the Probation Service? What sorts of changes should be proposed to improve the effectiveness of community sentencing? How can we modernize probation practice? Can community sentences be a real and effective alternative to short- or medium-term imprisonment for some offenders? All these questions are difficult to answer at this point. Nevertheless, they point to the importance of moving from a social work model of probation practice towards a more empirical-based social work criminal justice practice. The evidence-based practice encourages the probation officers or social workers to be critical towards their own intervention with offenders and to continue to look for better alternatives for offenders who are often marginalized and excluded from society.

Note

1 In addition to the probation order and community service order, post-release supervision order for prisoners or parole is considered one form of community sentence. It will be discussed fully in Chapter 12.

Review questions

1 What are the major justifications for community sentences?
2 To what extent do you agree that qualified social workers should be appointed to deal with offenders in the community? Give reasons to justify your answer.
3 What are the advantages and disadvantages of putting offenders on community sentences as opposed to imprisonment?

4 If you were to evaluate the effectiveness of community sentences, how would you measure recidivism?

References

Andrews, D.A., Bonta, J. and Wormith, J.S. (2006) 'The recent past and near future of risk and/ or need assessment', *Crime and Delinquency*, 52 (1): 7–27.

Andrews, D.A. and Dowden, C. (2005) 'Managing correctional treatment of reduced recidivism: A meta-analytic review of programme integrity', *Legal and Criminological Psychology*, 10 (2): 173–87.

Ashworth, A. (2007) 'Sentencing', in M. Maguire, R. Morgan and R. Reiner (eds) *The Oxford Handbook of Criminology* (4th edn) (pp. 990–1023). Oxford: Oxford University Press.

Barry, M. (2000) 'The mentor/monitor debate in criminal justice: 'What works' for offenders', *British Journal of Social Work*, 30 (5): 575–95.

Bernfeld, G.A., Farrington, D.P. and Leschied, A.W. (eds) (2001) *Offender Rehabilitation in Practice: Implementing and Evaluating Effective Programs*. Chichester, West Sussex: John Wiley & Sons.

Bottoms, A.E. and McWilliams, W. (1979) 'A non-treatment paradigm for probation practice', *British Journal of Social Work*, 9 (2): 159–202.

Brownell, P. and Roberts, A.R. (2002) 'A century of social work in criminal justice and correctional settings', *Journal of Offender Rehabilitation*, 35 (2): 1–17.

Chan, W.T. (1996) 'Social work and services for offenders', in I. Chi and S.K. Cheung (eds), *Social Work in Hong Kong* (pp. 98–111). Hong Kong: Hong Kong Social Workers Association.

Cherry, S. (2005) *Transforming Behaviour: Pro-social Modelling in Practice*. Cullompton, Devon: Willan.

Chui, W.H. (1999) 'Residential treatment programs for young offenders in Hong Kong: A report', *International Journal of Offender Therapy and Comparative Criminology*, 43 (3): 308–21.

Chui, W.H. (2002) 'Social work model of probation supervision for offenders in Hong Kong', *Probation Journal*, 49 (4): 297–304.

Chui, W.H. (2003a) 'Experiences of probation supervision in Hong Kong: Listening to the young adult probationers', *Journal of Criminal Justice*, 31 (6): 567–77.

Chui, W.H. (2003b) 'What works in reducing re-offending: Principles and programmes', in W.H. Chui and M. Nellis (eds) *Moving Probation Forward: Evidence, Arguments and Practice* (pp. 56–73). Harlow, Essex: Pearson Education.

Chui, W.H. (2004) 'Adult offenders on probation in Hong Kong: An exploratory study', *British Journal of Social Work*, 34 (3): 443–54.

Chui, W.H. (2006) 'Factors associated with the one-year probation outcome: A self-report study in Hong Kong', *Asian Journal of Criminology*, 1 (2): 155–71.

Chui, W.H. and Nellis, M. (eds) (2003) *Moving Probation Forward: Evidence, Arguments and Practice*. Harlow, Essex: Pearson Education.

Clear, T. and Dammer, H.R. (2003) *The Offender in the Community* (2nd edn). Belmont, CA: Wadsworth.

Corrections Section (1994) *Basic Guide for Practice in Probation Service*. Hong Kong: Social Welfare Department (unpublished).

Davies, M., Croall, H. and Tyrer, J. (2005) *Criminal Justice: An Introduction to the Criminal Justice System in England and Wales* (3rd edn). London: Longman.

Director of Social Welfare (various issues, 2002–5) *Annual Report*. Hong Kong: Government Printer.

Director of Social Welfare (2007) *Services for Offenders*. Hong Kong: Social Welfare Department. Available at: http://www.swd.gov.hk/en/index/site_pubsvc/page_offdr/sub_introducti/

Fleet, F. and Annison, J. (2003) 'In support of effectiveness: Facilitating participation and sustaining change', in W.H. Chui and M. Nellis (eds) *Moving Probation Forward: Evidence, Arguments and Practice* (pp. 129–45). Harlow, Essex: Pearson Education.

Gaines, L.K. and Miller. R.L. (2007) *Criminal Justice in Action* (4th edn). Belmont, CA: Thomson Wadsworth.

Gregory, M. (2007) 'Probation training: Evidence from newly qualified officers', *Social Work Education*, 26 (1): 53–68.

Harris, R. (1992) *Crime, Criminal Justice and the Probation Service*. London: Routledge.

Harris, R.J. and Lo, T.W. (2002) 'Community service: Its use in criminal justice', *International Journal of Offender Therapy and Comparative Criminology*, 46 (4): 427–44.

Hollin, C.R. and Palmer, E.J. (2006) 'Criminogenic need and women offenders: A critique of the literature', *Legal and Criminological Psychology*, 11 (2): 179–95.

Home Office (2003) *Restorative Justice: The Government Strategy*. London: Home Office.

Huang, T.P. (1970) 'A Mini Memoir of Days Gone By', *Hong Kong Probation*, 1 (2): 2–9.

Israel, M. and Chui, W.H. (2006) 'If 'Something Works' is the answer, what is the question?: Supporting pluralist evaluation in community corrections in the United Kingdom', *European Journal of Criminology*, 3 (2), 181–200.

Klapmuts, N. (1976) 'Diversion from the justice system', in S. Schafer (ed.) *Readings in Contemporary Criminology* (pp. 222–33). Reston, Virginia: Reston Publishing.

Law Reform Commission of Hong Kong (1983) *Report – Community Service Orders (Topic 7)*. Hong Kong: Law Reform Commission of Hong Kong.

Lee, S.M. (1973) 'The Probation Service in Hong Kong', *International Journal of Offender Therapy and Comparative Criminology*, 17 (1): 90–4.

Lo, T.W. and Harris, R. (2000) *Research Report on the Operation of Community Service Orders*. Hong Kong: Youth Studies Net, City University of Hong Kong.

Lo, T.W. and Harris, R.J. (2004) 'Community service orders in Hong Kong, England, and Wales: Twins or cousins', *International Journal of Offender Therapy and Comparative Criminology*, 48 (3): 373–88.

Lo, T.W., Wong, D. and Maxwell, G. (2006) 'Community support and diversionary measures for juvenile offenders in Hong Kong: Old legacy, new age', *Asian Journal of Criminology*, 1 (1), 9–20.

Mair, G. (2000) 'Research on community penalties', in R.D. King and E. Wincup (eds) *Doing Research on Crime and Justice* (pp. 259–83). Oxford: Oxford University Press.

Mak, W.H. (1973) 'Reminiscence of the Early Probation Work in Hong Kong', in Social Welfare Department (ed.) *Open Day Special Issue* (pp. 7–9). Hong Kong: Social Welfare Department.

Maltz, M.D. (1984) *Recidivism*. Orlando, FL: Academic Press.

McDonald, D. (1986) *Punishment Without Walls: Community Service Sentences in New York City*. New Brunswick, NJ: Rutgers University Press.

McGuire, J. (ed.) (2002) *Offender Rehabilitation and Treatment: Effective Programmes and Policies to Reduce Re-offending*. Chichester, West Sussex: John Wiley & Sons.

McIvor, G. (1992) *Sentenced to Serve: The Operation and Impact of Community Service by Offenders*. Aldershot: Avebury.

McWilliams, W. (1987) 'Probation, pragmatism and policy', *Howard Journal of Criminal Justice*, 26 (2), 97–121.

Nellis, M. (2000) 'Re-naming probation', *Probation Journal*, 47 (1), 39–44.

Nellis, M. (2003) 'Probation training and the community justice curriculum', *British Journal of Social Work*, 33 (7), 943–59.

Pollock, J.M. (2004) *Ethics in Crime and Justice: Dilemmas and Decisions* (4th edn). Belmont, CA: Wadsworth/Thomson Learning.

Raynor, P. and Vanstone, M. (2002) *Understanding Community Penalties: Probation, Policy and Social Change*. Buckingham: Open University Press.

Reynolds, K.M., Dziegielewski, S.F. and Sharp, C. (2004) 'Serving mentally ill offenders through community corrections: Joining two disciplines', *Journal of Offender Rehabilitation*, 40 (1/2): 185–98.

Robinson, G. (2003) 'Risk and risk assessment', in W.H. Chui and M. Nellis (eds) *Moving Probation Forward: Evidence, Arguments and Practice* (pp. 108–28). Harlow, Essex: Pearson Education.

Rumgay, J. (2003) 'Partnerships in the probation service', in W.H. Chui and M. Nellis (eds) *Moving Probation Forward: Evidence, Arguments and Practice* (pp. 195–213), Harlow, Essex: Pearson Education.

Sluder, R.D., Sapp, A.D. and Langston, D.C. (1994) 'Guiding philosophies for probation in the 21st century', *Federal Probation*, 58 (2), 3–10.

Social Welfare Department (various issues, 2003–6) *Social Welfare Services in Figures*. Hong Kong: Government Printer.
Taylor, A. (2001) 'Criminal justice social work in prison and community settings', in M. Connolly (ed.) *New Zealand Social Work: Contexts and Practice* (pp. 193–205). Auckland, New Zealand: Oxford University Press.
Trotter, C. (2006) *Working with Involuntary Clients: A Guide to Practice* (2nd ed.). St Leonards, NSW: Allen & Unwin.
Underdown, A. (1998) *Strategies for Effective Offender Rehabilitation: Report of the HMIP What Works Project*. London: Home Office.
Vass, A.A. (1990) *Alternatives to Prison: Punishment, Custody and the Community*. London: Sage.
Ward, T. and Melser, J. and Yates, P.M. (2007) 'Reconstructing the risk-need-responsivity model: A theoretical elaboration and evaluation', *Aggression and Violent Behavior*, 12 (2), 208–28.
Ward, T. and Stewart, C. (2003) 'Criminogenic needs and human needs: A theoretical model', *Psychology, Crime and Law*, 9 (2), 125–43.
Whitehead, P. and Thompson, J. (2004) *Knowledge and the Probation Service: Raising Standards for Trainees, Assessors and Practitioners*. Chichester: John Wiley & Sons.
Willis, A. (1986) 'Help and control in probation: An empirical assessment of probation practice', in J. Pointing (ed.) *Alternatives to Custody* (pp. 162–82). Oxford: Blackwell.
Worrall, A. and Hoy, C. (2005) *Punishment in the Community: Managing Offenders, Making Choices*. Cullompton, Devon: Willan.
Yip, T.C. (1973) 'The role of a probation officer', in Social Welfare Department (ed.) *Open Day Special Issue* (pp. 8–12). Hong Kong: Social Welfare Department.

Legislation cited

Community Service Orders Ordinance (Cap. 378)
Criminal Procedure Ordinance (Cap. 221)
Dangerous Drugs Ordinance (Cap. 134)
Juvenile Offenders Ordinance (Cap. 226)
Probation of Offenders Ordinance (Cap. 298)
Reformatory Schools Ordinance (Cap. 225)
Weapons Ordinance (Cap. 217)

Useful websites

Law Reform Commission of Hong Kong	http://www.hkreform.gov.hk/en/index/index.htm

National Probation Service (Home Office, England and Wales)	http://www.probation.homeoffice.gov.uk/output/Page1.asp
National Offender Management Service (Home Office, England and Wales)	http://www.noms.homeoffice.gov.uk/
Social Welfare Department	www.swd.gov.hk

Chapter 11

Custodial sentences and correctional services

T. Wing Lo

Introduction

Custodial sentences are run by the Correctional Services Department (CSD), formerly the Prisons Department before 1982, which is responsible for the secure, safe, and humane custody of all persons detained under the *Immigration Ordinance* (Cap. 115), and persons committed or sentenced by the courts under the *Criminal Procedure Ordinance* (Cap. 221), *Prisons Ordinance* (Cap. 234), *Detention Centres Ordinance* (Cap. 239), *Rehabilitation Centres Ordinance* (Cap. 567), *Training Centres Ordinance* (Cap. 280), and *Drug Addiction Treatment Centres Ordinance* (Cap. 244). The vision of the CSD is to become an internationally acclaimed correctional service, with the upholding of five values: integrity, professionalism, humanity, discipline, and economy (CSD 2005). While the CSD provides multi-level intervention to rehabilitate offenders, during daily operations its major duties are summarized into two main categories: prison management and rehabilitation of offenders.

Radzinowicz and Hood (1990) remarked that the modern prison has emerged as its functions changed from being primarily custodial-coercive to punitive, and offenders are now sent to prison 'as a punishment, not for punishment' (Ruck 1951: 23). As such, the loss of personal freedom due to incarceration is already a punishment, and the conditions inside prisons should be as humane and rehabilitative as possible to maintain the dignity of individual prisoners. Inside correctional institutions, the CSD provides inmates with basic necessities, comprehensive medical, psychological, and welfare services, opportunities to engage in useful work, and a decent and healthy living environment. It maintains order and control to minimize the chance of escapes and acts of indiscipline. To correct inmates' criminal behaviour, its programmes emphasize self-control and discipline, provide education and vocational training, drug addiction treatment, community reintegration programmes, and aftercare and support services. It protects the public and helps reduce crime but simultaneously promotes community acceptance of, and support for, rehabilitated offenders through public education, publicity, and community involvement.

Current situation

In 2004 and 2005, 30,070 and 25,525 inmates served sentences in CSD institutions, with a total annual expenditure of HK$2,441 million and HK$2,372.3 million respectively. This amounts to between HK$81,000 and HK$93,000 per inmate per annum in 2004/5. When the average daily number of inmates (11,869 and 10,983) is taken into account, the expense spent on each inmate was between HK$205,600 and HK$215,900 (see Table 11.1). Overcrowding continued to be a problem, with the average daily number of inmates in CSD institutions being greater than the stipulated capacity (further discussion below). Inmates were allowed to spend time out of their cells for a significant proportion of the time. Concerted acts of indiscipline were extremely low in 2004/5, with no escapes and abscontions. As shown in Table 11.1, the number of inmates engaged in welfare and counselling services, education, vocational training, and community reintegration programmes reflects the rehabilitative elements of CSD programmes.

Significant breakthroughs in the correctional services

In 1996, the government commissioned a research team at City University of Hong Kong to review all of the rehabilitation services for young offenders in Hong Kong. The team interviewed over 500 young offenders and 30 staff from CSD, as well as 38 magistrates who had experiences of sentencing young offenders. Based on the findings, the team recommended a number of measures (Lo *et al.* 1997). The government responded positively by making a number of improvements in correctional services. The following are two significant breakthroughs.

Table 11.1 Prison management and rehabilitation statistics

Prison management	2004	2005
Total inmates in all institutions	30,070	25,523
Average daily no. of inmates	11,869	10,983
Total expenditure	$2,441M	$2,372.3M
Occupancy rate (%)	123.1	114.5
Average no. of hours an inmate out of cell/dormitory	11.4	11.5
No. of escapees and absconders	0	0
No. of concerted acts of indiscipline	12	7
Average daily no. of young inmates engaged in correctional education (including vocational training)	919	880
No. of cases under aftercare supervision	2,866	2,889
Average daily no. of inmates under re-integration-cum-supervision programmes	1,607	1,650
No. of counselling/welfare sessions	316,220	280,753

Source: CSD 2005, 2007

Service gaps and the new rehabilitation centres

Some magistrates expressed concerns about young offenders who were not physically fit but where the detention centre was considered the most appropriate sentencing option. The detention centre requires young offenders to be physically fit in order to undergo the harsh training, such as hard work, physical training, and foot drills. The research team found some young offenders, who were not fit enough to attend detention centre but to whom the community-based treatment programmes were too lenient, were forced to receive long-term rehabilitation in training centres due to the absence of a suitable alternative. In addition, the inadequacy of rehabilitative programmes for young female offenders was another issue raised by magistrates. They expressed the need to provide short-term rehabilitative programmes because the detention centre was not an option available for them, and the sentencing period in training centres was too long.

Having identified the service gaps, the research team recommended another form of short-term rehabilitative programme for both young male and female offenders. In addition to the emphasis on discipline, deportment, and hygiene, it was recommended that the programme incorporate social training and counselling services for young offenders. The recommendations were accepted by the government and the *Rehabilitation Centres Ordinance* (Cap. 567) was enacted in 2001 and implemented in 2002, in response to service gaps identified in the aforesaid review.

A new division of rehabilitation

The mission of the CSD is the correction and rehabilitation of offenders. Since the 1980s, the CSD has developed and introduced a whole range of rehabilitative programmes, including pre-sentence assessment, educational and vocational training, community re-integration programmes, psychological services, aftercare and welfare services, and the Release Under Supervision Scheme. New services developed in the mid-1990s included sentence planning, a Post-Release Supervision Scheme, a statutory review of long-term prison sentences, and so on. However, the research team was concerned with the organizational structure, in that the Assistant Commissioner (Operations) had to direct and oversee all matters relating to penal operations and rehabilitation. This arrangement was viewed as being manifestly inadequate since operations and security concerns would continue to take precedence over rehabilitation matters (Lo *et al.* 1997). In order to achieve better co-ordination of policies and programme development related to rehabilitation, the research team recommended a split of Operations and Rehabilitation in the CSD line management, and for the whole area of rehabilitation to be placed under a new Rehabilitation Division headed by a new post of Assistant Commissioner (Lo *et al.* 1997).

This recommendation was later fully adopted and the Division of Rehabilitation was formally set up in 1998. It has functioned effectively since its inception, as reflected by the modernization of vocational training facilities, provision of social work training to frontline staff, and the development of a systematic risk-assessment tool and various treatment programmes for inmates. The rehabilitative programmes and functions, previously under the direction of the Operations Division, were restructured or reorganized. Since then, the CSD has gradually made substantial developments in the following strategic directions (Pang 2007):

- specialization of treatment services;
- modernisation of educational programmes;
- accreditation of vocational training;

- reinforcement of drug abuse prevention;
- restoration of parent–inmate relationships;
- promotion of cultural activities;
- enhancement of community partnerships; and
- appeal for community support.

Types of institutional regimes

There are five types of regime: prisons, drug addiction treatment centres, training centres, a detention centre, and rehabilitation centres, with the latter three centres being targeted solely at young offenders (see Table 11.2). The CSD also runs remand centres and a detention centre for Vietnamese illegal immigrants, which currently has no inmates. The remand centres receive inmates from, and deliver them to, the courts while they are waiting for assessment reports, trials, and sentencing.

With the exception of prisons, inmates of all the other regimes have undetermined sentences. Their exact date of release is determined by the administration of each institution rather than by the court. Under a progressive system set by each regime, inmates can be promoted through several grades, with the promotion giving inmates more opportunities and fewer restrictions. The point of release is determined by the superintendent or senior superintendent on the advice of a review board of the institutions concerned. The regimes are introduced below:

Detention centre

The US-style boot camp for teenagers has been increasingly used as a sentencing option in its own right (Lee 2001). The Hong Kong detention centre is an example of such use. It places an emphasis on physical training, where '3S' ('short, sharp, shock') training is the core element for male offenders who have never been institutionalized. The 'short' in 'short, sharp, shock' refers to the sentencing period; youth offenders aged between 14 and 20 are detained for between 1 and 6 months, while young adults aged from 21 to 24 are detained for terms of 3 to 12 months. 'Sharp' refers to the high physical requirements of the training in which inmates are required to do hard labour. 'Shock' refers to the impact of the training aimed to make inmates realize the consequence of committing crimes within the short training period of institutionalization. Due to the emphasis

Table 11.2 Regimes of correctional services

Programmes	Age	Period of Institutionalization	Supervision Period	Special Supervision Conditions
Detention Centre (male only)	14–20 21–24	1–6 months 3–12 months	One year	Under curfew and must stay at home overnight
Rehabilitation Centre	14–20	3–9 months	One year	Under curfew and must stay at home overnight
Training Centre	14–20	6–36 months	Three years	Long-term supervision
Drug Addiction Treatment Centre	14 or above	2–12 months	One year	Must have urine sample checked regularly
Youth Offenders Scheme (Youth Prison)	14–20	Determined by the court	One year	—
Prison	21 or above	Determined by the court	—	—

on strict discipline, hard labour, and body and foot training, offenders must be physically and mentally fit to participate in the vigorous activities. It is expected that after the tough training, offenders will come to understand the consequences of committing crimes and breaking the law. The progress of the inmates is regularly monitored by the Review Committee, which decides on when to discharge inmates. Before their discharge, inmates need to have found suitable employment or a school placement. Following discharge, inmates are subject to one year of aftercare supervision.

Rehabilitation centres

Those young offenders who are not fit enough to endure the harsh training in the detention centre may be placed in a rehabilitation centre. The whole programme comprises two phases and provides 3 to 9 months' training for inmates. Phase I of the programme is 2 to 5 months in duration, with an emphasis on disciplinary training. Inmates attend half-day basic work skills training and half-day educational or counselling programmes. The aim is to develop offenders' self-control ability and regular life pattern. Phase II consists of a 1 to 4 month community-based reintegration programme. Offenders are permitted to go out to work, attend training and educational courses, or participate in community services, and are subject to one year of aftercare supervision following discharge.

Training centres

Offenders between the ages of 14 and 20 are the target of training centres. The period of training varies from 6 months to 3 years, progressing through three stages. All inmates are required to undergo half-day educational training and half-day vocational training daily, commensurate with their previous educational attainment and work experience. The centres also organize various types of activities for inmates who have behaved satisfactorily and are physically fit. Activities such as volunteer service, boy scouts and girl guides, outreach training, and lion dances are all aimed at helping youths reintegrate into society. When inmates have satisfied the centres' requirements, and employment or schooling arrangements are in place, the Review Committee will approve inmates' discharge. Most inmates are released after serving around 15 to 18 months. After discharge, youths undergo three years of aftercare supervision.

Drug addiction treatment centres

Drug abusers who have been convicted of an offence must undergo compulsory drug treatment at the Hei Ling Chau Drug Addiction Treatment Centre (male) or the Chi Ma Wan Centre (female). The treatment period lasts from 2 to 12 months, depending on the progress and improvement of individual offenders. The treatment centres detoxify and restore inmates' physical health. A variety of therapeutic and treatment programmes, including work therapy, personal counselling, outdoor physical activities, and discipline training, are provided to wean inmates from drug dependence. Inmates attend a Relapse Prevention Programme to prepare them psychologically for their release. Upon release, inmates must stay in a halfway house for 6 to 8 weeks and receive one year of aftercare supervision.

Prisons/Youth prisons

Prisons provide safe and humanitarian confinement to inmates; the terms of imprisonment are decided by the court. Young inmates aged between 14 and 20 are separated from adult inmates. Although the emphasis is on confinement, those youths who behave well, who have good skills, and who have not completed primary education may receive half-day education and half-day vocational training. Vocational training is not aimed at developing offenders' skills, but at helping them to use their time constructively, to cultivate work habits, and to set positive life goals. Adult male prisons are classified into maximum, medium, and minimum security establishments. Inmates with psychiatric or related problems are housed in the Siu Lam Psychiatric Centre. Rehabilitative programmes previously catering solely for young inmates are now extended to include voluntary adult inmates aged below 35 who have shown interest in participating in educational programmes and vocational training. Unlike adult inmates, young inmates are required to receive one year of statutory supervision after release.

Supervision schemes for inmates

The CSD runs five supervision schemes, or parole, for inmates, largely adults, with the aim of enhancing inmates' reintegration into the community (see Table 11.3). The decision is not solely determined by the CSD, but also involves other departments such as the Police and Social Welfare Department. Final approval of application for the schemes rests with independent Boards whose members are appointed by the Chief Executive of Hong Kong. Operation of the schemes is quite similar to a proposal made in the *Halliday Report* (Home Office 2001) published in England and Wales that suggests all custodial sentences should involve discharged prisoners being subject to supervision until the expiry of the sentence, with the possibility of recall to prison in case of breach of supervision conditions. However, the Hong Kong model does not involve all prisoners.

The first two supervision schemes, launched in 1988, aim at helping suitable inmates serve their sentences in the community. The Release under Supervision Scheme provides an opportunity for successful applicants who have served half of their sentence of imprisonment of 3 years or more or 20 months, whichever is longer, to be discharged from prison and receive aftercare supervision in the community (see *Prisoners (Release Under Supervision) Ordinance* (Cap. 325)). Similarly, the Pre-release Employment Scheme allows those successful applicants, both adult and youth inmates, who are within 6 months of the expiry of their imprisonment of 2 years or more, to have an earlier discharge on the condition that they engage in appropriate employment. Discharged inmates of both schemes reside in a halfway house with aftercare services upon release.

Two other schemes target long-term prisoners serving a determinate sentence of 10 years or more, prisoners with an indeterminate sentence, juvenile prisoners who have been convicted of murder when they are under 18 years of age, and prisoners detained at Executive discretion. The Conditional Release Scheme allows selected inmates to be released under supervision for a period of not more than 2 years before the Long-term Prison Sentences Review Board makes recommendations on whether to convert their indeterminate sentences to determinate ones. Once the sentences are converted, the Board may order the inmates in question to receive post-release supervision under the Supervision after Release Scheme.

The largest scheme, in terms of participant numbers, is the Post-Release Supervision of Prisoners Scheme, launched in November 1996 under the same ordinance passed on 31 May 1995. This scheme involves adult inmates serving a prison sentence of 6 years or above and those sentenced to 2 years or more for specific offences, such as violent crimes, sexual offences, and triad-related crimes. About 35 per cent of adult inmates were eligible for this scheme in June 2005 (Post-Release Supervision Board 2005). In making a decision of whether to grant the supervision as well as its length, the Post-Release Supervision Board will consider the inmate's age, previous convictions, nature of offence, sense of remorse, behaviour in prison, family support, and physical and mental health. Since for prison sentences a system of one-third remission for good behaviour is in place, the supervision period will be no longer than the remitted part of the inmates' sentence. This normally ranges from 6 to 24 months and on very rare occasions the Board will impose a longer period of supervision. If discharged inmates breach the supervision conditions regarding residence, employment, good behaviour and meeting with supervising officers, or commit an arrestable offence, they may be recalled to serve the remainder of the unexpired period in jail.

Previously, inmates enjoyed one-third automatic remission for good conduct on all determinate sentences. However, after the introduction of the Post-Release Supervision of Prisoners Scheme, discharged inmates are now required to undergo supervision for a specific period of time decided by the Board within the remission period. This controversial move is unwelcome because inmates believe they are not free after their discharge. The *Post-Release Supervision of Prisoners Ordinance* (Cap. 475) was challenged in court in 1999 by a prisoner sentenced before the enactment of the Ordinance. The prisoner was given a supervision order which he thought imposed a heavier penalty on him than a treatment given to him at the time he committed the offence. He claimed the Ordinance contravened Article 15(1) of the *International Covenant on Civil and Political Rights* (ICCPR) and Article 12(1) of the *Hong Kong Bill of Rights Ordinance* (Cap. 383), to no avail. The court ruled that the imposition of supervision orders is essentially a rehabilitative measure and does not constitute a 'heavier penalty' within the meaning of Article 15 of the ICCPR or of Article 12(1) of the *Hong Kong Bill of Rights Ordinance*, and the provisions of the Ordinance are accordingly not in breach of Article 30 of the *Basic Law* (see *Lui Tat Hang Louis v The Post-Release Supervision Board & Another* [1999] HCAL 154/1999). The Ordinance was further challenged on similar grounds in 2000 and 2002 but the legality of the application of the Scheme to prisoners who were sentenced before the commencement of the Ordinance was reaffirmed (see *Chan Chung Kan v The Post-Release Supervision Board* [2000] HCAL 1149/2000; Post-Release Supervision Board 2003).

Rehabilitative programmes provided by the regimes

Education

Education is mainly provided to young offenders who are unmotivated learners, or have gone through frustrating experiences in normal schools, or left school when they were very young (Morgan 2002). The curriculum is precisely designed to meet with the characteristics of penal education, not only in that inmates have different attainment levels, but they are admitted at different times, different rates, stay for different lengths of time, and that their social maturity outstrips their education attainment. In view of this diversity, the CSD has to find a balance in achieving three different objectives: skills attainment, knowledge enhancement and moral education. The first objective is to provide inmates with practical subjects so that they can learn useful skills to find employment in society post-discharge. The second objective is to enhance inmates' academic knowledge so as to prepare them for public examination or further studies. Moral education, the third objective, is expected to play a role in reconstructing inmates' characters and life goals.

To achieve the first two objectives, classes, with standards ranging from primary to secondary levels, are conducted by qualified school masters, with an inspectorate system run by the CSD itself. The curriculum is close to, but not the same as, mainstream education, modified to suit inmates' needs and academic levels. More time is devoted to the teaching of practical subjects, such as computer application, language, management, and accountancy. Teaching materials are tailor-made and more innovative, and lively teaching styles are introduced, for example learning English and Mandarin through listening to pop songs. Inmates dedicated to continuing their studies, or with the will to learn, are helped to fit in the nearest level of normal schools. Arrangements are made for able inmates to sit public examinations that can bridge their further studies, such as Pitman and Test of English as a Foreign Language.

It is the strategy of the CSD to achieve the above two objectives in training centres because of the longer period of detention. Since the detention centre emphasizes physical training and the period of detention is very short, education is not a primary task. All inmates attend a half-hour remedial class each week, focusing on moral education. At youth prisons, inmates' sentence length varies and education is not mandatory because most inmates have low motivations to study. Having a definite sentence, inmates are not afraid of teachers complaining of class misconduct, and it is difficult for teachers to control class discipline. Nevertheless, education can be provided if requested by inmates, both youth and adult. The main focus of education in youth prisons is on moral education but a small number of able inmates are helped to achieve success in public examinations. In 2006, inmates sat 1,850 examination papers, with a pass rate of 80%. Since 2004, volunteer instructors and lecturers from the Open University and City University of Hong Kong have regularly provided continuing education for selected inmates in prisons.

Vocational training

Research suggests that there is a high correlation between crime and unemployment (Britt 1995; Collins and Weatherburn 1995). In correctional institutions, a variety of industrial activities are offered, such as metalwork, fibreglass, bookbinding, carpentry, and laundry services, etc. The objectives embodied in vocational training are three-fold. Firstly, to help inmates cultivate good working habits. Secondly, to gain self-confidence and learn positive working attitudes, such as getting along with others, and following rules and regulations. The third objective is to help inmates learn specific trade-skills to suit their aptitude and capacity, enabling them to experience a sense of achievement and compete for relevant employment upon discharge. It is expected that discharged inmates with stable employment will adjust to society more readily and refrain from a deviant way of life.

Most of the aforementioned vocational training programmes for young offenders are carried out in training centres. However, not all inmates can be offered the chance to enrol for special trade-skills training within training centres because of limited places, or because the courses demand inmates to have possessed specified academic attainments. Another consideration is the variation in the length of the sentence. The reality of the situation in the CSD is that both physical and human resources are always limited, so the CSD gives priority to those inmates best able to benefit from the more favourable training. For those discharged inmates who are willing to continue vocational training, the CSD will help them seek placements in accredited training programmes with the Vocational Training Council and Construction Industry Training Authority.

Compared with their counterparts in training centres, inmates in other institutions have fewer opportunities to attend special trade-skills training. For instance, the unique '3S' training in the detention centre does not allow room for vocational training. In rehabilitation centres, although inmates attend half-day basic work skills training, the aim is more on promoting positive work habits and attitudes rather than learning a specific trade because the time of detention is too short. Similarly, the objective of vocational training in youth prisons is mainly to kill time and promote work habits rather than train in job skills. The work programme in drug addiction treatment centres helps addicts to improve their health and develop better work habits.

An encouraging recent development is the launch of an Enhanced Reintegration Programme in 2006 for voluntary male adult prisoners below the age of 30. Inmates can attend full-time vocational training on a voluntary basis if they have completed junior secondary education and have a remainder of 6 to 18 months in jail. They can learn Chinese cooking, clerical and office work, hair design, air-conditioning, electrical maintenance, and painting. The CSD actively looks for opportunities for their training courses to be recognized or accredited by external authorities, such as the Vocational Training Council. For example, after completing a Food and Beverage Course in one of the institutions, inmates will obtain a certificate recognized by Commonwealth countries. Such recognitions aim to arouse inmates' interest, enhance their self-confidence, and increase their job opportunities.

Community reintegration, religious, and cultural activities

Activities are organized to help inmates develop potential, discipline, leadership, and resilience, such as the Hong Kong Award Scheme, Boy Scouts, Girl Guides, adventure-based counselling, and Outward Bound. Other cultural activities such as lion dance classes, marching band, and Chinese orchestra and band are organized for inmates. Writing is encouraged and a prison newspaper is printed once every three months for young offenders, and every six months for adults. Participation in religious activities is highly encouraged. Regular visits to prisons are paid by a number of religious organizations and their volunteers.

Voluntary work is an effective means to achieve social reintegration. Community services provide opportunities for inmates to connect with people from all walks of life, and help reduce the social stigma of prisoners. Feeling that they have the ability to serve society, inmates gain a sense of accomplishment and a more positive self-image. Such satisfaction cannot be obtained through committing an offence or in their former life of deviance. When they see the struggle of the deprived and underprivileged, it is hoped that inmates will realize they are not the most unfortunate individuals. This encounter motivates inmates to face personal problems optimistically and appreciate the chances they are given in rehabilitation.

However, it is impossible to engage all inmates in such activities because of the limited opportunities provided to inmates by the organizing bodies. The financial implications for inmates to participate in costly activities, and the risks and physical demands involved in some activities are also major concerns. Furthermore, not all inmates are entrusted or permitted, on security or medical grounds, to go out of the centres, for example those on escapee lists or on medical officers' lists. Due to limited places, only those with good performance are given a priority to participate in these activities. Thus the activities are seen as an incentive or reward for good behaviour. Inmates have to take turns and very often fair performance does not guarantee a chance, not to mention those with behaviour or adjustment problems.

Aftercare services

Discharged inmates of the detention centre, rehabilitation centres, training centres, drug addiction treatment centres, and various 'Release Under Supervision' schemes will face a period of statutory supervision provided by aftercare officers. Individuals are recalled if they fail to observe the conditions of supervision. The CSD adopts the principle of 'throughcare' (Lo *et al.* 1997; Kwok 2007). That is, aftercare service begins inside the institutions so that a relationship built on trust can be established between aftercare officers and inmates and their families at an early stage. This includes helping newcomers adjust to the environment of the institution and observe rules and regulations, encouraging inmates to participate in community reintegration activities and become law-abiding citizens, and preparing them for discharge. Pre-release therapeutic courses and information are provided to help individuals deal with problems they may experience upon discharge. After their release, officers will visit ex-offenders in their hostel, home, or workplace to give further support and guidance.

Family work

Family work is regarded as one major means of rehabilitation. Aftercare officers not only have to provide guidance to inmates but sometimes also to their families, because without adequate family support the rehabilitation inmates have undergone would be in vain. Family contact is a continuous process. Officers normally keep close contact with the inmates' family from immediately after their admission up until just prior to their discharge. Parents are invited to visit the centre in order to understand its programmes and operation. Family members are invited to attend the inmate's birthday party. Parent groups or parent-inmate programmes are held to improve the relationship and communication between inmates and their families. A parent–inmate centre has been formed in the Tai Tam Centre. However, since not all family members are co-operative and supportive, or attend meetings, aftercare officers often encounter difficulties in offering effective services.

Psychological services

Psychological services are provided to all inmates and family members who need assistance in coping with emotional and behavioural problems, and to promote psychological well-being. Psychological services are provided by a team comprising of one clinical psychologist and an officer. The officer is responsible for providing supportive counselling and organizing group activities for inmates. In the 1990s, a perpetual shortage of clinical psychologists was a common problem in a variety of disciplines in Hong Kong, and the CSD was no exception. For instance, in 1996 only 60 per cent of clinical psychologist staff vacancies could be filled (Lo *et al.* 1997). This shortage issue has been much alleviated today. However, it is still an ideal to achieve the target of one clinical psychologist per institution.

Compared to the 1990s there has been substantial development in the assessment and treatment programmes in which psychologists have played an active and significant role. An integrated procedure for evaluating and managing the risks and needs of offenders has been developed and implemented. The protocol for the rehabilitation of offenders has been refined. A number of quality treatment programmes have been put in place, such as a Sex Offender Evaluation and Treatment Programme, Offending Behaviour Programme, Inmate–Parent Programme for young offenders, Violence Prevention Programme for adult offenders, and Substance Abuse Awareness and Recidivism Prevention Programme for drug addicts.

Halfway houses

To facilitate inmates' adjustment into society after a period of incarceration, discharged inmates of the detention centre, rehabilitation centres, training centres, or drug addiction treatment centres are placed in a halfway house, such as Phoenix House, Bauhinia House, and Pelican House, for a period of 6 weeks to 4 months. They either study or work in the community and learn to readapt to society. Aftercare workers at the halfway houses provide guidance, organize interest and social groups, and encourage inmates to engage in more contacts with their families throughout this transitional period. Collaboration between aftercare officers of the halfway house and discharged inmates' mother institutions exists. Aftercare officers of the latter pay regular visits to discharged inmates residing in the halfway house and continue to provide supervision as soon as the discharged inmates move back to stay with family.

Community partnerships and service initiatives

In recent years the CSD has been proactive in strengthening community partnerships with NGOs and in developing various service initiatives for the community. In the 1990s the CSD was in collaboration with fewer than 10 NGOs, but by 2006 there were close to 60 NGOs (Pang 2007). Three NGO forums have been organized to let the partners exchange views, expectations, and experiences. The Committee on Community Support for Rehabilitated Offenders, which draws members from all walks of life, was formed to provide guidance for the CSD. In 2004 a CSD Rehabilitation Volunteer Group was formed to provide training and services to inmates in correctional institutions. The Group comprises people from all walks of life, such as professionals, university students, housewives, and retired persons. Most of them have attained post-secondary education. A variety of community education and publicity actions, such as a drama series and concerts, have been organized to appeal for community acceptance of, and support for, rehabilitated offenders.

A common phenomenon is that inmates released from CSD institutions are still at risk of reoffending if they do not have sufficient support in the community post-discharge, as many inmates maintain frequent contact with their deviant friends, indulging in pleasure-seeking activities, running an imbalanced lifestyle between work and leisure, and encountering difficulties in adjustment after institutionalization. In 1998, one non-governmental organization launched Project Dawn to help discharged inmates of the detention centre through intensive group activities, training, and supportive programmes in the community. In the first few years, the response of the CSD was relatively passive, as reflected from the small number of referrals to the project. With increasing attention to community support and partnership in recent years, the CSD has, under the auspices of the Continuing Care Project, extended its scope to include seven NGOs and provide community support services to inmates of nearly all correctional regimes (Kwok 2007).

Since 1993, the CSD has been organizing the Personal Encounter with Prisoners Scheme for marginal and school youths to visit designated correctional institutions. Through the visits and meetings with inmates who have reformed themselves, they witness the hardships of correctional life and the pain that inmates suffer from the loss of liberty. The purpose is to enable these youths to understand the serious consequences of crime, and to deter them from committing crimes. Similarly, in the Green Haven Scheme young people visit drug addiction treatment centres to learn about the harmful effects of drug abuse from inmates' personal experiences and feelings about being placed in custody. They also go through a closing ritual declaring their determination to remain drug-free. Both schemes have drawn very good responses.

Other issues of concern

Prison population

Variations in the rate of imprisonment can be explained by many factors, such as crime rates, considerations in public policy, the supply of prison places, unemployment, and changing fashions in punishment philosophy, demography, and economic activities (Zimring and Hawkins 1991). In Hong Kong the population of adult and youth prisons has been on the rise since the turn of the century. In 1996, the total prison population was 14,343; this number rose to 18,513 in 2001 and reached its peak with 27,930 inmates in 2004, falling slightly to 23,199 in 2005. Looking at the differences between male and female prisoners, the female population has increased threefold from the mid-1990s to the mid-2000s (see Figure 11.1). This is largely a result of the influx of illegal immigrants from mainland China prostituting in Hong Kong. This trend is similar to the rise of the female prison population in England and Wales throughout the 1990s due to the growth in the number of female foreign nationals convicted of drug trafficking (Morgan 2002). Drug addiction treatment centres have maintained a population of below 2,000 since 1997.

The trend among the population of detention, rehabilitation, and training centres is quite different to that of prisons. The population for training centres, which provide longer periods of institutionalization, declined steadily from 321 in 1996 to 135 in 2005 (see Figure 11.2). In contrast, the population of the detention centre rose sharply from 1999 to 2002, while the number of inmates in training centres had

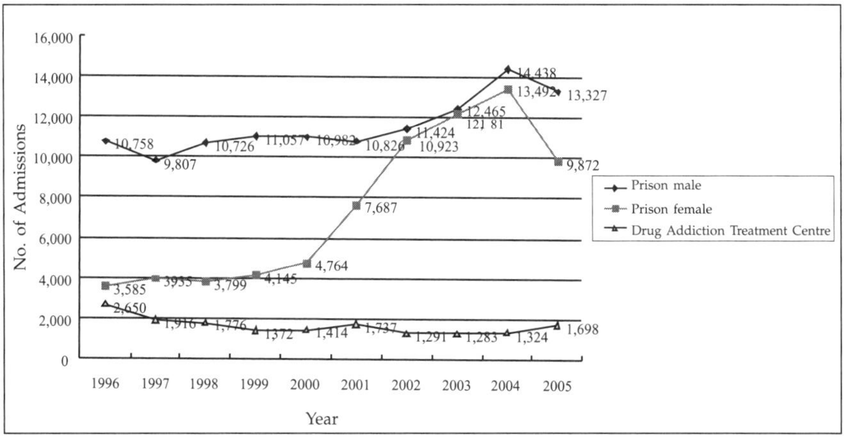

Source: CSD (1996–2005)

Figure 11.1 Population of Prison and Drug Addiction Treatment Centre

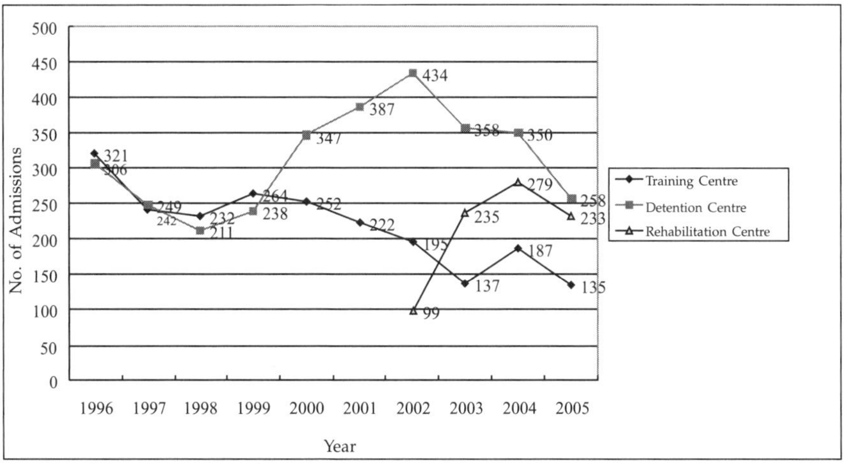

Source: CSD (1996–2005)

Figure 11.2 Population of Training Centre, Detention Centre and Rehabilitation Centre

dropped, reflecting the sentencing ideology of the courts at that time, that is, favouring shorter sentences.

While the detention centre was previously the most overcrowded institution in the early 1990s (Vagg 1991: 143), in recent years the population of the detention centre has begun to drop primarily due to two factors. Firstly, there has been an increase in the number of drug-using youth offenders who do not meet the 'physically fit' criterion of the detention centre. Secondly, the launch of rehabilitation centres in late 2002, which also provides short-term institutionalization for young offenders, has detracted potential targets of the detention centre. The combined population of detention and rehabilitation centres peaked at nearly 600 inmates in 2003, while the population of training centres dropped below the 200 level, strongly indicating that the courts favoured shorter sentences for young offenders.

Overcrowding

Overcrowding has been a common problem in correctional institutions over the last two decades. The CSD has described it as a 'perennial problem' (Asia and Pacific Conference of Correctional Administrators (APCCA) 2005). In the early 1990s Vagg (1991, 1994) claimed that the correctional system as a whole was holding approximately a third more inmates than it was designed for. In recent years the problem of overcrowding has been improved, but nevertheless it continues to be a concern for the CSD administration. The overall occupancy rates for all CSD institutions in 2004 and 2005 were 123.1 per cent and 114.5 per cent respectively, suggesting that overcrowding continues to be a problem despite it not being as serious as it was in the 1990s. As such, the CSD endeavours to seek long-term solutions to address the problems of overcrowding in penal institutions (CSD 2007).

Overcrowding is not spread equally across institutions. Some institutions experience more problems with overcrowding than others. For instance, it was 'highest [at 88 per cent] in the detention centre in 1991' (Vagg 1991: 143), and some institutions were holding over 50 per cent above their certified capacity (Vagg 1994). In 1996, Pik Uk Correctional Institution, with a standard capacity of 385, held over 500 inmates (Lo *et al.* 1997). In particular, overcrowding is more of a serious problem in female institutions. In 1997, Tai Tam Gap Correctional Institution held 81 per cent over its original capacity of 160 (Lo *et al.* 1997). However, the opening of the female centre at Chi Ma Wan later brought some relief to Tai Tam Gap's overcrowding problem. 2004 saw a record high in the imprisonment of female adults, and although the female penal population dropped to 8,775 in 2005, it still continued to exceed the certified accommodation (CSD 2005).

Overall, adult institutions and female institutions suffer overcrowding more than young male institutions. Since the number of offenders is far more than the original capacity in some institutions, facilities and manpower are thinly spread to meet inmates' needs; there is insufficient space for inmates and resources have been used to the maximum level. This may result in arousing conflicts among offenders and pressurize the CSD staff.

Table 11.3 Success rates of regimes and schemes

Regimes/schemes	2004 (%)	2005 (%)	No. of supervisions expired in 2005
Detention centre (non-conviction one year after discharge)	95.8	96.3	325
Rehabilitation centres (non-conviction one year after discharge)	96.6	95.0	258
Training centres (non-conviction three years after discharge)	68.1	68.2	242
Drug addiction treatment centres (non-conviction and drug-free one year after discharge)	63.6	59.7	1343
Youth prisons (non-conviction one year after discharge)	85.4	85.3	102
Release Under Supervision Scheme (non-conviction until latest date of discharge)	100	100	3
Pre-Release Employment Scheme (non-conviction until earliest date of discharge)	100	100	18
Post-Release Supervision Scheme (non-conviction during supervision period)	89.1	88.0	443
Conditional Release Scheme (non-conviction during supervision period)	100	No expired case	0
Supervision After Release Scheme (non-conviction during supervision period)	100	100	3

Source: CSD (2005, 2007)

Hong Kong is a very crowded city and electronic monitoring (Whitfield 1997) is not a viable option to monitor offenders' activities in the community. As such, the failure to use electronic monitoring or, specifically, incapacitation achieved through electronic tagging, adds to the issues of overcrowding in prisons. In addition, the extensive use of recalls to prisons (Vagg 1991) for those who breach supervision conditions is another direct cause of overcrowding. In 2005 alone, 791 recall orders were issued.

Success rates

To measure the recidivism of offenders is a sophisticated issue, involving both static and dynamic factors (Zamble and Quinsey 1997). The success rates officially published by the CSD are monolithic and measured only by non-conviction of a criminal offence (as well as remaining drug-free for drug addiction treatment centres) within the period of statutory aftercare supervision. Since there is no supervision period following imprisonment, no statistics have been published on the success rate for prisons. As shown in Table 11.3, four of the Release Under Supervison Schemes have 100 per cent success rates because of the small number of cases under supervision, when the sample is large, as in the case of the Post-Release Supervision Scheme, the success rate drops to 88–89 per cent. For the five regimes outlined in Table 11.3, the detention centre and rehabilitation centres have the highest success rate (95–97 per cent) followed by youth prisons (85 per cent), mainly because the period of aftercare supervision is shorter (one year), compared to a three-year supervision period for discharged inmates of training centres, which have lower success rates (68 per cent).

The success rates achieved are relatively high throughout the different regimes and schemes, with an overall success rate of around 77 per cent. However, there is a significant difference between the overall success rate and overall recidivism rate, which is around 49 per cent (APCCA 2005). The latter is measured by the percentage of readmission of local offenders to a CSD facility within a three-year period from release, excluding convictions resulting in probation or fines. Vagg (1991) suggested that the high success rates were attributed in part to the extensive use of recall to prison. Similar to Western research (Caulkins and Reuter 1998), many of those who reoffend are related to the availability of drugs and price variations in the drug market (Pang 2007). Because of the limitations associated with the monolithic measurements aforementioned, readers should be cautious when interpreting the success rates.

Conclusion

The CSD claims that the Hong Kong prison model is similar to the one promoted by Mathiesen (1990) but modified to suit the local cultural context with five main strategies: strict discipline training, timely and appropriate rehabilitation services (including education, vocational training, cultural activities, and psychological services), comprehensive aftercare services, public support and acceptance of rehabilitated offenders, and strengthening co-operation with NGOs (Kwok 2007). Such a model has in fact emerged from a few decades of trial and error, with a staff force with low academic qualifications, insufficient resources, and poor community support.

To conclude the development of correctional services in Hong Kong, in the 1970s the CSD tended to emphasize coercive custody and neglect the importance of rehabilitation and treatment of offenders. In the 1990s, increasing attention was paid to the rehabilitation and reintegration of offenders. By 2000, the appeal for community support and the formation of community partnership became the CSD's focal concern. Today the professionalization of correctional services not only witnesses the development of various treatment and assessment programmes; the CSD has more staff with bachelor and master degrees than ever before. Despite the fact that difficulties still arise in providing quality education, vocational training, and rehabilitative programmes to all inmates, the CSD has found its vision, mission, and values of corrections as well as different intervention and treatment approaches. Such sound philosophical and practice frameworks of corrections should be shared by members of the 6,600-strong staff force from top management to frontline operation staff.

Review questions

1 Are custodial sentences expensive means in the rehabilitation of offenders? If they are, what are the major justifications?
2 What are the daily programmes offered to prisoners in correctional institutions? Do you think they can achieve the goal of rehabilitating offenders and prepare them to be reintegrated into the community after discharge?
3 In recent years the CSD has become more active in promoting community participation in helping discharged inmates. What other community programmes do you think CSD should be organizing to further engage community and business organizations in helping the discharged?

4. How would you measure the success rates of correctional services? What are the limitations of the current practices adopted by the CSD?

References

Asia and Pacific Conference of Correctional Administrators (APCCA) (2005) *25th APCCA Conference Report*, Seoul, Republic of Korea: APCCA. Available at: http://www.apcca.org/main-publications/publications.html

Britt, C.L. (1995) 'Reconsidering the unemployment and crime relationship: Variation by age group and historical period', *Journal of Quantitative Criminology*, 13 (4): 405–28.

Caulkins, J.P. and Reuter, P. (1998) 'What price data tell us about drug markets', *Journal of Drug Issues*, 28 (3): 593–612.

Collins, M.F. and Weatherburn, D. (1995) 'Unemployment and the dynamics of offender populations', *Journal of Quantitative Criminology*, 11 (3): 231–45.

Correctional Services Department (CSD) (1996–2005, various issues) *Annual Report*. Hong Kong: Correctional Services Department.

CSD (2007) *Controlling Officer's Report, 2006–07*. Hong Kong: Correctional Services Department.

Home Office (2001) *Making Punishments Work: Report of a Review of the Sentencing Framework for England and Wales*. London: Home Office.

Kwok, L.M. (2007) *Services for Rehabilitated Offenders provided by the Correctional Services Department of Hong Kong SAR*. Hong Kong: Correctional Services Department (in Chinese).

Lee, M. (2001) 'Diversion', in E. McLaughlin and J. Munice (eds) *The Sage Dictionary of Criminology* (pp. 102–3). London: Sage.

Lo, T.W., Wong, S.W., Chan, W.T., Leung, S.K., Yu, C.S. and Chan, C.K. (1997) *Research on the Effectiveness of Rehabilitation Programmes for Young Offenders: Full Report*. Hong Kong: Government Printer.

Mathiesen, T. (1990) *Prison on Trial: A Critical Assessment*. London: Sage.

Morgan, R. (2002) 'Imprisonment: A brief history, the contemporary scene, and likely prospects', in M. Maguire, R. Morgan and R. Reiner (eds) *The Oxford Handbook of Criminology* (3rd edn) (pp. 1113–67). Oxford: Oxford University Press.

Pang S.Y. (2007) Public Lecture on Correctional Services in Hong Kong: 1971 to 2006, delivered by the former Commissioner of Correctional Services at City University of Hong Kong on 6 March 2007 (unpublished).

Post-Release Supervision Board (2003) *Post-Release Supervision Board 2001–2003: Fifth Report*. Hong Kong: Post-Release Supervision Board.

Post-Release Supervision Board (2005) *Post-Release Supervision Board 2003–2005: Sixth Report*. Hong Kong: Post-Release Supervision Board.

Radzinowicz, L. and Hood, R. (1990) *The Emergence of Penal Policy in Victorian and Edwardian England*. Oxford: Clarendon Press.

Ruck, S.K. (ed.) (1951) *Paterson on Prisons: Prisoners and Patients*. London: Hodder and Stoughton.
Vagg, J. (1991) 'Corrections', in H. Traver and J. Vagg (eds) *Crime and Justice in Hong Kong* (pp. 139–52). Hong Kong: Oxford University Press.
Vagg, J. (1994) 'The Correctional Services Department', in M.S. Gaylord and H. Traver (eds) *Introduction to the Hong Kong Criminal Justice System* (pp. 145–60). Hong Kong: Hong Kong University Press.
Whitfield, D. (1997) *Tackling the Tag – The Electronic Monitoring of Offenders*. Winchester: Waterside Press.
Zamble, E. and Quinsey, V.L. (1997) *The Criminal Recidivism Process*. Cambridge: Cambridge University Press.
Zimring, F.E. and Hawkins, G. (1991) *The Scale of Imprisonment*. Chicago: Chicago University Press.

Legislation cited

Criminal Procedure Ordinance (Cap. 221)
Detention Centres Ordinance (Cap. 239)
Drug Addiction Treatment Centres Ordinance (Cap. 244)
Immigration Ordinance (Cap. 115)
Long-Term Prison Sentences Review Ordinance (Cap. 524)
Post-Release Supervision of Prisoners Ordinance (Cap. 475)
Prisoners (Release Under Supervision) Ordinance (Cap. 325)
Prisons Ordinance (Cap. 234)
Rehabilitation Centres Ordinance (Cap. 567)
Training Centres Ordinance (Cap. 280)

Cases cited

Chan Chung Kan v The Post-Release Supervision Board [2000] HCAL 1149/2000
Lui Tat Hang Louis v The Post-Release Supervision Board & Another [1999] HCAL 154/1999)

Useful websites

Hong Kong Correctional Services	http://www.csd.gov.hk/eindex.html
Long-term Prison Sentences Review Board	http://www.sb.gov.hk/eng/links/ltpsrb/index.htm
Post-Release Supervision Board	http://www.sb.gov.hk/eng/links/prsb/prsb.html
Release Under Supervision Board	http://www.sb.gov.hk/eng/links/rusb/index.htm

Chapter 12

Crime prevention

Lena Y. Zhong

Introduction

As the proverb goes, prevention is better than cure. It is much better to stop crime before it is committed by taking preventive measures, for example by residents installing anti-burglary doors to prevent burglary. Crime prevention is an important component in criminal justice. Firstly, the benefits of crime prevention are in parallel to those of disease prevention. A sound public health system should provide education and guidance on how to prevent cancer rather than just treat cancer after patients are diagnosed with cancer. In terms of crime, however, many popular media accounts of crime, both real-life and fictional, convey the message that the most effective way to control crime is to arrest offenders. This reactive approach to crime is no more than closing the stable door after the horse has bolted. Secondly, it has demonstrated in the extant literature that a small number of people commit a disproportionate amount of crime, and that a criminal history is a significant factor in future reoffending (see, for example, Zamble and Quinsey 1997). It follows logically then that 'preventing' people from having a criminal record in the first place has substantial effects on recidivism, and therefore overall crime in society. Thirdly, crime prevention has economic benefits. Simply put, crime prevention could save money and therefore put to greatest use the resources allocated to the criminal justice system (Swaray 2006). Last but not least, a particular crime involves a network including the offender, the victim, their family members, and the whole community.

To prevent the crime from ever occurring spares the whole network of the impact and damage from crime.

Hong Kong is among the safest cities around the world, both in terms of official crime statistics and crime victim surveys (see Chapter 3 of this volume). While this high level of safety could be attributed to a wide range of factors, the crime prevention efforts made by the law enforcement agencies (particularly the police) and the community at large should not be discounted. This chapter aims to highlight the various crime prevention programmes and initiatives in Hong Kong in the context of the development of crime prevention internationally. It is organized into three sections: definitions of crime prevention, classifications of crime prevention, and selected local crime prevention programmes and initiatives.

Definition of crime prevention

According to Lab (1988, 2004), crime prevention entails any action designed to reduce the actual level of crime and/or the perceived fear of crime. Van Dijk (1990) referred to crime prevention as 'the total of all policies, measures, and techniques, outside the boundaries of the criminal justice system, aiming at the reduction of the various kinds of damages caused by acts defined as criminal by the state' (1990: 205). The targets of most crime prevention programmes include not just crime *per se*, but also behaviours associated with incivility and disorder, an essence of the 'broken windows' theory[1] (Kelling and Coles 1996; Wilson and Kelling 1982). Crime prevention also entails the reduction of any harm or suffering that may result from crime, including the fear of crime. Some crime prevention programmes such as Neighbourhood Watch also strive to strengthen community cohesion and informal social control in the hope of defending against crime (Rosenbaum 1988). An even broader definition of crime prevention includes reduction of risk factors for crime (such as gang membership) and increases in protective factors (such as completing high school) (see Sherman, Gottfredson, MacKenzie, Eck, Reuter, Bushway, in collaboration with members of the Graduate Program 1997).

Crime prevention is not the sole responsibility of the criminal justice system. The role of other government agencies (such as labour and welfare) and the general public is crucial (see Garland 1996). In contrast to the traditional compartmentalized response to crime (especially the police solution to crime), a holistic approach of fostering partnership is employed to prevent crime (see Zhong and Broadhurst 2007). In Hong Kong crime prevention is regarded as a multi-agency business. The Hong Kong Police Force (HKPF) has a Crime Prevention Bureau (CPB) at the Police Headquarters and Regional Crime Prevention Units at each of the six regions. The Police Public Relations Branch (PPRB) also engages in publicity of crime prevention. The community is organized to prevent and fight crime, as evidenced by the establishment of the Fight Crime Committee (FCC) and the Mutual Aid Committees (MACs), and by the active involvement of various faith organizations and non-governmental organizations (NGOs) such as the Chinese Young Men's Christian Association of Hong Kong, the Evangelical Lutheran Church of Hong Kong, and the Society of Rehabilitation and Crime Prevention, Hong Kong.

Sometimes crime prevention and crime control are used interchangeably. Strictly speaking, the two concepts should be distinguished from each other. Lab (1988) differentiated them by arguing that 'crime prevention' is an attempt to eliminate crime either prior to the initial occurrence or before further activity, while crime control is the maintenance of a given or existing level and the management of certain behaviour by authorized regulating and coercive institutions.

Classifications of crime prevention

Many theoretical models have been offered to classify crime prevention interventions and programmes. This section introduces the three models of crime prevention which are prevalent in the literature and which are of relevance to the Hong Kong context.

Public health model

This model draws on the approaches utilized in disease prevention. Based on the principal population target, crime prevention is distinguished between primary, secondary, and tertiary prevention. According to Brantingham and Faust (1976), primary prevention targets the general population and intends to prevent crime from ever occurring, secondary prevention aims to prevent crime among an at-risk population based on the prediction of their predispositional or probalistic risk factors, and tertiary prevention aims to prevent known offenders from committing further offences.

The public health model does not draw boundaries 'outside' or 'inside' the criminal justice system. In spite of its heuristic value, this model lacks sufficient explanation of the different philosophical, ideological, and political assumptions underlying different crime prevention initiatives (Crawford 1998). It fails to take into account who does the preventive action, and ignores the fact that a particular party such as the police can engage in all three levels of the prevention activities (Graham and Bennett 1995). Furthermore, it seems to primarily address crime or criminality of offenders, potential or known. As demonstrated, crime can be prevented through changing the behaviour of potential victims or the characteristics of the community where both the offenders and the victims usually reside.

Social/situational approach

This approach addresses the nature of the intervention. Social crime prevention is concerned with measures aimed at tackling the root causes of crime and the disposition of individuals to offend (Crawford 1998; Rosenbaum, Lurigio and Davis 1998). Currie (1996) advocated the strategies of social crime prevention at both the macro and micro levels of the social structure. At the macro level, he proposed three policies: a supportive labour market; a concerted, unapologetic strategy to reduce extremes of social and economic inequality; and an active supportive child and family policy. At the micro level, he pointed out the three most urgent interventions of social crime prevention in American society: (a) comprehensive child and family support programmes, (b) a youth intervention strategy that focuses on the expansion of tangible opportunities, and (c) a 'user-friendly' approach to drug abuse prevention and treatment.

Whereas social crime prevention addresses the root causes or *ultimate/push* factors of crime, situational crime prevention involves the management, design, or manipulation of the immediate physical environment so as to tackle the *proximate/pull* factors of crime with the aim of reducing the opportunities for specific crimes (see, for example, Clarke 1995, 1997; Crawford 1998). Thus the underlying rationale for social crime prevention is that crime is the product of complex social, economic, and cultural processes, while for situational crime prevention crime is opportunistic and can be controlled through the manipulation of the physical environment.

Tonry and Farrington's four–level model

In Tonry and Farrington's typology (1995), crime prevention is classified into four categories: law enforcement, developmental, community, and situational prevention. Crime prevention by law enforcement emphasizes the general prevention in enacting and implementing the criminal law. It achieves the goal indirectly through effects on socialization and directly through deterrence, incapacitation, and rehabilitation. On the basis of a series of research studies in the United States, Tonry and Farrington (1995) argued that even pre-adjudication criminal processes, such as mandatory arrest policies for domestic violence, could produce preventive effects.

Situational crime prevention, as referred to earlier, is based on the premise that a large proportion of crime is contextual and opportunistic. Therefore crime can be blocked by adopting target hardening measures such as locking the door, shuttering the windows, purchasing dogs, installing alarm systems. But of concern are the consequences of the 'fortress society' (Blakely and Snyder 1997). In terms of its effectiveness, 'displacement' is the Achilles heel (Crawford 1998), while 'diffusion of benefits' shows the hidden benefits in that efforts to prevent one crime cause the unintended prevention of another, and crime control efforts in one locale reduce crime in other untargeted areas (Clarke and Weisburd 1994).

Community crime prevention refers to actions intended to change the social conditions that are believed to sustain crime in residential communities. It is premised on the insight that individuals' criminality is related to the community where they live and therefore changing the community may change the behaviour of its residents. This initiative can be dated back to the pioneer work of Shaw and McKay's Chicago School of Criminology, which focused on ecological and community explanations for crime and promoted the crime prevention role played by community organizations. This ecological approach has gained a revival in recent years and is further developed by scholars along its tradition (for example, Bursik and Grasmick 1993; Sampson, Raudenbush and Earls 1997; Sampson 2002). Prevention efforts under the community approach have been focused on altering the physical and social organization of communities such as community organizing; tenant involvement; resource mobilization; and community defence (Hope 1995). Apparently there are overlaps between community crime prevention and situational crime prevention.

The last category in Tonry and Farrington's typology is developmental prevention. Through locating the risk factors and protective factors in childhood, the links between developmental processes and later delinquency are clarified. Thus interventions in children's development process, by decreasing risk factors and increasing protective factors, can have either delinquency-reducing effects or beneficial effects on other indicators such as school performance, hyperactivity, and impulsivity that are associated with reduced offending probabilities.

Selected local crime prevention programmes and initiatives

The selected programmes and initiatives are grouped into three areas: youth crime prevention, situational crime prevention and community crime prevention. Youth crime is always a concern in the local community and indeed a lot of resources are devoted to its prevention (Wong 2000). Thus various efforts to prevent youth crime in Hong Kong are introduced. Given the wide use of situational crime prevention worldwide, several local initiatives along that line are introduced. Initiatives of community crime prevention are described to illustrate the partnership between the government and the public in crime prevention.

Youth crime prevention

Crime by young people is always high on the agenda of the local community (Choi and Lo 2004). The official crime statistics show that shop theft and serious assaults were the most common crimes committed by young people under the age of 18 in Hong Kong in recent years (*South China Morning Post*, 7 February 2007). According to Mr Ambrose Lee, Secretary of Security, the government adopts a strategy of deterring first-time offenders and reducing recidivism.[2] This strategy is implemented through a multi-agency holistic approach. This section reviews the following schemes: the Police Superintendent's Discretion Scheme, Junior Police Call, Police School Liaison Scheme, Working with Gangs, Anti-school Bullying, Personal Encounter with Prisoners Scheme, and Youth Ambassador Against Internet Piracy Scheme.

Police Superintendent's Discretion Scheme (PSDS)
PSDS is designed to divert young offenders from the criminal justice system with the aim of preventing their future criminal activity (Laidler 2005). As an initiative of diversion, it is classified as a secondary crime

prevention in the public health model. Under PSDS, a police officer of the rank of superintendent or above may, at his or her discretion, caution a young offender instead of initiating a criminal prosecution against the offender. The following guidelines are used to assess the eligibility of juvenile offenders for PSDS: (1) at the time the caution is administered, the offender is under the age of 18; (2) the offender has no previous criminal record; (3) the evidence available is insufficient to support a prosecution; (4) the offender voluntarily and unequivocally admits the offence; and (5) The offender and his parents or guardians agree to the caution (Fight Crime Committee 1997–2006).

If the police superintendent holds the view that aftercare is necessary in addition to caution, the offender will be referred to one or more of the following organizations for follow-up: Juvenile Protection Section (JPS), Community Support Service Scheme (CSSS), Social Welfare Department (SWD), and Education and Manpower Bureau (EMB). Table 12.1 shows the number of juveniles arrested and cautioned from 1996 to 2005, and Table 12.2 shows the distribution of the referrals among the four organizations from 1997 to 2005.

Junior Police Call (JPC) scheme

The JPC scheme[3] was launched in 1974. Its objectives are to encourage and improve communication and mutual understanding between the police and the youth, to foster police–youth partnership in the fight against crime, and to provide a wide range of activities and training

Table 12.1 Juveniles* arrested and cautioned under PSDS

Year	No. Arrested	% eligible for PSDS	No. Cautioned	% Arrested/ Cautioned
1996	9,898	54.2	3,884	39.2
1997	8,810	54.5	3,256	37.1
1998	8,708	52.0	3,190	36.6
1999	8,646	54.7	3,216	37.2
2000	9,173	54.5	3,760	41.1
2001	8,732	53.5	3,585	41.0
2002	8,156	54.7	3,345	41.0
2003	7,918	50.4	3,012	38.0
2004	7,566	51.9	2,929	38.7
2005	6,821	55.6	3,026	44.4

*As of 1 July 2003, the minimum age of criminal liability was raised from 7 to 10.

Source: Fight Crime Committee (1997–2006, various issues)

Table 12.2 Referrals for juveniles cautioned under PSDS

Year	Juvenile protection section (JPS)	Community support service scheme*	Social welfare department	Education department	Total in number
1997	85.8%	11.3%	2.7%	0.2%	2,258
1998	74.6%	24.1%	1.0%	0.3%	2,761
1999	77.0%	20.6%	2.2%	0.2%	2,724
2000	73.9%	22.5%	3.2%	0.4%	3,702
2001	73.2%	21.6%	5.1%	0.1%	3,500
2002	54.6%	43.2%	1.5%	0.7%	3,952
2003	48.9%	48.2%	1.5%	1.4%	3,576
2004	42.1%	55.9%	1.5%	0.5%	3,730
2005	46.1%	53.3%	0.5%	0.1%	4,056

*The referrals to CSSS have seen a rapid growth since 2002. This may be due to the fact that in 2001 three more units of CSSS run by three non-governmental organizations were set up in Hong Kong (see Lee 2005).
Source: Fight Crime Committee (1997–2006, various issues)

for young people in order to equip them as future leaders and develop their potential leadership. JPC is operated on a district basis by the Police Community Relations Officers (PCRO). A chief inspector of the PPRB supervises and monitors all JPC and youth activities, and the superintendent in charge of the Community Relations of PPRB oversees the entire scheme (Lo and Cheuk 2004).

With its membership expanding rapidly over the years, JPC has become one of the largest youth organizations in the world with strong police ties. Since 1974 over 900,000 young people have joined JPC as members. As of 30 April 2007, it has 160 JPC advanced leaders 19,657 JPC leaders, and 125,420 JPC members. Since 1975, JPC has striven to develop School Clubs in primary and secondary schools in order to recruit JPC members, disseminate the anti-crime message within school, promote JPC activities within schools, train students to perform crowd control duties in school, and provide suitable students for the school prefect system. Presently, the number of School Clubs is 821, including 451 in primary schools and 370 in secondary schools.

Police School Liaison scheme (PSL)

PSL[4] was first introduced in 1974 by HKPF as part of the strategy on community policing. In the first 10 years the function was performed by police officers appointed as School Liaison Officers (SLO). In 1984,

SLO's function was integrated into the duties of Neighbourhood Police Co-ordinators who also had the overall responsibility for community relations. However, given the rising juvenile crime, 25 SLO posts were re-established in September 1995 in all police districts except those lacking student populations (for example, the airport and rail districts), in order to focus efforts on police–school liaison. As part of a comprehensive programme of support services for youth at risk, 33 Secondary School Liaison Officer (SSLO) posts at the rank of sergeant were created in August 2001 to strengthen police commitment in juvenile crime prevention work with secondary school children. One of the primary objectives is to give schoolchildren an understanding of the role of the police and a respect for law.

Working with gangs

Based on the information provided by 153 frontline social workers (Lee 2005), in Hong Kong the average number of youth gang members ranged from five to eight. The members are predominantly male and even in gangs of mixed genders males outnumber females with females assuming an inferior and subordinate role. Triad affiliations are quite common among youth gangs. As early as 1979, outreach social work services were provided to street gangs and deviant youth as a government policy on social welfare. Three approaches were used by many outreach teams to work with street gangs: gang work, groupwork and casework. If the gang was a delinquency-oriented one, social workers would reduce the gang's cohesiveness, thus controlling the delinquent behaviour of its members; otherwise, the aim was to transform it into a formal youth club. Social workers also handle their personal problems through casework (Lo 1986).

Anti-school bullying

School bullying has gained broad attention in the local community with the wide media coverage of two high-profile school bullying cases in December 2003 and February 2004 (*South China Morning Post*, 17 February 2004). Surveys conducted by Wong *et al.* (2002) and Wong (2004a) showed that school bullying is common among students in both primary and secondary (or high) school in Hong Kong. For instance, Wong *et al.* (2002) found that about 31.7 per cent of 7,025 primary school students reported being bullied physically. Wong's (2004a) survey found that 18.3 per cent of 3,297 secondary school students were victims of physical school bullying. However, Wong and Lo (2002) were dismayed with the fact that so little was done in local schools after a survey with 905 teachers.

Wong (2004b) argued strongly that unresolved school bullying problems are often a precursor of school violence and delinquency, and hence called for the deployment of a comprehensive anti-bullying strategy instead of suppressive tactics such as reprimanding bullies and suspension. For example, Wong and Lee (2005) advocated the use of a whole-school approach to tackle school bullying in Hong Kong. The theoretical underpinning of the whole-school approach is team-building and communication theories, which involve all parties, including parents, teachers, social workers, and students. Applying this approach, Wong and Lee (2005) introduced a pilot anti-bullying programme in a secondary school, a first of this kind in Hong Kong. The objective of this pioneer programme was to create a peaceful and happy learning culture among students, to enhance students' interpersonal skills, and to decrease the number of bullying incidents. The students, teaching staff, and school principals viewed this programme very positively and positive changes were observed among the students, such as improved self-discipline, greater concern for others' feelings among some troubled students, and a better sense of belonging and decreased number of bullying cases. This whole-school approach involves all the 'stake-holders' implementing a multiple-element strategy. Research has shown that such complex prevention programmes have a greater chance of being effective in reducing offending than programmes based on only one type of prevention technique (see Tonry and Farrington 1995).

Personal Encounter with Prisoners Scheme (PEPS)

PEPS has been launched since 1993 by the Correctional Services Department to target at-risk students or school drop-outs at the age of 13 to 18 in response to rising youth crime. Through 'encounter' with inmates, the students experience the atmosphere of custodial life, feel the pain of the inmates who have lost freedom because of committing crime, correct their misconception of triad members as heroes, and reflect on their own lifestyles. The scheme aims to strengthen participants' determination in leading a crime-free life and is promoted as 'an integrated effort in crime prevention'. It consists of a site visit to prison facilities and discussions with selected prisoners in a group meeting in the company of the school teachers, disciplinary school officers, or social workers.

Sy (1996) did an evaluation of the scheme. Fifty students in three groups were administered pre- and post-visit questionnaires on their attitudes and self-reported delinquency. There were changes in attitudes among the students: after the visit the students showed less approval for delinquent behaviour but tended to be less afraid of prisons. Sy (1996) observed that 'without adequate follow-up, changes in behavior will not be realised and "at-risk" students may be less fearful of the consequences' (1996: 83). This finding is not surprising. Schemes under the roof of 'Scared Straight' demonstrated similar results. Petrosino, Petrosino and Buehler (2006) did an extensive review of 'Scared Straight' and other juvenile awareness programmes conducted over a quarter-century in eight different jurisdictions and involving nearly 1,000 participants. They found that these programmes are not effective as a stand-alone crime prevention strategy. On the contrary, the empirical evidence showed that these programmes result in an increase in criminality in the experimental group when compared to a no-treatment control group. Notwithstanding the harmful effects, as Petrosino, Petrosino and Buehler (2006) pointed out, 'Scared Straight' and its derivatives continue in use. The 'Personal Encounter with Prisoners' Scheme shows no signs of abating according to Sy's (1996) study.

Youth Ambassador Against Internet Piracy Scheme (Youth Ambassador Scheme)

The Youth Ambassador Scheme aims to enlist the youth in protection of intellectual property rights (IPRs).[5] It encourages young people aged 9 to 25 to report online copyright infringements to the authorities via a website. Initiated by Hong Kong Customs and Excise Department in co-operation with the Intellectual Property Department, it was one of the main campaigns in a series of publicity and educational programmes for IPRs protection launched by the Commerce, Industry and Technology Bureau on 29 May 2006. The Scheme has three main objectives: promoting the importance of IPRs, expanding the avenues for monitoring illegal internet activities by involving young people, and reducing the flow of infringing BT seeds on the internet. In February 2006, a pilot programme was launched, and during the five months to 18 July 2006 a total of 1,200 reports of suspected BT seeds involving pirated copyright work were made. Among them, over 60 per cent of such infringing BT seeds had been removed, less than 1 per cent of cases were under investigation, and the remainder had been invalidated. Mr Timothy Tong, Commissioner of Customs, hailed the scheme as manifesting the success of 'tripartite cooperation' in that it 'pools together the Government, copyright industry and the community for combating illegal file sharing activities of pirated movie and music files by BT software in local websites'. However, the Scheme has raised eyebrows in the local community concerning privacy and the role of children in law enforcement. Suggestions were made that the government is recruiting young people to spy on others.

As the above youth crime prevention programmes show, a multi-agency approach has been adopted to prevent youth crime. In particular the Police work closely with the community and the schools. In fact in the Police there is a section dedicated to juveniles: Juvenile Protection Section (JPS), as referred to earlier in PSDS. Since late 2004, the services of the JPS have been extended to children below the age of 10. At the district level, innovative initiatives were made to reach out to schoolchildren. For example, Tuen Mun District and Lingnan University jointly rolled out a police-school network website in 2005,[6] and Wan Chai District and the University of Hong Kong jointly rolled out a police–school website in 2006.[7] Such initiatives, together with the Youth Ambassador Scheme, also show the deployment of high technology in youth crime prevention. Moreover, in the Youth Ambassador Scheme, compared with traditional crime prevention programmes, the young people play a different role: they are not just the recipients of a crime prevention service; they help to prevent crime.

Situational crime prevention

The following section reviews three situational crime prevention programmes, namely the Police publicity and education campaign in opportunity reduction, crime prevention in the Hong Kong subway system (Mass Transit Railway, MTR), and the use of surveillance cameras: the closed circuit television (CCTV).

Police publicity and education campaign in opportunity reduction

The Police, through the Crime Prevention Bureau (CPB), adopt a wide range of measures to educate the public that taking sensible, common-sense, and usually simple measures could prevent crime. For example, Announcements in the Public Interest (APIs) are periodically made by the Police through television and radio broadcasts for crime prevention tips. The CPB officers educate the public, especially the elderly, on how not to fall prey to street scams, such as spiritual blessing scams (*South China Morning Post*, 22 April 2007). They organize displays, exhibitions, seminars, and lectures. They visit business and residential premises to give advice to occupants. The Mobile Exhibition Centre (Display Bus) visits various locations, including public housing estates, with exhibitions of security equipment and crime prevention advice. Robotcop is equipped with an LCD monitor and an advanced digital and electronic audio-visual system. It visits schools, family days and festivals to teach schoolchildren civic responsibility and personal safety, with an emphasis on the prevention of shop theft and triad recruitment in schools.[8]

Sometimes it proves frustratingly difficult for the CPB officers to persuade the public, especially the merchants, to use common sense and install opportunity reduction devices. For example, the refusal of goldsmith shops to install unbreakable glass and steel grilles and to examine customers before staff open doors to let them into shops has frequently led to robberies. Apart from the loss of millions of dollars, violent gangsters sometimes shot policemen and killed innocent bystanders while escaping from the scene of robberies. So the CPB officers persuade the owners of jewellery outlets to heed the advice, coupled with action from the insurance industry. The CPB also has a display room featuring a wide range of security-related products and equipment.

It is common in Hong Kong that housing estates, whether private or public, employ security guards to watch the entrance. It is to provide capable guardians according to the routine activity theory suggested by Cohen and Felson (1979). The Security and Guarding Services Industry Authority was established on 1 June 1995 under the *Security and Guarding Services Ordinance* (Cap. 460) to administer a licensing scheme to regulate the security industry.

Crime prevention in the MTR

The MTR provides a vivid illustration of how to 'design out' crime. A senior police officer was involved in the whole planning process of the subway system. From the construction planning stage, concepts were introduced to 'design out' anything that would facilitate crime. Stations were designed to minimize dark corners, dangerous niches, and unseen spots, thus denying potential criminals hiding places and points of ambush. Where such places could not be eliminated, as in multi-level station access tunnels and bends in corridors, mirrors and closed circuit television were installed. There are no public toilets in the MTR, no fast-food facilities, and no left luggage lockers where bombs or drugs can be planted.

Gaylord and Galliher (1991) attributed the design to the suggestions made by the Hong Kong Police: (1) a key ingredient of the effective policing in the MTR is the communications system; (2) stations have been designed to promote easy observation; (3) stations offer a limited number of entrances and can therefore be sealed off quickly should a crime or other incident occur; (4) 'Exact fare' systems obviate cash transactions;[9] and (5) building on the abovementioned principles, the MTR has been designed to act as a 'physical policeman'. Good planning pays out: the safety standard on the system is the best in the world. Since its inception, there has never been a rape, armed robbery, serious mugging, or murder on the MTR.[10]

The use of closed circuit television (CCTV)

CCTV cameras are very popular in some countries as a situational crime prevention measure. For example, in England and Wales it is the single most heavily funded non-criminal justice crime prevention measure. A meta-analysis of the 19 CCTV evaluations with solid research designs shows that crimes decreased by 21 per cent in experimental areas (installation of CCTV) compared to control areas (Welsh and Farrington 2006).

CCTV is also widely used in Hong Kong by public and private sectors such as the MTR, as referred to earlier. The CCTV systems in the public sectors are under the purview of the following departments: Transport Department (TD), Housing Department (HD), and the Leisure, Cultural Services Department (LCSD), and HKPF. The CCTV systems of TD are for traffic surveillance, control, and management purposes, and the cameras are generally installed at strategic locations to provide real-time traffic conditions to TD's Area Traffic Control (ATC) Centres. For HD, two types of CCTV systems are installed in public housing estates and shopping centres: a security system inside the lifts and a Falling Object Monitoring System at the facade of the domestic buildings. LCSD operates CCTV systems at the airport and stadiums and its other facilities. However, the HKPF has not installed CCTV systems at fixed locations in public places. Separately, CCTV systems have been installed in the land boundary of Hong Kong for security purposes, particularly for the detection of illegal immigrants.

It is not known how many CCTV systems are currently used in Hong Kong, in either the public or private sectors.[11] While CCTV surveillance cameras are widely used in the private sector, its limited use by the HKPF in public places on a temporary basis for law and order purposes is so different from other jurisdictions such as in England and Wales. HKPF has only used temporary CCTV systems in crowd management operations during major festivals and events such as Millennium celebrations, Christmas Eve and Lunar New Year Firework Display events, and large-scale international conferences.

In 2002, the then Deputy Police Commissioner announced a pilot scheme to permanently install CCTV cameras in Lan Kwai Fong for crime prevention and crowd control purposes. The proposal attracted widespread media coverage and a public debate on the possibility of infringing personal data privacy and 'big brother' surveillance. It roused strong objections at the Legislative Council, and the proposed scheme was withdrawn at a late stage (Legislative Council 2002; Office of the Privacy Commissioner for Personal Data 2003). It is unknown to what extent temporary cameras used by the Police are effective in preventing crime. As for the cameras used in private and public housing estates, anecdotal evidence shows that they help to prevent crime, for instance through quick identification of a suspect.[12]

Community crime prevention

The Fight Violent Crime Committee was established in March 1973 to tackle rising crime from the early 1970s. Its terms of reference were to plan, organize, and co-ordinate government and public efforts to assist the Police to combat violent crime. In 1975 the Fight Violent Crime Committee was renamed the Fight Crime Committee (FCC), with its membership expanded to include non-official members. In May 1983 the FCC was tasked to draw up plans to reduce crime, to co-ordinate efforts in fighting crime, to monitor the results, and to report progress to the then Governor.

The FCC consists of 16 members: eight are members of the public appointed by the Chief Secretary for Administration and eight are heads of relevant government policy bureaus and departments. There are two sub-committees under the FCC: Standing Committee on Young Offenders and Publicity Sub-committee. The FCC holds an average of five meetings every year, in order to examine the crime situation, monitor progress of the PSDS, implement the fight crime publicity work, and oversee the work of District Fight Crime Committees. Apart from that, at the meetings the FCC also addresses issues of major concern to the community. For example, in 2005 the committee revisited the strategies on the war against drugs and money laundering, and discussed the strategies and measures to prevent and tackle crime related to domestic violence.

District Fight Crime Committees (DFCCs) are established in the 18 districts of the territory in Hong Kong and comprise official and non-official members. They play an important part in promoting the fight against crime and in encouraging public participation at the district level. They have cross-membership with District Councils and are the only committees that are directly concerned with law and order issues in each of the districts. The DFCCs meet every two to three months to monitor the state of crime and significant trends in district crime statistics and address law and order issues specific to the individual districts. The FCC and DFCCs are supposed to serve as an important bridge between the community and the government, but it is unknown to what extent they have fulfilled such a role, apart from the studies conducted in the 1990s (see, for example, Chau 1992; Wai 1995) to assess the effectiveness of FCC and DFCCs in crime prevention.

Mutual Aid Committees (MACs) are another form of community crime prevention. They are voluntary self-help organizations formed by residents of individual buildings. They are under the purview of the Home Affairs Department (HAD) through the HAD District Offices and Liaison Officers. MACs were initially promoted in private multi-storey buildings, and then quickly extended to public housing estates, industrial buildings, temporary housing, and squatter areas. By February 2007, there were 2,983 MACs in Hong Kong. The primary aims of MACs are to promote a sense of neighbourliness, mutual help, and responsibility among residents, and to promote better security, a better environment, and generally more effective management within the building. They serve as an important channel of communication between the government and the residents on matters affecting the well-being of the individual and the community and also provide opportunities for residents to participate in community activities.

Government departments such as the HAD and Food and Environmental Department actively engage the MACs on issues of concern to the residents. For example, the HAD addresses notices to the MACs to advise and guide the property owners on building management, such as purchasing third-party liability insurance to minimize losses to the property owners.[13] The Food and Environmental Department sent notices to the MACs on how to deal with rodents and how to maintain a clean and hygienic environment.[14] As the 'broken windows' thesis demonstrates, the focus on physical environment could have enormous implications for crime and fear of crime at the neighbourhood level (Kelling and Coles 1996). Moreover, opportunities are provided to MAC members to better deal with conflicts and disputes at the neighbourhood level, for example through training on 'professional mediation service'.[15]

With the pace of urbanization and industrialization accelerating, there is an outcry that the old community spirit is lost: people living in the high-rise buildings seldom get to know their neighbours next door and the old proverb 'it takes a village to raise a child' simply does not apply anymore. But research along the line of neighbourhood and informal social control demonstrates that the community, i.e. where you live, still matters a lot. For example, a large-scale study entitled Human Development in Chicago Neighbourhoods demonstrated that 'collective efficacy', defined as social cohesion among neighbours combined with their willingness to intervene on behalf of the common good, is linked to reduced violence at the neighbourhood level. The effects remain after individual-level characteristics, neighbourhood characteristics, and prior violence at the neighbourhood level are taken into account (Sampson, Raudenbush and Earls 1997). It attests to the importance of grassroots organizations such as the MACs as they are important media for promoting 'collective efficacy' and ultimately law and order at the community level.

Conclusion

While a wide range of policies and initiatives are adopted in Hong Kong to prevent crime, they are seldom evaluated, with a few exceptions. Indeed, not all crime prevention programmes are proved to be effective. Some crime prevention initiatives continue to receive widespread social and political support despite their limited usefulness, such as DARE (Drug Abuse Resistance Education), a school-based anti-drug programme in the United States and other countries (see Lab 2004). Hence ideally crime prevention should be based on the best possible evidence. The most appealing approach to evaluating crime prevention programmes is an experimental or quasi-experimental design (Sherman *et al.* 1997). Evaluations of crime prevention increasingly stress the employment of both process and output (outcome) evaluations (Ekblom and Pease 1995). The mechanisms presumed to underpin the causal relationships of crime reduction should be established and tested (Pawson and Tilly 1994). Effectiveness of crime prevention goes beyond the question of 'does it work' to questions of 'what works' and 'at what price', as reflected in costs measurement and cost-benefit analysis (see Welsh and Farrington 2000; Swaray 2006).

Crime prevention in Hong Kong involves a multi-agency approach, and all facets of the society are organized to pursue the common goal of preventing crime and maintaining law and order. Some prevention measures are common sense, such as locking up and watching out, but whether they will be adopted entails consciousness, sensibility, and sensitivity on the part of the individuals and merchants. Other measures are not so straightforward, and involve resolve, dedication, and perseverance on the part of the multiple agencies involved in the process. Some strategies are demonstrated to work effectively. For some strategies, effectiveness is still unknown. Some are demonstrated to be harmful elsewhere, but are still in use locally. Some strategies invoke concerns in the local community, although their effectiveness is demonstrated elsewhere.

Notes

1 The 'broken windows theory', as developed by Wilson and Kelling (1982), suggests that physical disorder (for example, broken windows, accumulated trash) and social disorder (for example, vandalism, rowdyish youth) in a neighbourhood could lead to crime in the neighbourhood, because 'one unrepaired broken window is a signal that no one cares, and so breaking more windows costs nothing' (1982: 3).

2 Source: Press release on 8 February 2006 titled 'LCQ8: Effective strategies formulated to handle juvenile crime', available at http://sc.info.gov.hk/gb/www.info.gov.hk/gia/general/200602/08/P200602080211.htm

3 Source of the JPC section: please refer to the website of the Hong Kong Police Force, available at http://www.police.gov.hk/hkp-home/english/jpc/index.htm. JPC also has its own website as a registered society, available at http://www.hkpjpc.org.hk/

4 Sources: Press release on 17 October 2001 titled 'LCQ10: Secondary School Liaison Officers Programme', available at http://www.info.gov.hk/gia/general/200110/17/1017180.htm; Press release on 19 September 2001 titled 'Secondary School Liaison Officers Help Curb Juvenile Crime', available at http://www.info.gov.hk/gia/general/200109/19/0919238.htm

5 IPRs are vigorously protected in Hong Kong. This is reflected in the conviction, after appeal to the Court of Final Appeal, of a man nicknamed 'Big Crook' for attempting to distribute movies using BitTorrent peer-to-peer file-sharing technology, a case hailed as unprecedented worldwide (*South China Morning Post* 19 May 2007).

6 Source: 'Tuen Mun District rolls out first police–school website', *Offbeat*, Issue 803, 20 July to 2 August 2005, available at http://www.info.gov.hk/police/offbeat/803/eng/n20.htm. The police–school website is www.ln.edu.hk/tmpol.schnet

7 Source: 'WCHDIST rolls out first police–school website', *Offbeat*, Issue 833, 11 October to 24 October 2006, available at http://www.info.gov.hk/police/offbeat/833/eng/n04.htm. The police–school website is www.hkuspace.hku.hk/wchpol-schlink

8 Source: the website of the Crime Prevention Bureau, available at http://www.police.gov.hk/hkp-home/english/cpb/mobile.htm

9 Gaylord and Galliher (1991) spoke highly of the use of the 'magnetized single- or return-journey ticket about the size of a credit card' (1991: 21) at their time of writing. They would be amazed with the widespread use of the Octopus cards nowadays in Hong Kong.
10 See the website of the Crime Prevention Bureau, available at http://www.info.gov.hk/police/hkp-home/english/history/history_09.htm
11 The number of CCTV cameras used by the government as of 7 November 2001 was revealed in the following source: Press release on 7 November 2001 titled 'LCQ12: Closed circuit television cameras in public places', available at http://www.info.gov.hk/gia/general/200111/07/1107179.htm
12 See an example: 'Kwun Tong anti-burglary team scores more success', available at http://www.info.gov.hk/police/offbeat/777/eng/n08.htm, *OffBeat*, 777, 16 June 2004 to 29 June 2004.
13 See the notice, available at http://www.buildingmgt.gov.hk/file_manager/tc/documents/macnother_letter.pdf
14 See the notice, available at http://www.fehd.gov.hk/events/rodent2003/letter03c.pdf
15 A workshop 'Professional Mediation Service' was run by the Home Affairs Department's Building Management Resource Centre (New Territories East) and priority was given to the MAC members to enrol. See details at http://www.buildingmgt.gov.hk/en/whats_new/2_3_69.htm

Review questions

1 What aspects should a sound definition of crime prevention include?
2 How should crime prevention be classified?
3 Try to use the three typologies of crime prevention to classify every local initiative of crime prevention.

References

Blakely, E.J. and Snyder, M.G. (1997) *Fortress America: Gated Communities in the United States*. Washington, DC: The Brookings Institution and Lincoln Institute of Land Policy.

Brantingham, P.L. and Faust, F.L. (1976) 'A conceptual model of crime prevention', *Crime and Delinquency*, 22 (3): 284–96.

Bursik, R.J. and Grasmick, H.G. (1993) *Neighborhood and Crime*. New York: Lexington Books.

Chau, A.K.Y. (1992) *An Assessment of the Work of the Fight Crime Committee* (unpublished Master of Public Administration thesis). Hong Kong: The University of Hong Kong.

Choi, A. and Lo, T.W. (2004) *Fighting Youth Crime: A Comparative Study of Two Little Dragons in Asia* (2nd edn). Singapore: Eastern University Press.

Clarke, R.V. (1995) 'Situational crime prevention', in M. Tonry and D.P. Farrington (eds) *Building a Safer Society: Strategic Approaches to Crime Prevention* (pp. 91–150). Chicago: University of Chicago Press.

Clarke, R.V. (ed.) (1997) *Situational Crime Prevention: Successful Case Studies* (2nd edn). Guilderland, NY: Harrow and Heston Publishers.

Clarke, R. and Weisburd, D. (1994) 'Diffusion of crime control benefits: Observations of the reverse of displacement', in R. Clarke (ed.) *Crime Prevention Studies, Vol. 2* (pp. 165–83). New York: Criminal Justice Press.

Cohen, L.E. and Felson, M. (1979) 'Social change and crime rate trends: A routine activity approach', *American Sociological Review*, 44 (4): 588–608.

Crawford, A. (1998) *Crime Prevention and Community Safety: Politics, Policies and Practices*. London: Longman.

Currie, E. (1988) 'Two visions of community crime prevention', in T. Hope and M. Shaw (eds) *Communities and Crime Reduction* (pp. 280–92). London: Home Office Research and Planning Unit.

Currie, E. (1996) 'Social crime prevention strategies in a market society', in J. Muncie, E. McLaughlin and M. Langan (eds) *Criminological Perspectives: A Reader* (pp. 343–54). London: Sage.

Ekblom, P and Pease, K. (1995) 'Evaluating crime prevention', in M. Tonry and D.P. Farrington (eds) *Building a Safer Society: Strategic Approaches to Crime Prevention* (pp. 585–662). Chicago: University of Chicago Press.

Farrington, D.P. (2000) 'Explaining and preventing crime: The globalization of knowledge – The American Society of Criminology 1999 presidential address', *Criminology*, 38 (1): 1–24.

Fight Crime Committee (1997–2006, various issues) *Fight Crime Committee Report*. Hong Kong: Government Logistics Department.

Garland, D. (1996) 'The limits of the sovereign state: Strategies of crime control in contemporary society', *British Journal of Criminology*, 36 (4): 445–71.

Gaylord, M.S. and Galliher, J.F. (1991) 'Riding the underground dragon: Crime control and public order on Hong Kong Mass Transit Railway', *British Journal of Criminology*, 31 (1): 15–26.

Graham, J. and Bennett, T. (1995) *Crime Prevention Strategies in Europe and North America*. Helsinki: European Institute for Crime Prevention and Control Affiliated with the United Nations.

Hope, T. (1995) 'Community crime prevention', in M. Tonry and D.P. Farrington (eds) *Building a Safer Society: Strategic Approaches to Crime Prevention* (pp. 21–90). Chicago: University of Chicago Press.

Kelling, G.L. and Coles, C.M. (1996) *Fixing Broken Windows: Restoring Order and Reducing Crime in Our Communities*. New York: Touchstone.

Lab, S.P. (1988) *Crime Prevention: Approaches, Practices and Evaluations*. Cincinnati, OH: Anderson.

Lab, S.P. (2004) 'Presidential address: Crime prevention, politics, and the art of going to nowhere fast', *Justice Quarterly*, 21 (4): 681–92.
Laidler, K.A.J. (2005) 'Police diversion measures for juveniles at risk', in F.W-L. Lee (ed.) *Working with Youth-at-Risk in Hong Kong* (pp. 53–74). Hong Kong: Hong Kong University Press.
Lee, F. W-L. (2005) 'Service programmes for "youth-at-risk" in Hong Kong', F.W-L. Lee (ed.) *Working with Youth-at-Risk in Hong Kong* (pp. 7–14). Hong Kong: Hong Kong University Press.
Legislative Council (2002) *Legislative Council – Official Record of Proceedings*, 3 July 2002. Available at: http://www.legco.gov.hk/yr01-02/english/counmtg/hansard/cm0703ti-translate-e.pdf
Lo, T.W. (1986) *Outreaching Social Work in Focus: Report of An Outreaching Social Work Project for Street Gangsters in Tung Tau*. Hong Kong: Outreaching Service, Caritas.
Lo, C. W-H. and Cheuk, A. C-Y. (2004) 'Community policing in Hong Kong: Development, performance and constraints, *Policing: An International Journal of Police Strategies and Management*, 27 (1): 97–127.
Office of the Privacy Commissioner for Personal Data (2003) *Community Perceptions Towards Surveillance Cameras in Public Places*. Hong Kong: Office of the Privacy Commissioner for Personal Data. Available at: https://www.pco.org.hk/english/publications/files/Summary%20Report%20pt1.PDF
Pawson, R. and Tilley, N. (1994) 'What works in evaluation research?', *British Journal of Criminology*, 34 (3): 291–306.
Petrosino, A., Petrosino, C-T. and Buehler, J. (2006) 'Scared straight and other juvenile awareness programmes, in B.C. Welsh and D.P. Farrington (eds) *Preventing Crime: What Works for Children, Offenders, Victims, and Places* (pp. 87–102). Dordrecht: Springer.
Rosenbaum, D.P. (1988) 'Community crime prevention: A review and synthesis of the literature', *Justice Quarterly*, 5 (3): 323–95.
Rosenbaum, D.P., Lurigio, A.J. and Davis, R.C. (1998) *The Prevention of Crime: Social and Situational Strategies*. Belmont, CA: West/Wadsworth.
Sampson, R.J. (2002) 'Transcending tradition: New directions in community research, Chicago style', *Criminology*, 40 (2): 213–30.
Sampson, R.J., Raudenbush, S.W. and Earls, F. (1997) 'Neighborhoods and violent crime: A multilevel study of collective efficacy', *Science*, 277 (5328): 918–24.
Sherman, L.W., Gottfredson, D., MacKenzie, D., Eck, J., Reuter, P., and Bushway, S. in collaboration with members of the Graduate Program (1997) *Preventing Crime: What Works, What Doesn't, What's Promising (A Report to the United States Congress)*. Maryland: Department of Criminology and Criminal Justice, University of Maryland. Available at: http://www.ncjrs.gov/works/index.htm
Swaray, R. (2006) 'Economic methodology and evaluations: The costs and benefits of criminal justice interventions', in A.E. Perry, C. McDougall and

D.P. Farrington (eds) *Reducing Crime: The Effectiveness of Criminal Justice Interventions* (pp. 143–62). West Sussex: John Wiley & Sons.

Sy, M.L.J. (1996) *An Assessment of the 'Personal Encounter with Prisoners Programme' of CSD* (Unpublished MSocSc thesis). Hong Kong: University of Hong Kong.

Tonry, M. and Farrington, D.P. (1995) 'Strategic approaches to crime prevention', in M. Tonry and D.P. Farrington (eds) *Building A Safer Society: Strategic Approaches to Crime Prevention* (pp. 1–21). Chicago: University of Chicago Press.

van Dijk, J. (1990) 'Crime prevention policy: Current state and prospects', in G. Daiser and H-J. Albrecht (eds.) *Crime and Criminal Policy in Europe: Criminological Research Report (Vol. 43)* (pp. 205–20). Freiburg: Max Planck Institute.

Wai, W.H-C. (1995) *Crime Prevention: The Role of the District Fight Crime Committees* (unpublished MSocSc thesis). Hong Kong: University of Hong Kong.

Welsh, B.C. and Farrington, D.P. (2000) 'Monetary costs and benefits of crime prevention programs', in M. Tonry (ed.) *Crime and Justice: A Review of Research (Vol. 27)* (pp. 305–62). Chicago: University of Chicago Press.

Welsh, B.C. and Farrington, D.P. (2006) 'CCTV and street lighting: Comparative effects on crime', in A.E. Perry, C. McDougall and D.P. Farrington (eds) *Reducing Crime: The Effectiveness of Criminal Justice Interventions* (pp. 95–104). West Sussex: John Wiley & Sons.

Wilson, J.Q. and Kelling, G. (1982) 'The police and neighborhood safety: Broken windows', *Atlantic Monthly*, 127 (March): 29–38.

Wong, S.W. (2000) 'Juvenile crime and responses to delinquency in Hong Kong', *International Journal of Offender Therapy and Comparative Criminology*, 44 (3): 279–92.

Wong, S.W. (2004a) 'School bullying and tackling strategies in Hong Kong', *International Journal of Offender Therapy and Comparative Criminology*, 48 (5): 537–53.

Wong, S.W. (2004b) *School Bullying and Responding Tactics: A Life Education Approach* (2nd edn). Hong Kong: Arcadia Press (in Chinese).

Wong, S.W. and Lee, S.S-T. (2005) 'Strategies for tackling school bullying: A whole-school approach', in F.W-L. Lee (ed.) *Working with Youth-at-Risk in Hong Kong* (pp. 39–52). Hong Kong: Hong Kong University Press.

Wong, S.W. and Lo, T.W. (2002) 'School bullying in secondary schools: Teachers' perceptions and tackling strategies', *Educational Research Journal*, 17 (2): 253–72.

Wong, S.W., Lok, D.P., Lo., T.W. and Ma, S. (2002) *A Study of School Bullying in Primary Schools in Hong Kong*. Hong Kong: Department of Applied Social Studies, City University of Hong Kong (in Chinese).

Zamble, E. and Quinsey, V.L. (1997) *The Criminal Recidivism Process.* Cambridge: Cambridge University Press.

Zhong, L.Y. and Broadhurst, R.G. (2007) 'Building little safe and civilized communities: Community crime prevention with Chinese characteristics?', *International Journal of Offender Therapy and Comparative Criminology*, 51 (1): 52–67.

Legislation cited

Security and Guarding Services Ordinance (Cap. 460)

Newspaper articles cited

'Schools must face up to bullying problem', *South China Morning Post*, 17 February 2004.

'Theft, assault "most common youth crimes"', *South China Morning Post*, 7 February 2007.

'Is Hong Kong wising up to the con men?', *South China Morning Post*, 22 April 2007.

'Internet film pirate sent to jail after appeal fails', *South China Morning Post*, 19 May 2007.

Useful websites

Customs and Excise Department	http://www.customs.gov.hk/eng/content_e.html
Fight Crime Committee Report (various issues)	http://www.sb.gov.hk/eng/pub/index.htm
Hong Kong Police Force	http://www.police.gov.hk
Intellectual Property Department	http://www.ipd.gov.hk/eng/home.htm
Mutual Aid Committees, Home Affairs Department	http://www.had.gov.hk/en/public_services/district_administration/mutual.htm
National Criminal Justice Reference Service – Crime Prevention (USA)	http://www.ncjrs.gov/App/Topics/Topic.aspx?TopicID=49
National Crime Prevention Council (USA)	http://www.ncpc.org
Security and Guarding Services Industry Authority	http://www.sb.gov.hk/eng/links/sgsia/index.htm
Security Bureau	http://www.sb.gov.hk/eng/about/welcome.htm

Index